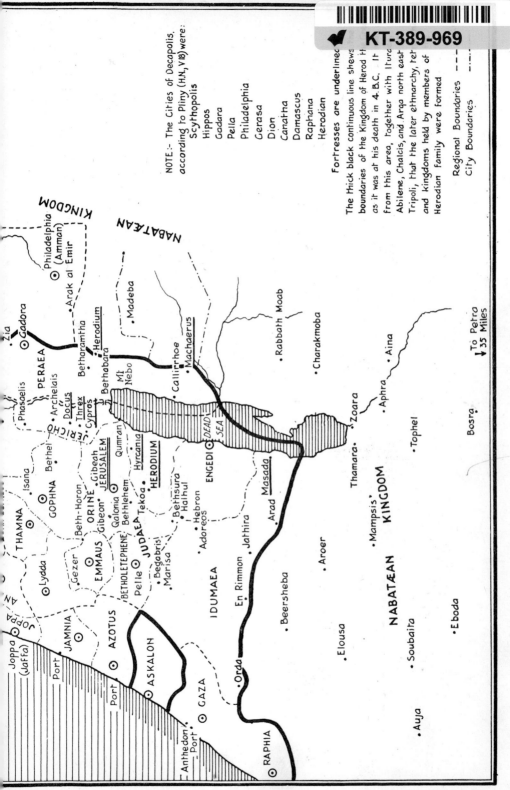

NOTE:- The Cities of Decapolis,
according to Pliny (H.N., V18) were:
Scythopolis
Hippos
Gadara
Pella
Philadelphia
Gerasa
Dion
Canatha
Damascus
Raphana
Herodian

Fortresses are underlined

The thick black continuous line shews
boundaries of the Kingdom of Herod H
as it was at his death in 4.B.C. It
from this area, together with Itura
Abilene, Chalcis, and Arqa north east
Tripoli, that the later ethnarchy, tet
and kingdoms held by members of
Herodian family were formed

Regional Boundaries   ---
City Boundaries   -·-·-

PHILADELPHIA
KINGDOM

NABATÆAN
KINGDOM

Philadelphia
(Amman)
Arak al Emir

Zia
Gadora
PERAEA
Betharamtha
Herodium
Madeba
Rabbath Moab
Charakmoba

Phasaelis
Archelais
DOCUS
Threx
Cypros
Mt Nebo
Betharbara
Calirrhoe
Machaerus
Zoara
Aphra
Aina

JERICHO
Isana
Bethel
Qumran
Gibeah
JERUSALEM
Hyrcania
HERODIUM
ENGEDI
DEAD SEA
Thamara
Tophel
Bosra

THAMNA
GOPHNA
Beth-Horon
ORINE
Gibeon
Bethlehem
Tekoa
Bethsura
Halhul
Hebron
Adoreos
Arad
Masada
Mampsis
NABATÆAN KINGDOM

Lydda
Gezer
EMMAUS
BETHOLETEPHENE
Pelle
Begabris
Marisa
Qalonia
JUDAEA
Jathira
En Rimmon
Aroer
Beersheba
Elousa
Soubaita
Eboda
Auja

JOPPA
Joppa
(Jaffa)
Port
JAMNIA
Port
AZOTUS
Port
ASKALON
Port
GAZA
Anthedon
Port
RAPHIA
Orda
IDUMAEA

To Petra
35 Miles

"Render therefore unto Caesar the things which are Caesar's; and unto God the things that are God's" (Matthew xxii. 21).

This picture, which was chosen by Mr. Berenson as the most eloquent representation of its subject, was painted by Titian for the Duke of Ferrara about 1514, when Titian was thirty-eight. It is now in the Dresden Gallery.

THE
LATER HERODS

THE POLITICAL BACKGROUND OF
THE NEW TESTAMENT

by

Stewart Perowne
M.A., F.S.A.

HODDER AND STOUGHTON

*Printed in Great Britain for Hodder and Stoughton Ltd., by
The Camelot Press Ltd., London and Southampton*

SOURCES AND ACKNOWLEDGMENTS

IN a book called *The Life and Times of Herod the Great*, published by Messrs Hodder and Stoughton in 1956, I tried to trace the course of events in Palestine which ended with Herod's death in the year 4 B.C. The present book is an attempt to continue the story, and to give some account of Palestine in the first century of our era. In that sense, and that sense only, it is a sequel to the former book; it does not in any way presume that those who wish to read *The Later Herods* will have read its predecessor. At the cost of some repetition, the present book has been designed as a single and self-contained study.

The sources for it are largely those which were used for *The Life and Times of Herod the Great*. It is not necessary to recapitulate them; but the following comments are appropriate. First, Josephus is more than ever the essential guide, particularly when he comes to relate the events in which he himself played a part. No ancient historian has left us a more detailed or vivid story. When, at the end of the narrative, we arrive at a period beyond that of which Josephus wrote, we realize our loss. It is like crossing the line between the sown and the desert.

Secondly, when dealing with things Roman, we now step into the circle of fierce light which Tacitus, in his *Annals* and *Histories*, has cast upon the events of the first century. "By far the most complete and the most trustworthy author that we possess for the early Principate" is the verdict of the *Cambridge Ancient History*. It is tantalizing that his *Histories* take us only to the opening stages of the siege of Jerusalem: the rest of the work is lost. Suetonius, also, is of great value. His *Lives of the Twelve Caesars* are as racy as anything in Roman literature; and much of the flavour is preserved in the translation made by Philemon Holland in 1606. As an historical source Suetonius is not to be compared with Tacitus, but he has recorded a great many things that we should not otherwise know. For the latter years of the century, we are particularly dependent on Dio Cassius, a Roman citizen of Greek descent, a distinguished public servant (he was twice Consul), who published a history of Rome in eighty books in about A.D. 200. These are our three chief classical sources. Others to whom we owe information on some particular point—often of considerable importance—are

vii

mentioned in the text, Juvenal, Eusebius, Photius among them.

Coming now to modern works, to those named at the outset of *The Life and Times of Herod the Great*, two in particular may be added. The first is Mr John Allegro's *The Dead Sea Scrolls* (Pelican Books, 1956), which not only gives the story of the discovery of the scrolls, obtained from some of those who found them, but also an interpretation of their meaning by one who is actually at work on them. The second is Jérôme Carcopino's *Daily Life in Ancient Rome*, translated by E. O. Lorimer with Professor Henry T. Rowell's bibliography and Notes. This, too, is now available in a Pelican Books edition, from which I have quoted it. As an introduction to Roman society, religion and manners, it is not likely to be surpassed. It describes Rome in the second century, but illustrates equally Rome of the first.

Finally, I must once again record my complete dependence on the late Père Abel's *Histoire de la Palestine depuis la conquête d'Alexandre jusqu'à l'invasion arabe*. Almost every page of my book bears the impress of Abel. I have followed him to the point of plagiarism; but, where a task has been perfectly performed, it would be arrogant to attempt to do it differently. I have once again adopted Abel's chronology, in particular with regard to the siege of Jerusalem. His figures for its dating and duration are supported by H. St J. Thackeray; they do not widely or sufficiently vary from that of other scholars.

For the illustrations, I thank Mr David Brewster, the Directors of the British Museum and the Bibliothèque Nationale, the Librarian of Corpus Christi College, Cambridge, Mrs Reifenberg, my brother Leslie, Mr Rothenberg, the Munich Museum, the Beirut Museum, Messrs Anderson, Alinari, N. V. Uitgeversmaatschappij Elsevier, Fr R. Grollenberg, O.P., and the Director of the Institut Français d'Archéologie in Beirut, M. Henri Seyrig, who has also given me the benefit of his deep knowledge of Syrian archaeology. Professor Bentwich has once again given me unstinted help on a number of points. To the Rev. Arthur Shepherd, Vice-Dean of Worcester Cathedral, Fr Seraphim Zarb, O.P., the Librarians of the Royal Malta Library and the Library of the Royal Malta University, Dr F. Rumford and Mr Milton Gendel I am also grateful for help. Mr Bernard Berenson gave me his counsel and encouragement at every stage of the work.

The Master and Fellows of Corpus Christi College, Cambridge, have once again allowed me the privilege of living in College during the Long Vacation of 1956; and later in the year Mr

Frederick Maxse invited me to continue my work in his house in Kyrenia. To them and to him I am deeply grateful.

Mr Geoffrey Woodhead, the Classical Praelector of the College, although engaged on a year's special study at the Institute for Advanced Study, Princeton, New Jersey, offered yet again to read the whole of my manuscript. Him too, last but not least, I thank.

As in *The Life and Times of Herod the Great*, I have taken £500 sterling as a modern equivalent of the talent.

S. P.

CONTENTS

ILLUSTRATIONS

MAPS

[*D. Brewster.*

1. The northern terrace of the South Palace which Herod the Great built at Jericho. It was burned down after his death in 4 B.C. and sumptuously restored by Archelaus (page 32). Archelaus was banished in A.D. 6. The work, therefore, cannot be later than that date: the *opus reticulatum*, or *network*, so called from the arrangement of the bricks, e.g. below and behind the seated figure, is notably fine for so early a date and so far from Rome. The colonnettes and niches, alternately round and square-topped, suggest an Eastern influence.

[*Alinari.*

2. The Empress Livia (58 B.C.-A.D. 29) as a priestess, from a statue in
the National Museum, Naples. Compare the portrait of her great-grand-
daughter, Agrippina (Plate 24). Both shew the same hard, cynical mouth,
beneath a calm, broad brow.

Note the protruding ears, a marked feature of the later Julio-Claudians,
e.g. Claudius, Agrippina and Nero. It seems probable, from this statue,
that it was Livia who brought them into the family.

INTRODUCTION

"THEN went the Pharisees, and took counsel how they might entangle him in his talk. And they sent out unto him their disciples with the Herodians, saying, Master, we know that thou art true, and teachest the way of God in truth, neither carest thou for any man: for thou regardest not the person of men. Tell us, therefore, What thinkest thou? Is it lawful to give tribute unto Caesar, or not? But Jesus perceived their wickedness, and said, Why tempt ye me, ye hypocrites? Shew me the tribute money. And they brought unto him a penny. And he said unto them, Whose is this image and superscription? They say unto him, Caesar's. Then said he unto them, Render therefore unto Caesar the things which are Caesar's; and unto God the things that are God's."

These famous words from the Gospel of St Matthew (xxii. 15-21), state the dominant problem of the first century of our era, and announce its solution. Until our own day, while the problem has remained, the solution has proved for many men, and in many times and places, unattainable. In fact, there have been very few epochs in which true harmony has been achieved between the claims of the state and those of God. Our own age is notoriously not one of them.

The problem is now universal; but it was in its origin Jewish. It was the Jewish discovery that God is not only one God, but an omnipotent God, that brought the dilemma into being. In the pages of the Old Testament, we can discern the conflict gradually developing, from the days of Balaam to those of Daniel. Balaam and Daniel were individual men. With the advent of Israel's Greek overlords, first the Ptolemies and then the Seleucids, the problem became a national issue. It reached its first crisis in the year 168 B.C., under the megalomaniac Antiochus IV Epiphanes, who arrogated divine attributes to himself, and tried to subvert Judaism. The Maccabean revolt, which his folly generated, gave the Jews the semblance of independent statehood under the rule of sovereign pontiffs, until the coming of Rome, in the person of Pompey, in 63 B.C.

A headlong collision with Rome seemed inevitable; but it was averted or rather postponed by the political genius of a man who, although he was a Jew by religion, was by race an Idumaean, and of that man's son—of Antipater and Herod. Herod became King of Judaea, as a client of the Romans. So long as he lived, whatever charges might be brought against him of internal oppression, he had undeniably enhanced the reputation of the Jews in the world at large, and above all he had kept the Jewish polity free from Roman interference. With Herod's death, the whole scene was transformed. His children would try, to the second and third generation, to maintain the precarious balance between the claims of Rome and those of the God of Israel. They would fail. Finally, many of the Jews themselves, unable to find a way of living as servants of God and as subjects of Rome, would abandon both their religion and their temporal allegiance, falling away to the Moloch of nationalism. By one of the awful ironies of history, it was to be Rome itself, Caesar, who, by crushing the nationalist rebel, would force upon Jewry the recognition that the worship of the One God was their true destiny.

During this same period, which covers the first century of our era, yet another religious revolution was to be born, for in this very epoch occurred the ministries of John the Baptist, Jesus of Nazareth and Paul of Tarsus. The infant Faith almost at once incurred the odium and hostility both of Jewry and of Rome: for what other purpose, indeed, than to ensnare its Founder did the Romanizing Herodians and the Nationalist Pharisees who hated them ever make common cause? Nevertheless, the sovereign words which are cited above were to form the guide of a system which would assimilate the religion of the Jews and the might of the Romans, releasing all men from the limitations of either.

In the conflicts and clashes of this unique time, the children, grandchildren and great-grandchildren of the first Herod played a prominent and important rôle. They were throughout the century the titular if not substantive sovereigns of their people, and in that capacity formed the link between Judaea and Rome. To them, therefore, it fell to try to achieve the *modus vivendi* which was essential to the happy survival of their people. That they failed does not make them any the less interesting; and it is the story of the lives of them and of their people, and of Jewish policy, leaning now to Rome, now to nationalism, never reconciling the two irreconcilables, and of the final and inevitable outcome that this book will try to tell.

Chapter I

PAX ROMANA

ROME, in the year 4 B.C., had known peace for nearly thirty years. It was unheard of, and it was wonderful. Always, Rome had been at war—in Africa, in Gaul, in Spain, in Britain, in the north and in the east; and in the terrible days which so many men still remembered, there had been war in Rome itself. The horrors of the civil wars, of the slave rebellion, finally of the proscriptions, when rival dynasts playing for the stakes of empire had traded human lives like gamblers' counters—men preferred not to recall those tribulations. Almost every home had been afflicted by them. But now a whole generation had grown up which had known nothing but absolute peace—peace abroad, peace in the provinces, and, greatest boon of all, peace throughout Italy and in Rome itself.

And this was the gift, said the Romans, of one man. Ever since, at the battle of Actium in September of 31 B.C., Octavian, the great-nephew of Julius Caesar, had defeated the combined hosts of Antony and Cleopatra, he had been hailed by his countrymen as a deliverer. He was called *Princeps*, First Citizen, *Augustus*, Worshipful. He was given supreme and individual power to rule Rome and the Romans. The republic was still there in name; but as Cicero had complained half a century before, the Romans had lost not only the blood and vigour of the republic, but even the form and colour of it. Nobody wanted it back: they wanted peace and quiet. Augustus had given them that. Helped by a minister of outstanding genius, Marcus Vipsanius Agrippa, the Princeps had completely overhauled the administration, eradicating the rapacity and corruption which had undermined it. He largely rebuilt Rome, and encouraged the inhabitants of the provinces to enlarge and adorn their cities for their greater comfort and amenity. The temple of Janus had been closed in 29 B.C., to signify that Rome was at peace; and this had happened only twice before in the history of Rome. Twenty years later, in 9 B.C., Augustus had dedicated his great Altar of Peace, the sculptures of which still expound to us the sense of almost divine blessing which Augustus had diffused throughout the Roman world.

Trade flourished, particularly with the East. This traffic had formerly been in Arab hands, for it was the Arabs who controlled the Red Sea, and it was through Arabia that the caravans bore from Arabia Felix to Petra the spices of the south and the riches of India and Ceylon. All this was to change. Augustus had despatched an expedition into Arabia in 25 B.C. It had been a failure, but the knowledge it had gained had been of use. Then at last an Alexandrian sea-captain, Hippalus, discovered the secret of the Monsoon, and the Arab monopoly of navigation was broken. As we learn from Strabo, who was writing at the end of the first century B.C., the Red Sea trade increased to such an extent that whereas in the days of the Ptolemies not twenty ships a year dare pass the straits of Bab-el-Mandeb, in his day 120 would sail annually to Somalia and India, returning with valuable cargoes which paid double dues, for import and export, at Alexandria. Nevertheless, although the Arab monopoly was thus invaded, Petra, the former clearing-house of the landborne cargoes, continued to expand and to flourish more than ever—so great was the demand in Rome for spices and other oriental products. This trade with India and Africa grew naturally in the atmosphere of the imperial peace. It was the work of merchants, not ministers. As Rostovtzeff puts it (*Social and Economic History of the Roman Empire*, Ch. III, note 18): "We must not exaggerate the importance of governmental measures, and we have not the slightest ground for supposing the existence of any economic policy on the part of the emperors of the first century." Nevertheless, to the city of Rome, and to the man who ruled it, this trade was of prime importance, and contributed to the concern which he must always have for the East and its affairs, as a powerful factor in Roman felicity.

Assured as this now appeared to be, there was, of course, another side to the medal, both for Rome and for Augustus. The age which Augustus had made possible, the great Augustan Age, was barren. It produced no great spirits. Great men lived in it, such as Virgil, the greatest of them all, and Horace his friend; but they were not of it. They had been born into the republic, of which they were the last living legacy. They and their like were dead now. No one had replaced them—neither poet, nor thinker, nor philosopher, nor artist, nor priest, nor prophet. None of the types by which the characters of men are moulded and their spirits elevated appeared in Augustan Rome. Its civilization was material, its outlook on life negative and static. Even in practical, mechanical matters no real progress was made. To cite but one instance: all Roman cities, like their Greek prototypes, used enormous quantities of water; it was one of their most commendable virtues. This water had to be conveyed, as often as not, from considerable distances, over undulating ground. Yet the Romans never learned how to cast iron, so as to manufacture cheap iron pipes; nor did they ever widely employ the common pump. But why worry, when unlimited slave labour could be used to construct endless high-level aqueducts? Such was the mental inertia, the spiritual *incuria* of the time. Strangely enough, Virgil had realized this trait in the Roman character, and had even appeared to praise it. Let the Romans leave the arts and sciences to others, he sang; their task in the world was to govern. A nation of bureaucrats would not now be accounted a very enviable or praiseworthy people; but that is the ideal which was held out to the Romans by their laureate, and realized by Augustus and his generation. Morally, they were an ailing stock. Not because they submitted to the rule of one man. It must always be borne in mind that representative government, as we know it to-day, was unknown in antiquity: the principate, beyond question, was accepted by mankind. But the age was ungentle. Revolting cruelty was a commonplace, the tone of Roman society was coarse, lewd and ostentatiously vulgar. In rural Italy, families of strong, decent peasants were still to be found. But for a century or more the yeomanry had been on the decline, the urban proletariat, the demanders of "bread and circuses", on the increase. Here, neither Augustus nor any of his ministers could find a remedy. They were wholly at a loss, when it came to character.

To Augustus himself, the years had brought personal sorrow and disappointment. He had no son to succeed him. His saintly sister, Octavia, was dead. So was her son Marcellus, the wonder-child, poisoned, it was said, by the empress. Dead, too, was Agrippa, whom Augustus had compelled, by means of a heartless political divorce, to marry his daughter Julia. He had no joy of it. When Agrippa died, the Princeps, by yet another cruel separation, had forced Tiberius, his stepson by his third and present wife, Livia, to put away a woman to whom he was devoted and in his turn to marry Julia. Tiberius soon retired to Rhodes in disgust. Julia abandoned herself to a course of profligacy which was to lead two years later to her banishment. Another stepson, Drusus, had died in 9 B.C. Augustus, now rising sixty, was a lonely man.

But he still had work to do. Men would remember him by the
new city of his creation—he had found it brick, he said, and left it
marble (the famous quarries of Carrara had recently been opened)
—and by the monuments with which he had embellished it,
some of which survive to our own day, the temples, the grandiose
new forum, the three new aqueducts, the theatre begun by Julius
Caesar and finished by Augustus in memory of Marcellus, the
neighbouring portico of Octavia, where the spectators could
shelter from the rain, the family mausoleum down by the river,
the altar of Peace nearby, and Agrippa's great temple of all the
gods, the Pantheon. He would be remembered, too, as the friend
of poets, who repaid his patronage with immortal flattery. But his
real memorial is the great administrative machine which he had
built up, both in the capital and in the provinces, of highly com-
petent civil servants backed by brave and disciplined legions. For
though internally there was peace profound, on the frontiers of
the empire enemies still watched and waited. From two quarters
in particular experience had shown that danger might strike. The
first was the North, where beyond the Rhine and the Danube,
from the dim mists of outer Europe, wild and warlike tribes might
surge unheralded into the sunlit opulence of the civilized South.
It was from that quarter that Rome was to meet her doom, when
Alaric, and later Attila, swept down over the Alps to sack and to
slay. In the latter years of Augustus, the Roman peace was twice
broken by the men of the North (see pages 18 and 24).

The other area of anxiety was the East, which for the Rome of
those days meant the Levant. Beyond the Euphrates lived the
Parthians, the people who had built their empire on the débris
of the old Persian one. Rome had never overcome the Parthians:
on the contrary, the Parthians, in the year 53 B.C., had inflicted
on Rome one of the most humiliating defeats in her whole history.
They were still there, and would, as events were to prove, be a
constant source of disturbance and damage to Rome in the next
two centuries, as would be their successors, the Sassanians, after
them. It must, however, be recorded at the outset of this narrative,
in which Parthia and the Roman fear of Parthia will so often be
mentioned, that between Ventidius' victory over the Parthians in
38 B.C. and the second year of Marcus Aurelius, a period of two
centuries, no Parthian was ever seen west of the Euphrates, save
as a hostage, a captive or a suppliant. The title *King of Kings* was
an empty boast.

But the East held for Rome something more than danger.

3. This coin, of which M. Henri Seyrig has kindly supplied the photograph, was struck in the reign of Elagabalus (A.D. 218-222) and is now in the collection of the American Numismatic Society, New York. It shews Mount Lebanon, with the Grotto of Pan, in which stands a figure of Pan, leaning against a tree and playing the flute. On the mountain are trees.

Below the grotto is an arched enclosure, the sacred precinct which marked the source of the River Jordan. On the left, we see the *pedum* or shepherd's crook, the attribute of Pan; on the right, less distinct, a *syrinx* or pipe of Pan.

[*Henry Seyrig.*

[*R. Mouterde.*

4. With the ancient coin compare the photograph of the grotto as it is to-day, taken by Fr René Mouterde, S.J. The statue has long since disappeared, the foreground has become obstructed with débris dislodged by successive earthquakes; but the shrine and the arch are still there—striking testimony to the accuracy of the coin.

[*Dames de Zion.*

5. Part of the great stone pavement beneath the convent of the Dames de Zion, which covers a portion of the site of the Antonia. This pavement, which bears the marks of games such as Roman soldiers might have played, is held by many to be the Gabbatha, *lithostrotos* or *stone-paved* judgment-place of Pilate (see page 27).

The East was old, the East was august, the East was rich. In
the eyes of the ordinary Roman, the Levant possessed a prestige
which Italy could not attempt to rival. In the north of it stood
Antioch, formerly the capital of the Seleucids, the successors of
Alexander; in the south, Alexandria, the city which Alexander
had founded, and within which the first of the Ptolemies buried
him. These two cities were accounted the second and third of the
Roman world. They were only 500 miles apart, and the inter-
vening region was irradiated by both of them equally, so that it
became the portion of the empire in which, as in no other of
comparable size, learning and commerce, religion and philosophy
flourished and proliferated. Neither Italy nor Greece could compare with it. Then, too, the Levant was the gateway to even
richer lands, to the realms of Arabia, Ethiopia, India, Ceylon
and China, whose exotic and costly products a Rome at peace
would increasingly crave (see page 2).

The Levant thus held a triple claim to primacy in the eyes of
Rome and of Rome's master. It would, in fact, grow in importance
as time went by, until by the third century it had become the
epicentre of the storms that rent the imperial fabric. Already, in
the period to be covered by the present narrative, it will be apparent, it is hoped, how increasingly the East was to affect the
destinies of the West. Realization by western scholars of the
cardinal importance of the Levant in Roman days is of recent
origin. Europe had been so eminent for so long in every department of life, and the lands of the old Roman East had sunk so
low, that it was pardonable, in 1900, to assume that Europe had
been equally favoured in the days of Rome. As late as 1935, when
the volume of the *Cambridge Ancient History* dealing with the
Augustan age was published, a leading literary review could
write: "One serious criticism of Volume X is that the East receives
too much attention at the expense of the West." But the Cambridge scholars were sure of their ground, and few would now
question their scale of values.

To Augustus, certainly, as to his successors, the Levant was
the most sensitive area of the imperial body politic. He had
particular cause for disquiet, therefore, when in April of the year
4 B.C. bad news came from Palestine.

Here ruled one of his client kings—Herod, the first of that
name, known to history as Herod the Great. The son of an obscure
Arab civil servant and an Arab mother, this extraordinary man
had raised himself to eminence and a throne. For thirty-two years

now he had ruled in splendour and security. Augustus knew him well. He had met him in Rhodes, in Palestine and in Rome. Several of Herod's children had been brought up in Rome, his sister was the close friend of the empress. Herod had done well by Rome, whose eastern frontier he had kept. Now he was old, and ill. In April came the long-awaited, but dreaded, news that Herod was dead. It was the most fateful event that had occurred in Palestine for a generation—that is, if we except the birth, a few months before, of a child called Jesus to a couple from Nazareth. But no one took any notice of that.

Chapter II

THE SUCCESSION: ARCHELAUS

THE death of Herod the Great, in the spring of 4 B.C., left his country and family in chaos. The old king had been failing, both in mind and body, for some time. Assailed by gusts of rage, he had put his three eldest sons to death; and he had thrice altered his will, naming a different heir each time. He had, besides, aroused the vengeful resentment of the Pharisees, which he had ruthlessly repressed. His death was bound to be the signal for disorders.

At first, they were avoided by the address of Herod's only sister, Salome. She was the one survivor of that great generation, all Herod's three brothers having died before him. Throughout Herod's life, Salome, while quite unscrupulously advancing her own whims and fortunes, had contrived to be loyal to Herod. At the time of his death, which took place in Jericho, there was in that genial oasis a large assembly of notables from all over the country, who had been summoned by Herod (one account says to be killed at his death, but more probably as hostages), waiting in the hippodrome. Before the news could leak out, and the notables take matters into their own hands, Salome with her third husband Alexas went to them, calmly told them that Herod had changed his mind and bade them all go home in peace. Only when they had joyfully dispersed did Salome and Alexas summon the garrison and the people of Jericho to the amphitheatre, at the opposite end of the city from the hippodrome. Here Ptolemy, the late king's secretary, to whom he had entrusted his signet ring, after eulogizing the dead monarch, and exhorting the people to continue in their allegiance, read out, first, a letter from Herod to his army bidding them to be loyal to his successor, and then the fourth and final testament of Herod. This document announced that, always subject to the approval of Rome, which meant Herod's old friend the emperor Augustus, the kingdom which Herod had so laboriously assembled was to be broken up. There was to be no single successor. The old king's flair had remained undimmed to the end: he knew that Augustus would be unwilling to entrust the whole of the Judaean patrimony

7

to any one of Herod's surviving sons. For one thing, they were mere boys, now that their three elder brothers had been put to death. The eldest, Archelaus, was only eighteen. He was the son of Malthake, a Samaritan woman, so that he was no more Jewish than his father. If Herod's latest will were ratified he was to be king, but only of Judaea and the region of Samaria. Galilee and Peraea went to his full brother, Antipas, who would be a tetrarch. Their half-brother, Philip, whose mother was a Jerusalem Jewess called Cleopatra, would inherit the north-eastern annexes of the kingdom, Jaulan, Batanaea, Trachonitis and Panias. He, too, was to be a tetrarch. Aunt Salome, of course, did well by the settlement. She received Jamnia (Yebnah) and Azotus on the southern coast, and Phasaelis, the rich model farm north of Jericho, besides half a million drachmae (about £20,000) in cash. The remaining members of his family, two young boys and five girls, were given sums of money. The Emperor was to have various pieces of plate and one thousand talents, the equivalent of half a million sterling. The empress and the rest of the royal family and court were to divide about half that sum between them. Archelaus was charged to carry his father's ring to Caesar, together with all the state papers relevant to the administration of the kingdom, under seal; because the final word of assent or disallowance lay with Caesar.

The troops, who had received a handsome donative from Herod shortly before his death, surged forward with acclamations, and regiment by regiment took the oath of allegiance to the new king. They tried to place on Archelaus' head the diadem, the golden circlet which was the symbol of royalty. Archelaus prudently declined it, and set about the funeral. This was magnificent; and when the king had been laid in his chosen palace-tomb at Herodium, seven and a half miles south-east of Jerusalem, a week's court mourning was ordered, that being the sensible period enjoined by Jewish law. This was followed by a funeral banquet for the populace, "a Jewish custom", as Josephus says, "which reduces many to poverty", as many a Gentile has found in later centuries.

So far, all had gone well. Salome had been at hand to direct and guide, the army had been conciliated. But as soon as Archelaus had to act for himself, the trouble began. He was young, he was the son of an Idumaean father and a Samaritan mother, and, to make matters worse, he had spent most of his boyhood in Rome: he knew nothing of the temper of his compatriots. He

tried to ingratiate himself by playing up to what he thought were
their religious and national feelings. He put on a white robe,
entered the Temple, and, from a golden throne raised on a platform, addressed the people. He was received with cheers. He
thanked his subjects for the respect they had paid to his father's
obsequies, and for their loyalty to him. He could exercise no
authority, he said, because it was for Caesar to ratify Herod's
dispositions. He should have stopped there. Unfortunately, he
went on to say that he had every intention of making a full return
to the army and citizens for their devotion as soon as he was
confirmed in his kingship; and that he would earnestly and constantly try to treat them better than his father had done.

Instinctively and instantly the crowd sized up their man; he
was "sucking up" to them, he was weak. The clamour broke out—
demands for the reduction of taxes, for the abolition of purchase
tax, for the liberation of prisoners. Archelaus lost his head, and
agreed to grant all these demands. He then sacrificed and went
home. The crowd did not. Encouraged, as a Palestine crowd
always is, by the slightest display of weakness, they decided to
exact still more concessions. A demonstration was arranged for
the evening. During the past week, everyone had been mourning
for Herod; now they would show that they could mourn for some
of Herod's victims. Shortly before the old king's death, a group of
young fanatics, egged on by some malignant Pharisees, had, in
broad daylight, burst into the Temple, and hacked down a golden
eagle which adorned one of the gates. The ringleaders had been
burned alive, and others executed. They were now hailed as
"martyrs". A choir, directed by a conductor, intoned a dirge,
while shrieking and lamentation resounded throughout the city.
Herod's favourites must go, they shouted, and first among them
the reigning High Priest, Joazar.

Archelaus was in a difficulty. He was anxious to get away to
Rome as soon as he could, preferably sooner than his rivals, in
order to have himself confirmed in his inheritance; but he could
not possibly appear before Augustus as the would-be guardian of
a realm he had left in chaos. He tried more appeasement. He sent
the Temple commandant to reason with the demonstrators.
They stoned him before he could speak, and others whom
Archelaus sent after him. The populace were now completely out
of hand. To make matters worse, Passover was approaching, and
worshippers were pouring into the City from all over Palestine.
The organizers of the demonstrations were there in the Temple,

recruiting many of the peasants into their ranks. Too late, Archelaus swerved to firmness. He sent a battalion into the Temple Area to arrest the ringleaders. Most of the soldiers were killed by the indignant mob, and the commanding officer was wounded and only just escaped with his life. The rioters, as though the incident had been no more than a trivial interruption, went on with the service. Archelaus now turned out the whole garrison. The infantry swept down from the upper citadel through the narrow streets, across the viaducts which spanned the Tyropoeon valley and into the Temple; the cavalry went round outside the walls, and attacked the defenceless peasants who were encamped in tents to the north of the city. The rioters were trapped, many of them while still at the altar. About 3,000 were killed. The remainder were now in no mood to resist the order to disperse.

So ended the first Passover of the new régime. It had shown two things, the incapacity of Archelaus, and the virulent fanaticism of a section of the Jews. There was, of course, bound to be a reaction after Herod's death; but it is possible that had Archelaus shown more firmness from the outset, less zest for seeking the favour of the mob even at the cost of denouncing his own father, the slaughter might have been avoided. As it was, blood had been shed, new "martyrs" created, and the first step taken on the tragic road which was to lead to the destruction of the Holy City seventy-four years later. For all demonstrations, whatever their pretext, are demonstrations against government, and government, in the Palestine of 4 B.C., meant Rome.

To Rome Archelaus must now hurry. With him, he would take his mother, the Samaritan Malthake, and Herod's trusted minister Ptolemy, who had read the will, and Nicolaus of Damascus, the brilliant advocate and historian, who had served his father for so long and had the advantage of being a personal friend of Augustus. Antipas, the full brother of Archelaus, was a disappointed man. When Archelaus and his half-brother Philip had been at school in Rome, Antipas, who was left behind, naturally thought that it was they, not he, who were being trained for at least a part of the succession. He had therefore worked against them, with such good success, that Herod's third will had named Antipas sole heir. Now, by the fourth and final testament, he was to be dispossessed. He decided to dispute the will. He, too, set out for Rome. He had with him another Ptolemy, brother of Nicolaus, and a lawyer called Irenaeus. His mother appears to have backed him against her elder son. Salome pretended that she did, too;

but that old vixen was no doubt determined that, if there was to be any intrigue going, she would be in on it, preferably with the help of her dear friend the empress Livia. Other members of the family went on the trip for the same reason; no one could tell what perquisites there might be, and it would be a pity to miss them.

Just as Archelaus was at last about to embark at Caesarea, there was a further hitch. Sabinus, the procurator-fiscal of Syria, that is the imperial finance officer for the Levant, arrived on his way to Judaea, where, with the unimaginative rapacity of his kind, he announced that he intended to take possession of the entire fortune of the late king. Fortunately, P. Quinctilius Varus, the Governor of Syria, was an old friend of the family, and he had married a great-niece of Augustus. Archelaus, through his minister Ptolemy, at once asked him to come down from Beirut. Varus vetoed Sabinus' proposed raid on the castles and their treasure, and the disappointed functionary had to promise to wait until Caesar's pleasure was known. But he stayed in Caesarea, and no sooner had Varus gone back to Syria and Archelaus set out for Rome than he broke his word and went up to Jerusalem, where he occupied the palace. He then summoned the governors of the various forts to hand over the keys, and called for the ledgers and inventories. Archelaus' officers refused to yield, cleverly objecting that they were responsible to Caesar rather than to Archelaus. And of course Sabinus wrote a despatch to Rome, in which he did his best to prejudice Archelaus' cause. The activities of this dingy bureaucrat were to have terrible consequences.

In Rome, the court must have awaited the arrival of Herod's family with mixed feelings, in which embarrassment prevailed. Herod, the old king, had been a popular figure in the capital. He was likeable and he was reliable. He had been the friend of Caesar, and of Caesar's great minister, Agrippa, after whom one of his grandsons, now a boy of six, had been named. Four of Herod's sons had been brought up in Rome, and a fifth had lived there. All of them had moved in the highest circles. That the three eldest had met their deaths at their father's hands would hardly be regarded as strange in the Rome of that epoch.

Nevertheless, the circumstances of their condemnation, the comings and goings and the recourse to Caesar had undoubtedly been a nuisance. Yet here, instead of just one man in dispute with his sons, was the whole family, women and all, come to air a family row before the emperor. It was not in good taste; but since the Levant was so important (and the family so very rich), it must be put up with, and some sort of settlement reached. Old Salome now showed her hand: she decided to back Antipas, her reason probably being that the rest of the family were clearly on his side, and that, if they could secure the break-up of the kingdom, the pickings would be considerable. So that is the line they took: what they wanted was "self-government within the empire", they said. Failing that, they wanted Antipas as king. Archelaus on the other hand had sent in all the official papers, and his father's signet ring, in the most correct order. What would be the outcome?

Augustus had read Sabinus' report, and also a despatch from Varus, supporting Archelaus. He now called a council, and listened to the rivals' speeches. Salome's son, Antipater, who inherited some of his mother's guile, accused his cousin of having really arrogated to himself kingly functions already: all Archelaus had now come to ask for was covering authority, the shadow, not the substance of royalty. It was making Caesar a mere dispenser of words. Then there was all that drinking, when he pretended to be mourning for his father. And look at the number of innocent people he had already massacred. What would he do when he became king indeed? The relations were called on to support this harangue, point by point.

Nicolaus, who knew the cold Augustus as well as most people, simply contented himself with a restatement of the legal position. As for those who had been killed, they had met their ends in rebellion against the imperial government. Josephus' description of the scene, with the rhetorical tirade on the part of the provincials, and its colourless rebuttal by the administration's attorney, recalls many a court of enquiry into later colonial disorders. Archelaus said nothing. He simply came forward and fell in silence at Caesar's knees. Augustus raised him up, saying that he thought he was worthy to succeed his father; but he gave no final decision.

Before he could do so, alarming news arrived in fresh despatches from Varus.

[*N. V. Uitgeversmaatschappij Elsevier.*]

6. The north-west corner of the Temple area from the east. This part of the great enclosure was created by hewing away the living rock, traces of which appear in the photograph, both on the ground, where it has been levelled, and on the right, behind the trees, where it was dressed to form the *podium* on which stood the Antonia, 370 feet long, with corner towers of which three were 75 feet high and the south-east over 100. The fortress completely dominated the Temple.

QUMRĀN

[Grollenberg.

7. This picture is taken from the *Wadi Qumrān*, facing east. It shews, in the middle of the "V", just to the right of the tents, the remains of the so-called "monastery", or settlement (page 35). The dark cliffs in the foreground contain some of the caves in which many of the famous Dead Sea Scrolls were found. Fragments were also recovered from a hiding-place on the outskirts of the settlement itself. Beyond the Dead Sea rise the mountains of Gilead, or Peraea. The Jordan enters at the

Chapter III

THE WAR OF VARUS

VARUS, knowing the temper of the Jews, had realized that the situation was bound to be tense; so, before returning to Antioch, he had gone up to Jerusalem, and had left there one of the three legions he had brought with him from Syria. It was Sabinus who caused the outbreak. Not only did he use Varus' legionaries as inquisitors into Herod's property, but he armed a servile rabble of his own, and sent them out to seize what they could get hold of. The Feast of Pentecost, which fell that year on May 30th, was now imminent, and the Holy City was filling yet again with peasants from all the surrounding districts. Passover should have been a warning; but Sabinus disregarded it. He soon found himself and his troops besieged, the Jews having formed three camps, one on the north of the Temple, one on the south near the hippodrome, and a third on the west, just below the Palace. Sabinus was terrified. He was cut off from his troops, who occupied the barracks in the Antonia. He sent relays of messengers to Varus in distant Antioch. Worn down by the strain of waiting, he lost his nerve, and from the battlements of Phasael, the tower which dominated the citadel and the town, he signalled to the troops in the Antonia to attack the Temple. The soldiers omitted the first precaution necessary for quelling a riot in the Levant: they failed to occupy the roofs, which, being flat and continuous, form an ideal *place d'armes* for rioters. The insurgents ran along the tops of the Temple porticoes, raining missiles on the legionaries below. In desperation, the Romans set fire to them. The cedar wood, incrusted with gilded wax bas-reliefs, went up in flames. The improvised garrison were burnt to death, or fell upon the swords of the waiting soldiery. The treasury lay open. The soldiers helped themselves, and Sabinus was later reported to have secured £20,000 sterling. But he could not escape: he was still a prisoner in the palace.

The Jews were now determined and furious. The country fell to pieces; many of the local troops, even Herod's veterans, went over to the insurgents, except for the Sebastenians, that is battalions raised from the predominantly Greek population of the city of

Samaria-Sebaste, one of Herod's greatest creations. Rufus commanded the cavalry, and Gratus the infantry, each of whom, says Josephus, "was worth an army". Achiab, Herod's cousin, withdrew some of the loyal troops to safe positions in the hills. In the south, the north and the west the rebellion burned. A certain Judas, son of a brigand patriot whom Herod as a young man had executed, now sought revenge, and made himself master of Sepphoris, the capital of Galilee and an important arsenal. Simon, a burly royal slave from east of Jordan, attacked Jericho and would have looted the whole town, had not Gratus chased him off and killed him. Another body of insurgents from Peraea sacked Betharamtha, the farm colony at the foot of Mount Nebo. Finally, a sort of pseudo-Maccabee arose in the person of a shepherd called Athronges, who proclaimed himself king, and, together with his four brothers, organized regular commandos. They were so successful that they did not all capitulate until some time after the restoration of regular government.

This task fell to Varus. To rescue his beleaguered legion, he brought down with him from Syria his remaining two. He picked up another 1,500 auxiliaries at Beirut, and concentrated at Acre. Here he was joined by King Harith of Petra, interested, as the event quickly showed, less in the restoration of law and order than in the acquisition of loot. Varus acted briskly. Sending his second in command to subdue Sepphoris and to sell its rebellious citizens as slaves, he himself pushed on to Samaria, the citadel of Herodian loyalty. Harith took the opportunity to sack the two neighbouring villages of Haris and Safa, the former of which belonged to Ptolemy the chancellor, by way of getting his own back, if not on Herod, at least on his friends. Emmaus, where a Roman column had been cut to pieces by Athronges, was burned by Varus' orders. The two main roads to Jerusalem from the north and the west now lay open. At the approach of the legions, the commandos encamped round the city dispersed, and the inhabitants within took the very sensible and convenient line that they had been coerced by the rebels and were really on the side of the Romans. This was no doubt arranged by Joseph, Herod's nephew, who, in the absence of both Archelaus and (as will shortly appear) Philip as well, seems to have taken over the direction of affairs. The besieged legion together with Rufus and Gratus and the loyal Herodian troops met Varus outside the walls. The miserable Sabinus had slunk off to the coast, to be heard of no more. The ringleaders were soon rounded up, some imprisoned, and 2,000 crucified. Harith and his raiders were sent home. Achiab, Herod's cousin, negotiated the surrender of the 10,000 rebels, the hard core of the whole movement, who were still in arms in the south. Varus detained only the leaders, who were sent to Rome for trial, where Caesar pardoned all of them except those of Herod's family. It would never do to condone that sort of treason, which was ultimately a treason against Rome itself, so these few, but no others, were punished.

Thus ended the campaign. Considered purely as a military operation, it was brilliantly thought out, and speedily finished. Nevertheless the brutal toll of 2,000 crosses must chill our admiration; and it is not surprising that in Jewish eyes "the war of Varus" was to rank with the tyranny of Antiochus Epiphanes, and the invasion of Pompey, who had captured Jerusalem in 63 B.C.

Meanwhile, the political future of the country was being determined in Rome. Augustus had clearly been undecided how to dispose of Herod's dominions, and it was largely this indecision which had generated the disturbances. Augustus was partly to blame. Herod's death had come as no surprise, and Augustus was personally acquainted with both Archelaus and Philip. Neither time nor data had been lacking. His vacillation had placed him in a quandary. For, in addition to the various family claimants already in Rome, a deputation of fifty Jewish notables from Jerusalem now arrived. As a counterweight, Varus, always a friend of the Herods, sent Philip along with an escort to support his brother, and also, at least in Philip's view, to collect anything that might come his way.

The emperor received the parties in the new temple of Apollo on the Palatine, the sumptuousness of which must have reminded the Jews of their own great Temple. On one side were Archelaus, Philip and their supporters, on the other the fifty deputies. Salome and the rest of the family decided not to take sides, but to be ready to jump into the arms of the winner at the right moment. The fifty deputies were not alone. They were supported by 8,000 Jews of Rome. This fact has a twofold significance. In the first place it shows how large the Roman Jewish community had already become, and, in the second, how ready they were to appear before Caesar himself, in opposition to Caesar's friends and at the risk of incurring Caesar's displeasure, when it was a question of standing up for what they considered to be the rights of their brethren in Jerusalem and their holy religion. Once again, the delegation burst into a rambling tirade against Herod and

Archelaus—the forerunner of countless petitions and telegrams denouncing to the world at large the Palestine government of a later date. The gist of the demands was that the kingdom should be abolished and that Judaea should either become part of Roman Syria, or an autonomous region attached to it. Once again, Nicolaus calmly demolished the frothy contentions of his opponents, vindicating the actions of both Herod and Archelaus.

Augustus dismissed the assembly. He decided on a compromise. Palestine was to be partitioned. Archelaus was to keep Samaria, Judaea and Idumaea, that is the trunk of Herod's kingdom. He was to be called ethnarch only, ruler of the people, with the promise that he would be granted the title of king if he showed himself worthy of it. The remainder, about half of the total, was to be divided between Archelaus' full brother, Antipas, and his half-brother Philip. Antipas was to have Galilee, but without any access to the Mediterranean, and also Peraea, the fertile strip to the east of the Jordan. Philip received Batanaea, Trachonitis and Auranitis, that is the territory at the foot of Mt. Hermon and what is now the Hauran. Both were to be called tetrarchs. Salome was not forgotten. She received, in accordance with Herod's will, Jamnia and Azotus, on the southern coast of Palestine, and Phasaelis, at the foot of the Alexandrium in the Jordan valley, but administratively her holdings were to form part of Archelaus' territory. Augustus added the palace at Ascalon, an independent city, which Herod had bequeathed to him. The rest of the Herodian royal family received between them the half million sterling which Herod had left to Augustus. The emperor kept only a few works of art as a memento of his old friend. The Greek cities of Gadara and Hippos in the Decapolis and Gaza on the coast were detached altogether, and placed under the governor of Syria.

What had led Augustus to make this settlement? He must have realized that it was unsatisfactory and could not prove permanent. True, the fragmentation of territory, the allocation to Antipas of two regions which had no common frontier, and to Salome territories which were widely separated from each other did not matter: since client kingdoms and principalities were regarded as estates bestowed by the emperor, there was no more reason why they should form one territorial unit than the estates of a feudal duke, which they in many ways resembled. Nevertheless, there must have been some basic reason for the decision to disrupt a kingdom which during Herod's life had served Roman ends so well.

It appears to have been the following. Archelaus was a weakling: he had already shown it. Philip and Antipas were far more reliable, as they were to prove. But to give the whole kingdom, in its present mood, to any one of the three would be to provoke perpetual squabbles, and might, if the ruler lent his ear to nationalists, provoke yet another war. It would also exasperate Harith of Petra. At the same time, to annex the kingdom altogether would certainly cause strife, and that would imperil the frontier. For it was in terms of the frontier that the affairs of the Levant had always to be weighed. Rome never beat the Parthians. Parthia had beaten Rome, and although, in the torrent of praise which flowed from the pens of the court poets, the disgrace of Carrhae was officially deemed to have been washed away, it remained raw and angry in the heart of every Roman. The surest way to prevent the legions being once more humbled by the lords of the east was to ensure that they never met them. Thus, a collision-mat of buffer states was erected along the eastern marches. In the north, from the Crimean Bosporus, through Pontus, Armenia, Cappadocia, Cilicia and Commagene, to the shores of the Mediterranean, the line of client kingdoms stretched. Judaea and Arabia formed its south-east bastion. Only in the middle, where the desert intervened, and the immense riches of Syria proved irresistibly alluring, was direct rule imposed. To maintain this sheath of security on the eastern wall of the Mediterranean was therefore Augustus' prime object. A secondary one was to obviate a clash with the irreconcilable nationalism of at least a majority of the inhabitants of Judaea. The next century was to realize the achievement of the first but failure to attain the second.

In the actual allocation of territories, Nicolaus of Damascus no doubt had a large share; indeed, in one of the few fragments of his own memoirs which has come down to us directly, he describes the settlement and tells us that it was by his advice that Archelaus did not press for the retention of the Greek cities, which had for long chafed under what was to them an alien rule. Nicolaus was now sixty, and felt he would like to retire. He stayed on in Rome, loaded with honours by Augustus, whose biography he was to write. But we are the losers, because no longer could Josephus, our chief authority, make use of Nicolaus' history of his time, which had provided such a detailed account of the days of Herod. Henceforth, until we reach Josephus' own day—he was born in A.D. 37—our information is thin and scrappy.

The three brothers, Archelaus, Antipas and Philip, returned to a pacified Palestine. The "gentle-mannered" Varus, their old family friend, had returned to Antioch. He shortly afterwards left Syria, where, despite his nice manners, he had, so Velleius Paterculus tells us (II, 117), done very well for himself: "He entered a rich country as a poor man and as a rich man left a poor country." Varus appears in history only once more, ten years later, when he achieved a melancholy immortality as the general commanding a Roman army which was annihilated by the Germans. He committed suicide. It was the greatest, almost the only, military reverse of the Augustan age. When the news was told to the aging emperor he was heard to cry out, as he walked in the night alone: "Quinctilius Varus! give me back my legions."

Even now, the troubles attending the succession were not over. There was to be a curious Perkin Warbeck-like interlude. A young Jew, who had been brought up by a Roman freedman in Sidon, happened to bear some facial resemblance to Alexander, one of Herod's two sons by Mariamme the first, whom the old King had put to death three years before, in 7 B.C. The likeness was exploited by an unscrupulous intriguer, also a Jew, whose name we do not know. This rogue induced the young man to give out that both he, Alexander, and Aristobulus, his brother, had really not been executed at all, but smuggled out of the country alive. The imposture caught on among the local Jewish community, for whom Mariamme, as a Hasmonaean princess, and a woman of peerless beauty and purity killed by the Idumaean usurper, possessed a sentimental glory akin to that which, with less justice, Mary Queen of Scots was to hold for her doting countrymen in a later age. The pseudo-Alexander and his artful manager set out for Crete, where again the Jews rallied to him, and provided him with funds. From Crete they went to Melos, where the community proved even more lucratively gullible. Finally, he arrived, with high hopes, in Rome, where his fellow-Jews escorted him through the streets, carried in a litter, and adorned with the insignia of royalty. These proceedings came to the ears of Augustus. He knew Herod too well to suppose he would have made any mistake in so important a matter as the execution of his own children. He sent Celadus, one of his freedmen who had known the young men when they were in Rome, to bring the alleged Alexander before him. Celadus appears to have been deceived, but not so Caesar. He at once saw that the man was no gently-nurtured prince, but a horny-handed yokel. He asked him where Aristobulus was, to which the youth and his promoter both insisted on replying that he had been left in Cyprus, in case anything happened to the claimant—hardly a tactful excuse to make to the fountain of justice. Caesar then spoke to the lad in private, and told him that he would spare his life if he would say who he really was, and unmask the originator of the whole silly plot, because it was obvious that it must be the work of some older men. The youth confessed. He was sent to the galleys, where his strength would be put to good use. His exploiter was executed. The Jews of Melos were considered to have been punished enough already by their own credulity.

The story is significant, both as a tribute to Caesar's sagacity, and as showing the pathetic longing of the Jews, even of the Dispersion, and even thus early, that a ruler should arise from among their own people and from their own princes.

Chapter IV

ETHNARCH AND TETRARCHS

ON their return to Palestine, each of the three brothers adopted the family name "Herod", much to the confusion of the readers of the Gospels (see Tables I and II). But only Archelaus was entitled to add *ethnarch*. This title had been bestowed forty-three years before on Hyrcanus II, the last of the Hasmonaean priest-kings, by Julius Caesar, which was no doubt why Augustus now revived it. Julius Caesar had also granted to Antipater, Archelaus' grandfather, the coveted honour of Roman citizenship, which had descended to his heirs. They were members of Caesar's own *gens*, or clan, and were entitled to use the *Julian* name. Archelaus' full name therefore was Julius Herodes Archelaus. The title *tetrarch*, now conferred upon Antipas and Philip, originally denoted the ruler of a fourth part; but, just as our English word "quarter" has come to mean not necessarily one of four parts but any region or locality, so tetrarch came to mean a minor ruler, whether he had a chief or not. Here again, Augustus was reverting to precedent, because in 41 B.C., during the Second Triumvirate, Mark Antony had appointed Herod the Great and his brother Phasael tetrarchs. Financially, Archelaus was both a gainer and a loser. The revenues of Herod the Great had amounted to about half a million sterling—the revenues of his kingdom, that is: his private fortune was far greater. The total available to the three successors was £50,000 less, the diminution being caused by the separation of the three Greek cities, and Salome's inheritance. Archelaus, it is true, had the largest share, but it was only £300,000. Antipas received £100,000 a year, and Philip £50,000.

Of the three brothers, Philip is by far the most attractive character. But we know almost nothing about him. He was quiet, efficient and conscientious. He was in many ways, in fact, the prototype of the best sort of British colonial district commissioner. Instead of gadding to Rome or Beirut, like so many of his family, he lived in his own little principality. He would go on official tours with a modest staff, taking with him a portable judgment-seat. Whenever anyone came forward with a complaint or request,

Philip set up his court there and then, and gave his verdict on the spot. He brought to heel the chief of the Babylonian Jewish settlement which his father had installed in the Hauran, to protect the inhabitants from raids by their eastern neighbours. The Jewish military colony had been practically independent and tax-free. Philip by tact and firmness brought it under control without difficulty. There were no large towns in his tetrarchy. The temple which his father had built above one of the springs of the Jordan, at Panias, on the southern skirt of Mount Hermon, had already made it an important centre. Philip now enlarged it into a city, and called it Caesarea, after his patron. This is the Caesarea Philippi (as distinct from the great Caesarea on the sea coast) of the Gospels. The temple, with its four-columned portico, of glistening white stone, was a conspicuous monument. Philip was very proud of it, and put it on his coins. This caused no offence, because, although the temple was dedicated to Caesar, the great majority of Philip's subjects, it must be remembered, were pagans. He also enlarged another town at the north-east end of the Sea of Galilee, Bethsaida, which, in honour of Augustus' daughter, he called Julias. (The western shore belonged to Antipas, and the southern part of the east shore was divided between the Greek towns of Hippos and Gadara.) This must have been early in his reign, before Julia's disgrace and banishment in 2 B.C. Philip ruled his little principality for thirty-eight years, until his death in A.D. 34. He was soon forgotten, for though he had been married, he had no children to bear his name after him. His wife was a niece of his, such a union not being within the degrees of kinship forbidden by Leviticus and Deuteronomy (see Appendix I). She was called, after her great-aunt, Salome, and it is she, not her obscure and blameless husband, who is remembered, in splendid infamy, until this day (see Plate 16).

Archelaus, with his diminished kingdom and diminished revenue, should have done all in his power to re-establish tranquil government, to restore his realm so recently ravaged by war. He should have turned his back on personal pride and grandeur, in favour of sound and economical administration. If only he had been his brother Philip! Unfortunately, he had already proved himself to have inherited all the worst of his father's traits, the cruelty and the vainglory, without any of the charm and finesse which made Herod great. Instead of caring for his impoverished people, whom he had already done so much to harm, he spent large sums on rebuilding the Jericho palaces, which Simon had recently destroyed, on an even more magnificent scale than before (see Plate I). He then decided to enlarge his farms and groves. Salome had inherited Phasaelis, the agricultural settlement below the Alexandrium; so Archelaus laid out another between it and Jericho, at what is now the village of al-'Auja al Tahta. He called it after his own name, Archelais, and in the mosaic map on the floor of the Greek Orthodox church at Madeba, east of Jordan, which shows Palestine as it was in the fifth century, both Jericho and Archelais appear as flourishing and important localities. To increase the water available for the irrigation of his private groves, Archelaus appropriated half of the supply from a neighbouring village, an arbitrary piece of brigandage which must have ruined a number of his subjects. To the generality of townsmen and artisans, the cessation of the grand programme of public works started by his father Herod must have brought impoverishment and discontent.

It was clear that such a ruler would not qualify for the title of king, which he had been promised if he proved worthy of it. In addition, he was vindictive and revengeful. The parable of Luke xix, 12-27 is a clear reference to Archelaus, the opposition which he aroused and the ruthlessness with which he repressed it. And it was fear of Archelaus that caused Joseph to return from Egypt to Galilee without passing through Judaea (Matthew ii, 22).

The end was precipitated by his deposition of the High Priest Joazar, in whose room Archelaus appointed his brother, the silly pretext being that Joazar had sided with the insurgents, as though the brother-in-law of Herod the Great could have done any such thing (see page 38). The discarded pontiff and the extremists —now his allies—naturally sought an opportunity of revenge, and Archelaus provided them with an impeccable one. He was married to a certain Mariamme, probably a cousin, but is not known to have had any children by her. During a visit to the court of King Archelaus of Cappadocia, in what is now eastern Turkey, after whom he was named, he fell violently in love with Glaphyra, the king's daughter. This princess had first of all been married to Alexander, Herod's son by Mariamme. After his execution, she had married Juba II, the learned king of Mauretania in North Africa (whose first wife was Selene, daughter of Antony and Cleopatra). He later repudiated her. She was still young and attractive; but, by Jewish law, Archelaus might not marry her, because she had been his brother's wife, and had borne

Alexander three children. The law of the Levirate, as defined in Deuteronomy xxv, permits the marriage of a brother's wife only when the brother has died without issue, in which case it enjoins it solely for the purpose of raising up an heir to the dead brother, whose child the firstborn of the second union was deemed to be (see Appendix I). Nevertheless, Archelaus now divorced Mariamme and took Glaphyra to wife. She died soon after, reclaimed it was said by Alexander, who in a dream had reproached her for her infidelity.

Finally, in A.D. 6, Archelaus achieved the well-nigh unique distinction of uniting both Jews and Samaritans, who jointly denounced him to Caesar. The grounds of the accusation were that he had transgressed the injunctions of Caesar, in maltreating his subjects, and that he was morally reprobate. Augustus was very angry. He had known, of course, for some time that affairs were not going well in Palestine. Besides, he did not like the country or its people. He and his empress had presented vases to the Temple, and he had endowed a daily sacrifice therein. But that was a political move designed to enhance his own prestige. Nine years earlier, his grandson and heir, Caius, the child of his devoted minister Agrippa and his daughter Julia, then aged twenty, had visited the Levant, and, fired by the history of the Arabs which Juba had dedicated to him, may have contemplated a campaign against Arabia Felix or even the Nabataeans. On his way from Egypt to Parthia and Armenia (where he was to meet his death by treachery), Caius could easily have visited Jerusalem, as his father had done; but Augustus commended the young man for not doing so. The prattle of little Syrian and Moorish boys diverted the emperor's leisure hours; but he was never drawn to Jewry, and least of all to Archelaus. Herod had showered a thousand flattering attentions and presents on Augustus: the next generation seemed to neglect him.

When therefore the joint denunciation was delivered to Augustus he decided to put an end to a régime which had proved such a failure. He disdained to write to Archelaus. He summoned his chargé d'affaires in Rome, who was also called Archelaus, and curtly ordered him to go and bring his master to court. The messenger hurried away to Judaea, and arrived to find the ethnarch feasting with his friends. From the banquet Archelaus was hustled off to the waiting ship. He never returned to Palestine. Men remembered later that he had had a strange dream just before the débâcle, which had been interpreted, correctly as it proved, by Simon the Essene, as foretelling the end of his reign. Caesar, after a brief investigation, exiled Archelaus to Vienne, on the Rhône, the capital of the Allobroges. His fortune was confiscated. Eight years later he was dead.

It appears from a reference in Strabo that Antipas and Philip were also arraigned at the same time as Archelaus, but that they managed to clear themselves, and to return to their tetrarchies. Had Aunt Salome a finger in the plot? It seems probable that she had, and that for the last time this greedy and mischievous old woman successfully intrigued to enrich herself at the expense of her relations; because we find her inheriting Archelaus' new palm-groves, which so conveniently rounded off her own estate at Phasaelis.

The experiment had failed. Augustus was now an old man— he was nearly seventy—and disinclined to risk further innovations, particularly in an area so restless and so vital to Rome's security as Palestine. Direct administration seemed to be the only course open to the great administrator. Why, it might be asked, when Archelaus proved a failure, could not one of his tetrarch brothers be installed in his place? The answer is two-fold. First, whichever brother Augustus appointed would be the object of intrigues by the other, and Augustus had put up long enough with the bickerings of this singularly disunited family. Secondly, he trusted neither of them—they had come under suspicion equally with the now exiled ethnarch. And in this very year there occurred a serious revolt in Dalmatia and Pannonia, accompanied by a wholesale massacre of Roman residents, which seemed at one time to threaten Italy itself. For a moment it threw Augustus off his balance—it looked like Hannibal all over again. The danger was overcome; but such an event in the west must have made the emperor more than ever resolved to play for security in the east. So Judaea must, at long last, become a province.   *AD6*

Chapter V

THE ROMAN PROVINCE

THE Roman provincial empire had grown up, as the British was later to grow, piecemeal. In the latter part of the third century B.C., Rome had annexed first Sicily, then Sardinia and Corsica. Soon afterwards the legions occupied part of modern Spain, Northern Africa (after the fall of Carthage in 146 B.C.), Macedonia, part of Asia Minor and southern Gaul. Expansion, once started, continued by "manifest destiny", accelerated by the campaigns of the great *conquistadores*, Pompey and Julius Caesar, until, at the beginning of Augustus' régime, the territories subject to Roman rule comprised practically the whole of the known and lucrative areas within reach of the Mediterranean sea. Broadly speaking, the boundaries were the Rhine, the Danube, and the Black Sea in the north, the Red Sea, upper Egypt and the Sahara in the south, and the Atlantic and the English Channel in the west. Before Augustus, there was no regular or uniform provincial administration. The word "province" originally meant simply "assignment"—it might be a war or a government. Gradually it came to mean the government of a territory, and so that territory itself. These early provincial governments were constituted just as early British ones were to be—by edicts of the annexing general. Gradually a pattern of administration emerges, and by the time of Sulla, aristocrats who had held high office— again the English analogy holds—were sent out at regular intervals to govern provinces. Not seldom these men enriched themselves rapidly and shamelessly at the expense of their provincial subjects. Here the British have undoubtedly a better record than their Roman prototypes. In English history, pillage of provincials by colonial governors has been rare; among Roman republican governors it was the rule.

Augustus was the grandson of a banker, and he realized that a sound financial system must be the core of his imperial creation. And here we come to the two respects in which the Roman system differed from British: first, the Roman provinces were regarded not as trust territories, to become eventually self-governing sovereign states within or outside the empire, but as for ever and increasingly part of Rome's patrimony. Secondly, instead of being encouraged to improve their economic resources for their own benefit, entitled, like a modern British colony, to call upon the mother country for monetary help in welfare, development and cultural amenities, the Roman provinces were expected to pay tribute to Rome. Only a few favoured cities would be exempted; they were either old Greek foundations or restorations, by Romans for Romans. These little Romes overseas were called *colonies*—only to them was the word applied.

An efficient financial organization demanded an efficient system of control; and that was what Augustus set out to create. First of all, he rationalized frontiers and divisions, so that by the end of his career, counting the territories, of which Egypt was the most important, acquired during his reign, there were twenty-four or twenty-five provinces of the empire. Of these, he left under Senatorial control the richer and more settled ones, eleven in number. They needed no garrisons, and continued to be governed by ex-consuls or ex-praetors—*proconsuls*, as they all came to be called. The remaining provinces (with the exception of Egypt, for which the emperor devised a special régime, allowing no senator or knight to enter it without a visa), were governed by officers who were *delegated* by Augustus himself, and so were known generally as *legates*. These legates were members of the Senate, often ex-consuls. Thirdly, some of the smaller, less important, provinces were entrusted to men of an humbler order, the *knights*. These men were civil servants, who won promotion not by birth but by efficiency. They were known as *procurators*, or stewards. Judaea (by which is meant the whole ethnarchy of Archelaus) now became one of these third-class, procuratorial provinces. (Among the others were Corsica, Sardinia, the two Mauretanias in North Africa and Epirus, in Greece.)

"The salient fact," says Abel, "of the period of sixty years which followed the census of Quirinius is the maintenance in Judaea, except for an interval of three years, of a province of the third rank, founded in the year 6 and entrusted to a Roman procurator. Philip and Antipas continued to enjoy their tetrarchies, the former for twenty-eight years, the latter for thirty-three. Their remains later served to constitute the kingdom of their nephew Agrippa I, with the annexation thereto, for the term of three years, of the procurators' domain. His son, Agrippa II, had to be content with Philip's tetrarchy, enlarged by the Abilene of Lysanias, and three good cities of Galilee and Peraea."

As Abel adds, the fact that this was the political setting of the
Gospels and the Acts of the Apostles bestows on it an interest and
a fame which live to this day. It will be helpful, therefore, to
examine it in some detail. Just how was this province organized?

First of all, the capital of Judaea was no longer Jerusalem.
The new province was administered from Caesarea. From this
largely pagan and wholly princely seaport the procurator could
maintain communications by ship both with Rome and with
neighbouring provinces, particularly with Syria; for, although the
procurator was autonomous within his own frontiers, and
although his territory was separated from the province of Syria
by Galilee, which formed part of the tetrarchy of Antipas, it was
to the governor of Syria, with his three Roman legions, that the
procurator of Judaea must turn for advice and support in times of
stress. Caesarea, being a predominantly Hellenistic city, allowed
the expatriate Roman officials and their families to enjoy their
own way of life without constraint. There were no tiresome,
cramping traditions to be respected, because the city had been the
new and splendid creation of Herod the Great, who had designed
it as a gentile town, and had named it after his friend and patron
Augustus Caesar. Naturally, following precedent when other
client kingdoms had become provinces, the palace which Herod
had built for himself now became the residence of the procurator.
That is why in Acts xxiii, 35, we read that Paul was ordered to be
kept "in Herod's judgment hall" or *praetorium*. When, as for
instance on the occasion of a great feast such as Passover, the
procurator went up to Jerusalem so as to be on hand in case of
any disturbances, here, too, it was in Herod's palace that he and
his staff and suite found ample accommodation. This stood at the
western extremity of the Holy City, just inside what is now the
Jaffa Gate, and so afforded comfort and reasonable seclusion,
besides secure communication with the road to Caesarea. It was a
vast and sumptuous *Serai*, with barracks, and banqueting-halls,
baths and gardens within its massive walls. Down by the Temple,
and commanding it from the north-west corner, stood the castle
of Antonia, where Herod had lived for a time before he built his
new palace. This had thereafter become a purely military establishment, and remained one now. Was the judgment hall in which
Pilate condemned Jesus in the Palace or the Antonia? We may be
quite positive that it was in one or the other, but we cannot be
sure in which. Not even the learned Dominicans agree on this
question. Some of them, with Abel, relying on the testimony of

two contemporary authors, Philo and Josephus, hold that in the time of Pilate and of Gessius Florus (A.D. 66) the judgment hall was in the western palace. Vincent, their doyen, fortified by the remarkable *Gabbatha* or pavement (John xix, 13) recently brought to light beneath the Antonia, holds that it was there that the judgment took place (see Plate 5).

It was certainly in the Antonia that the procurator's garrison was housed, because there are many references in Josephus to its presence there. It was from the Antonia, too, that the soldiers came who rescued Paul from the violence of the mob (Acts xxi, 31). The procurator had no legions under his command, that is, no regular imperial troops, only auxiliaries. The Jews were exempt from military service, in accordance with a decree of Julius Caesar. (They made good soldiers, and individual Jews had risen to high rank under the Ptolemies, but their dietary rules and their dogged respect for the Sabbath made it impossible to integrate them in a pagan army.) Caesarea and Sebaste, Herod's other new Hellenistic foundation, built on the long-desolate site of ancient Samaria, provided plenty of pagan recruits, who were known generally as Sebastenians. As we have seen (page 14), this corps existed under Herod the Great, when it was commanded by Rufus and Gratus. It was about 3,000 strong. In the days of the procurators it was divided into five cohorts of 500 men each with a wing of cavalry of the same strength. It is natural to suppose that the *Augustan* cohort, one of whose centurions accompanied Paul to Italy (Acts xxvii, 1), was part of the Sebastenian regiment, *Sebaste* being the Greek for *Augusta*. That there were other troops in the country besides the Sebastenians is to be inferred from the mention of the Italian cohort in Acts x, 1; this cohort is mentioned also in an inscription from Philadelphia, but we know nothing of its identity. The normal garrison would be one cohort and a detachment of cavalry. The contingent which accompanied the procurator when he came to Jerusalem, "the soldiers of the governor" of Matthew xxvii, 27, so called to distinguish them from the resident troops, numbered about 200, including cavalry, and they lodged with the rest of the suite at the western palace.

Such was the armed strength that sustained the civil administration of the province. The procurator was the delegate of the *Princeps*, and as such shared in his *imperium* or authority. He was thus, for his subjects, the supreme fountain of justice, though in practice he took cognizance only of exceptional cases, whether civil or criminal. The empire, far more than the republic, took

pains to respect the local customs and codes, not only of its "free"
cities such as those of the Decapolis and its "colonies" such as
Beirut, but even of its subject regions. In Judaea, therefore, under
the Roman domination, we find the *Sanhedrin*, which, modelled
on the *synedrion*, or assembly, of the Greeks, had under the
Hasmonaeans become the supreme judicial and legislative body of
the Jews, once again—for under Herod it had been "purged" and
reduced to obsequious impotence—erected into vigorous pre-
eminence. The High Priest presided over the court, which had
full authority in civil and criminal cases. It possessed its own police
and could order arrests. It could even go so far as to find a Jew
worthy of death, but the actual *sentence* of death had to be pro-
nounced by the procurator. It was carried out by his soldiers,
generally by the *speculatores* or scouts of the praetorian guard, who
were armed with lances. That they were so armed at the Crucifixion of Jesus we know from John xix, 34. Over Roman citizens,
too, the procurator had judicial power; but, as in the famous
case of St Paul, it was always open to them to appeal to Caesar
(Acts xxv, 11), whereupon the procurator was bound to suspend
the proceedings.

The prime function of the provinces, in the eyes of their masters,
was to pay tribute to Rome. In every province, therefore, there
was an imperial finance officer. In the senatorial provinces he was
a *quaestor*, on the proconsul's staff, and he was responsible to the
public treasury. In the imperial provinces the finance officer was
answerable to Augustus alone. He, too, was called a procurator,
and it was his duty to see that the tribute was collected. To this
category of officials the lamentable Sabinus belonged. Even in
client kingdoms, or in any part of the empire where the emperor
had personal interests, his financial procurator would be found.

The inevitable corollary of this system was an accurate assessment of taxable income and of those who paid it; and whenever
the Romans took over a new province, they held a census. Such a
census was held in Judaea, when it in its turn became a province.
As St Luke tells us (ii, 1-5) this took place in the days when
Quirinius was legate of Syria. He says it was the "first census",
and so it was—of Judaea as a Roman province. But he also associ-
ates it with a census held at the time of our Lord's birth, which
took place in 5 B.C. As Abel has shown (*Histoire de la Palestine*,
Tome I, pp. 414 et seq.), there is good reason to suppose that
Sabinus had intended to make a new assessment as a prelude to
annexation, and by installing himself in the royal palace he may

already have seen himself as the first procurator of the new province. The governor of Syria at this time was not *Quirinius*, but, as we have seen, P. *Quinctilius* Varus, who would probably be known by the Greeks, and even more by the inhabitants of the country who rarely concede to anyone, especially a stranger, more than one name, as Quinctilius. In later recollection the two names, and the two similar censuses, may well have become confused.

The financial duties of the procurator included the collection of the taxes. These were, first, a land-tax, *tributum soli*, tribute of the soil, or, for those who possessed property other than land, *tributum capitis*, tribute of the head. This was the *tribute*, properly so called, and it was this which had to be paid to the Roman tax-collector, in the Roman coin bearing the effigy of the Roman emperor, in harsh contrast to the shekels and half-shekels, bearing Hebrew inscriptions and Jewish emblems, in which the Temple dues were paid. Then there was the *annona*, an annual contribution in corn and cattle which went to help feed the troops; for, though the Jews were exempt from military service, they were as liable as their Gentile fellow-subjects to contribute to its maintenance. Sales-tax, Customs dues, fees on the freeing of slaves, concessions for the use of public properties, exploitation of salt and such like—all these, being in principle exacted from everyone, and not, like the tribute, only from subject provincials, were known as the *publicum*. These taxes were farmed by companies of capitalists known as *publicani*, and the name of *publican* was handed on to their unpopular subordinates, the majority of whom, to judge by the story of Zacchaeus (Luke xix, 1-10: cf. xviii, 9-14, and from other sources) were Jews. Taken all in all, the sum of these exactions must have weighed heavily on the inhabitants of the new province, for in A.D. 17, only eleven years after its constitution, they complained, so Tacitus tells us, together with the people of Syria about their burdens to Tiberius. "To tax and to please, no more than to love and to be wise, is not given to men." The taxes were onerous; but it was the tribute that stung, because that was the brand of servitude, and the Jews were convinced that in reality, whatever appearances might be, they were the free people of God.

Chapter VI

HALF SLAVE AND HALF FREE

TAXES were the price of peace, and most men knew that peace was worth paying for, that it was the supreme good. Throughout the Roman world, therefore, the *imperium*, the authority of Rome, was accepted and indeed welcomed. Everywhere except in one small third-rate province: Judaea. Here, as the events recorded in the foregoing chapters have already shown, there was a fundamental restlessness, a basic malaise, which manifested itself in periodic outbursts against Rome and all things Roman. Again and again Rome would try to establish an understanding with the Jews, and on each occasion there would not be lacking Jews, men of principle and integrity, to reciprocate Gentile goodwill. But in the end the breach widened until it became an abyss which engulfed the whole of Jewry. What was the reason for this tragic decline? Why could not Jews be the same as others? Must they, even in their relations with Rome, be different?

The answer is that they must.

In an age when certain standards have for long been accepted as those which should govern society, it is hard, almost impossible, to imagine an era when these same standards were to the world at large unknown, when they were, in fact, the possession of an insignificant minority, called Jews. These Jews were in many respects like other dwellers in the Levant. As with their Syrian neighbours, while the bulk of the people were small farmers, many of them were traders, and had established themselves in Egypt, in Asia, and, as we have seen, in Rome itself. But they kept themselves to themselves. They were conscious of being different from other men. They were also conscious of being better than other men. In fact, if they observed their own proclaimed rules of conduct, they were. The Jews regulated their lives by a Law, which was ascribed to a single lawgiver, Moses (though it had, in fact, like most other codes, been evolved stratum by stratum), and by the teachings of certain Prophets. In its most condensed form, the Law is expressed in the Ten Commandments, though it had been elaborated so as to cover such diverse matters as, for instance, the digging of latrines by troops on active service, and the provision of safety-parapets on flat roofs. Decent Gentiles would have found themselves in agreement with many of these rules, though their own official law, particularly in the matter of the preservation of human life, would be far less humane; and many might read with admiration the sublime visions and admonitions of the Prophets. But to the majority the first three of the Ten Commandments would have seemed ridiculous and indeed blasphemous. Who were these Jews to claim that their god was not only better than anyone else's, but was the only God there was? Such a claim was outrageous: it implied that all the gods of Egypt, of Greece, of Asia and of Rome were phantoms, their images impostures, their temples empty sheds. That is precisely the claim which the Jews made. Later, it was to be vitally reinforced by Christianity and staunchly reaffirmed by Islam, until it has become generally accepted throughout the greater part of the world. It forms the moral atmosphere of civilized society.

There lies the fundamental difference between our days and those. Now, the great majority of Jews, spread over the face of the globe, live free and honourable lives among communities which, although Gentile, refer their conduct to much the same standards of conduct as their Jewish fellow-citizens. There is thus no need for separatism, and only a very small minority of world Jewry now chooses to live in self-imposed segregation in the Levant. In antiquity, it was the other way round: the majority lived in Palestine, and only minorities in the various Gentile lands. To themselves and to their brethren in Judaea, they were a *Diaspora*, or in Hebrew *Galuth*, a dispersion. They were bound to one another by their Law, by the rite of circumcision, by the worship of the Synagogue, in which prayer was offered and the Prophets read and expounded, and by their attachment to Jerusalem. Jerusalem was the fountain-head of their faith. Only in Jerusalem stood the Temple of the one God. It had been there for a thousand years, and had just been rebuilt by Herod the Great, so that it was famous throughout the world. It was also enormously rich, because Jews in every land sent their offerings to it. Here was a second factor which in those days rendered Judaea so much more important in Jewish eyes than the most sumptuous abodes of the Gentiles.

Josephus, the Jewish historian, was himself of priestly family, and so was well qualified to write not only a history of his people but also a defence of their religion. A certain Apion—he was a

[Alinari.

8. This bas-relief from the Arch of Constantine in Rome actually dates back to the reign of Marcus Aurelius, A.D. 161-180. It represents that emperor sacrificing in a military camp. He is the garlanded figure in the centre, and behind him are typical legionaries, with their standards, five of which can be distinguished. Of these five, it will be noted that only that on the extreme left bears Caesar's effigy. When therefore Josephus says (*Ant.* XVIII, iii. 1) that Pilate "introduced Caesar's effigies which were upon the ensigns, and brought them into the city; whereas our law forbids us the very making of images; on which account the former procurators were wont to make their entry with such ensigns as had not those ornaments", he is stating a very reasonable case (see page 51).

TIBERIUS

10. This is the silver *denarius* or "penny" of the Gospel story of the tribute-money. The "image" was that of Tiberius, the reigning emperor; the "superscription" reads: TI(BERIUS) CAESAR DIVI AUG(USTI) F(ILIUS) AUGUSTUS—Tiberius Caesar Augustus, son of the Deified Augustus. Both the representation and the wording would be anathema to pious Jews, the former as an infraction of the Second Commandment, the latter, of the First.

AUGUSTUS

9. The deified Augustus, from a dupondius (bronze) struck in the principate of Caligula, A.D. 37-41. It is inscribed DIVVS AUGUSTUS S.C. The last two letters stand for *Senatus Consulto* (by decree of the Senate), that body having retained the right of minting bronze coins. Gold and silver coins were issued by the Princeps or Emperor.

Note the spike-like rays (corona radiata) which spring from the head. They symbolize divinity.

N.B. The original coins from which this and some of the following illustrations are taken vary in size from just under to just over 1 inch in diameter. 1 inch is the diameter of a modern halfpenny.

grammarian trained in Alexandria—took upon himself to head a
deputation which went to Rome to complain to the emperor
Caligula against the Jews. He was loud-mouthed and vulgar:
Tiberius called him the world's drum. But we owe the story of
Androcles and the Lion to him, and also one of Josephus' most
illuminating works. Apion was not content with speaking against
the Jews, he wrote a book against them, which evidently must have
had some currency, since Josephus, who was a mere infant when
Apion started his campaign, found it desirable, as a grown man,
to refute the calumny. He therefore wrote a work in two books
called *Against Apion*, in which he sets out to prove both the
antiquity of the Jews and the spirituality of their religion.

It is a calm, able work, in the course of which Josephus points
out that the Jewish policy is unique, in that it "leaves all to God",
that it is—and here he coins the word—a *theocracy*. This attitude
was of deep and decisive importance. It placed the Jews, as
citizens and as individual men and women, in a wholly different
category from others. Those Jews who lived in foreign countries
were constantly offended by the sights, sounds and ceremonies of
what was to them pagan blasphemy. On the other hand, it was
but natural that those among whom they lived should resent
this withdrawal, this implication of moral superiority, and
that from time to time clashes should occur between Gentile
and Jew.

But in Judaea itself, in the hearth and homeland of their faith,
the Jews felt that they might hope to live a wholly Jewish life.
There were, it is true, a certain number of Gentiles in Palestine.
From Syria and from Nabataea, and from the Arabian south, came
merchants and camelmen; from the Decapolis came Greeks; and
Scythopolis (Beisan), the largest of all the Ten Cities, was actually
on the west bank of the Jordan. Then there were Herod's two
new creations of Caesarea and Sebaste, the former largely, the
latter almost wholly, pagan. In the district of Samaria—not to be
confounded with the city of that name—there were the Samaritans, who stubbornly refused to recognize the primacy of Jerusalem
and Judaism, and claimed that in their sacred mountain of
Gerizim above Shechem men ought to worship. But these alien
elements did not impinge upon the life of the ordinary Jew. He
could till his fields, for then, as now, the great majority of the
inhabitants of Palestine were farmers, sell or barter his produce,
breed and worship unmolested.

Until the coming of the Romans, that is. Once Rome had

D

entered into active possession of Judaea, this feeling of personality, of individuality that the Jews cherished so ardently for themselves and their land was irreparably compromised. No longer was it a land of God, under God's government. Caesar was there, all the time, everywhere. Every head of every family was numbered in his registers, and his tax-collectors exacted the tribute due to his pagan majesty. Within sight of the Temple itself the symbols of Gentile dominion were conspicuous. The same sun that illuminated the golden doors of the House of God was reflected from the helmets of the uncircumcised garrison which, from the Tower of Antonia, overlooked its courts. To avoid conflict between the Jews and the Romans would have been hard. But not impossible. Herod had done it, by making himself, as it were, the shock-absorber between Rome and Jewry. For all too brief a period his grandson Agrippa would do the same, with still greater success. Even after Agrippa's death there was hope; but developments within Jewry itself gradually extinguished it.

At this point it will be helpful to consider briefly the religious allegiances, or parties, in Judaea at the time when it became a province.

First, there were the Sadducees. They formed a comparatively small clique, composed of the rich and priestly families from which the High Priests had been appointed. They were traditionalists, who regarded themselves as the aristocracy of the nation. They disliked the Pharisees, and their playing up to the populace; and they rejected the new-fangled doctrines about angels and spirits and resurrection of the dead. They were quite content with the world, their world, as it was, and wanted no other either here or hereafter. They regarded the written Law as the one sufficient guide, and objected to the accretions of Pharisaic teaching. When they sat in judgment, they delivered stern sentences.

Opposed to the Sadducees was the popular party of the Pharisees. They had grown out of the *Hasidim*, or "righteous", who had organized themselves in support of the Maccabees, at the end of the second century B.C. Their name means *separate*, and they regarded themselves and were widely regarded by the people as being the spiritual élite of the nation. They had gradually evolved an elaborate formalism, far beyond what was required by the letter of the Law, with which the pages of the Gospels have made us familiar. As we know from the same source, the Pharisees did all they could to catch the public eye, and to keep themselves in it. They were undoubtedly the spiritual leaders of the people, particularly in that undefined realm between religion and politics which is always the danger zone in any country.

There was yet a third manifestation of Judaism, namely that of the Essenes. For the future history of religion these Essenes are of cardinal importance, far more important than the more familiar Sadducees and Pharisees, if only because it was among the Essenes that an attitude to God and mankind was developed and practised which made it easy for many of them to accept the teaching of Jesus of Nazareth, and so to contribute to the genesis of the primitive Church. It happens that we know a good deal about the Essenes, despite the fact that they lived, most of them, far from urban settlements. The elder Pliny, who visited Palestine shortly before the first revolt against Rome, in the sixties of the first century A.D., tells us that they lived a life of poverty and celibacy, recruiting their numbers from those who were tired of the world and its vanities. We have also the account of Josephus, who for a period during his adolescence attached himself to an Essene ascetic before joining the Pharisees. Finally, it is clear from Pliny's account that the Essenes possessed a settlement "above En Geddi" on the western shore of the Dead Sea on a site which corresponds to Qumrān, the complex of buildings which has been excavated in the last few years, and is now generally referred to as the "monastery" of Qumrān. Here are to be found relics of all the characteristic marks of the community—the baths for their frequent ablutions together with the conduits and tanks that brought the water from the neighbouring torrent bed during the winter storms, rare enough in that arid region, and stored it for ritual use; their refectory, the *scriptorium* wherein they wrote their books and treatises, their pottery, bakery and kitchen, their dormitories and their cemetery. The neighbouring caves, as is well known, have yielded thousands of fragments of the books they wrote and copied for their library.

Already a great deal has been written about the Qumrān settlement and its library, and much more will yet be written. For our purpose it is only necessary to say that, as in any theological college, the life its inmates led is more important than the books they wrote or acquired, and to stress four aspects of their rule of life. First, by their practice of the virtues of humility, purity and austerity, they set an example of godly living which was superior to anything that had yet been known either in Jewry or elsewhere. For them, the Law was not enough, the emphasis must be on the sublimer doctrine of the Prophets.

Secondly, they had evolved the idea of the communal religious life, the pattern of what was later to be monasticism. Indeed, to this day, a visit to the relics of Qumrān, followed by one to the house of the Trappist fathers at Latrun, on the other side of Jerusalem, imbues the visitor with a strange sense of continuity and fulfilment, as though in the living society of Latrun were projected and perfected the very principles which the Essenes first practised at Qumrān. Thirdly, although the majority of the Essenes lived a communal life remote from their fellow men, there were certain of them who lived the good life in the towns and villages. Some of them even married, but carnal intercourse with their wives was confined strictly to the minimum necessary for begetting children. It was thus possible for the belief and practice of the Essenes to be widely known and imitated. The Christian faith as it was originally conceived and transmitted is very far removed from the tenets of the Qumrān sect; nevertheless the diffusion of Essene piety must have created a moral atmosphere in which it was easy to pass from the Essene to the Christian society. Mr Allegro, in his book *The Dead Sea Scrolls*, suggests that the "great company of priests" who are mentioned in Acts vi, 7, as being "obedient to the faith" were in part Essenes. Another scholar has quite independently deduced from Acts ii, 41-44, that the "three thousand souls" who were among the very first adherents of the infant Church were Essenes, for who else would have imposed upon it the characteristically Essene communism which immediately followed this recruitment?

The fourth aspect of the Essenes which is of importance for the present study is their Messianism, their expectation that a deliverer would arise. For the Essenes, this deliverer was to be a priestly figure, a "Teacher of Righteousness" and an "Interpreter of the Law". The fact that even the Essenes, the most ethically sublime sect of contemporary Judaism, believed in the coming of a Messiah is of great significance. For if the Essenes held such a view, how natural it would be that, *a fortiori*, it should be held by the mass of the people, and that their conception should be considerably less ethereal than that of the Essenes? That is precisely what happened.

Messiah means *anointed*. In the Old Testament the ruling sovereign is the first to be called the Anointed One. When Samuel, as recorded in 1 Samuel x, 1, "took a vial of oil, and poured it upon his [Saul's] head, and kissed him, and said, Is it not because the Lord hath appointed thee to be captain over his inheritance?" he inaugurated a form of consecration of the sovereign of which the latest enactment took place in 1953, when Queen Elizabeth II was anointed in Westminster Abbey. By the ceremony of anointing the king became sacrosanct and inviolable.

Gradually the idea of the anointed one was stretched to include others than temporal sovereigns of Israel or Judah. Cyrus, for instance, who ended the Exile of the Jews, is called (Isaiah xlv, 1) God's anointed. The prophet Habakkuk, in his magnificent prayer, expands the concept still further and confers the title "anointed" on Israel itself. But, generally speaking, it was the idea of the anointed one as the *individual deliverer* that came to prevail. The well-known description of the ideal ruler in Isaiah xi, the righteous leader who inaugurates a régime of justice and gentleness not for the Jews only but for the Gentiles as well, although it contains no reference to the Messiah under that title, gives a lofty expression to the idea which underlay it.

The vicissitudes of the Maccabean age, and of the contact with Rome which followed it, greatly stimulated the belief in the coming of a Messiah; because, despite all the outward evidence, the Jews still could not regard themselves as a subject people. The intense Messianic longing of the age of Jesus of Nazareth is abundantly clear from the Gospels. The story of the pseudo-Alexander, related in Chapter III, shows how strong and widespread among Jewry was the belief, founded on that longing, that somehow, some time, a deliverer would arise. Both the Gospels and the earlier story show that in the popular mind the concept of a spiritual regenerator had been displaced and obliterated by that of a worldly lord. It was this belief which was to become more and more obsessive of the minds of men, until, as we shall see, it could even be adapted to their own ends by Gentile Romans.

"Lilies that fester smell far worse than weeds"—the corruption of the Messianic ideal, one of the loftiest that mankind had yet evolved, was to produce a breed of gangsters as vicious as any in later history.

Such is the background against which was to be played the tragedy of Jewish history which began in A.D. 6.

Chapter VII

THE FIRST THREE PROCURATORS— DEATH OF AUGUSTUS

DESPITE Augustus' deliberation, despite his administrative genius, corroborated now by nearly forty years of dazzling success, his new province of Judaea, from its very inception, bred nothing but frustration and failure.

The very first preliminary of regular administration, namely the census (Chapter V), stimulated the nationalist rancour to open defiance. The first procurator was called Coponius; but, as we have seen, for the census, so important was it esteemed, the Governor of Syria himself, Quirinius, came down to Judaea. He was charged not only with the census, but with the confiscation of Archelaus' property. This was large and lucrative, and included the famous groves of balsam and dates near Jericho in the Jordan valley. The Roman officials, bustling, officious and alien, were everywhere, their aim and object humiliatingly clear to every man and woman. They had come to enslave and impoverish the children of Israel, to exalt and enrich the ruler of Rome.

Fortunately, open insurrection was avoided. The High Priest, Joazar, was the son of a notable Sadducee, called Simon, whom Herod the Great had made High Priest, when he married his daughter, the second Mariamme. Simon was succeeded by Matthias; but in Herod's last days he had been deposed for the complaisance he had shown to certain malignants, and had been replaced by Joazar, who as Herod's brother-in-law could be relied upon to be loyal to Herod. This very quality had caused Archelaus to depose him, as related in Chapter IV, and to replace him by his brother. Nor did he last long, being replaced by Jesus son of See. But Joazar proved too strong for his opponents, and was now back again as High Priest. Being the staunch Herodian he was, he naturally counselled co-operation with Rome. The conciliatory spirit of the school of Hillel, the saintly and famous Rabbi, supported him. The people were persuaded that the census was not the prelude to slavery, as they had supposed, and there was no open revolt. The prestige of Hillel had helped, and so no doubt had the grim memory of the "War of Varus". But it was the initiative of Joazar which had averted bloodshed—an interesting indication of the power of the "Herodians" under the new dispensation. Little thanks did he receive for his loyalty. He was deposed yet again, this time by Quirinius, the very man he had helped, as a sop to the extremist Pharisees. He was succeeded by Ananos son of Seth, the ex-High Priest Annas of the Gospels. When in his turn he urged Pilate to appease the mob, at the expense of justice, did he not remember, with cynical satisfaction, the circumstances of his own elevation?

A still more sinister result flowed from this incident. As often happens in the Levant, the temporary triumph of common sense only inflamed extremist intransigence. An *exalté* Pharisee, who sprang, oddly enough, not from Judaea itself, but from the town of Gamala to the East of the Sea of Galilee, decided that only by implacable xenophobia could the national spirit be preserved · inviolate. His name was Judas, and he is generally called Judas the Galilean. He found an ally in a certain Saddoc, a Pharisee of the extreme, rigorist school of Shammai, the rival of Hillel. These two founded the party of the Zealots.

The Jewish historian Josephus, in the light of the terrible events which were to engulf his people sixty years later, and in which he himself had so large and prominent a part, rightly discerns that it was the Zealots who were in great measure responsible for the calamity. He does not call them "Zealots", *Qanna'im* in Hebrew, the name they themselves adopted, until he comes to the time of the war with Rome, but he describes them when dealing with the census, because it was then that the evil seeds were sown. They proclaimed that "taxation was no better than an introduction to slavery, and exhorted the nation to assert their liberty. . . . Men received what they said with pleasure and this bold attempt proceeded to a great height. All sorts of misfortunes also sprang from these men, and the nation was infected with this doctrine to an incredible degree; one violent war came upon us after another, and we lost our friends who used to alleviate our pain; there were also very great robberies and murders of our principal men. This was done in pretence indeed for the public welfare, but in reality for the hopes of gain to themselves, whence arose seditions, and from them murders of men, which sometimes fell on those of their own people. . . . The sedition at last increased so high that the very temple of God was burnt down by their enemies' fire." (This last charge is reinforced by the only mention of the Zealots in the Talmud, namely in *Aboth* of Rabbi Nathan, VI, who says that when Vespasian came to destroy Jerusalem, the *Qanna'im* attempted to burn everything with fire.) The Zealots, Josephus says, became a "Fourth Sect", in addition, that is, to the Sadducees, Pharisees and Essenes, and the infection spread particularly among the younger generation (*Ant.* XVIII, i, 4). Here we have, as it were, the blue-print of terrorism, which has become so disastrously familiar in our own day, the psychology of those who pass "the point of no return" into the void of fanaticism and hatred. Jewry was to be their first victim.

Rome without and dissension within—even this double assault was not to be enough for the infant province. The Samaritans decided to cause trouble. Under Herod's stern rule, their traditional rancour against the Jews had been denied an outlet; and recently they had even made common cause with the Jews—for the purpose of ridding themselves of a Jewish king, Archelaus, Herod's son (see page 23). Now they exploited the change of government to annoy and affront their ancient rivals, and they chose a mean and disgusting way of doing it. The gates of the Temple Area were in those days, as in our own, shut at dusk; but on the occasion of a Great Feast, they might be opened just after midnight for the convenience of the worshippers, many of whom had come long distances, and had no lodging in the city. It was Passover, and the people were in a state of ritual purity, which they must preserve at all costs (cf. John xviii, 28). Some Samaritans, determined to destroy the purity of the worshippers for the seven days' observance, slipped in through the open gates, and taking advantage of the darkness, scattered about the cloisters fragments of dead human bodies, which they had no doubt snatched from some cemetery in the suburbs. (Burial within the walls was forbidden.) The Samaritans were thereafter excluded from the Temple, which they had previously been allowed to visit for the Festivals, and the Temple guards were strengthened. Whether any other sanction was applied, we do not know; but the French scholar Jérôme Carcopino has suggested that a famous inscription found at Nazareth, in which (he claims) the emperor Augustus, apparently replying to a report from a procurator of Judaea, authorizes the death penalty for those who violate tombs, or transfer their contents elsewhere, was called forth by this incident. Coponius, after three years of office, was recalled, and replaced by Marcus Ambibulus (A.D. 9-11). It was under his administration that old Salome, Herod's sister, died. She was the last survivor of that great generation, which had seen the Idumaeans emerge from obscurity to brilliant eminence. In the process, Salome had played a commanding, if sinister, part. She had reaped a rich reward. During her life, she had cultivated the friendship of the empress, Livia, just as Herod had sought that of Augustus. The two women had more in common than the two men. They were both iron-willed careerists, who were resolved to let no scruple come between them and the attainment of their ambition, which was simply the enhancement of the power, dominion and glory of the men whose fortunes they had decided to promote, in Livia's case her husband's, in Salome's that of her brother. Salome now bequeathed almost her whole landed estate to Livia, omitting only Azotus, or Ashdod, the little port midway between Joppa and Gaza, with its top-archy. The empress received Phasaelis, the model farm-colony which Herod had laid out at the foot of the Alexandrium in memory of his brother Phasael, and the rich date groves of Archelais, the plantation that linked Phasaelis with the Jericho of Herod the Great. Jericho, with the rest of Archelaus' property, had already been confiscated to the imperial treasury. This fine estate, which extended for fifteen miles continuously, was now consolidated into one imperial holding. It continued to flourish. A century later, the poet Martial would write (X, 50) of Victory wearing Idumaean, i.e. Herodian, palms; and in the famous mosaic map of the fifth century at Madeba, in Trans-Jordan, both Jericho and Archelais are shown as well-built and populous towns.

Livia also received the toparchy of Jamnia (Yebnah), which lay between Joppa and Azotus. It, too, was rich. Pliny would note its affluence in his *Natural History* (XXXIV, 3). The toparchy could produce 15,000 soldiers. An inscription mentions a *servus Archelaianus*, who was no doubt the imperial official who was required to administer so great an inheritance as that which, by confiscation and bequest, had now enriched the Julian house. Jamnia was to acquire another, and more spiritual renown, as a centre of Jewish piety and learning after the destruction of Jerusalem. Across the river Jordan, just opposite Jericho, Herod had created another agricultural colony, Betharamtha, which was watered by the streams that flow from Heshbon and the foot of Mount Nebo. This now belonged to Antipas, who had already tactfully renamed it Livias, after the empress. When he learned, after Augustus' death, that Livia had formally, in his will, been affiliated (like his own grandfather, and so himself) to the Julian line, he amended the name to Julias.

Ambibulus had as his successor Annius Rufus (A.D. 12-14), and it was during his term of office, on the 19th August in the year 14, that Augustus died. He was in his seventy-sixth year. He had ruled for forty-four years since the day when the victory of Actium had made him lord of the Roman world, fifty-seven and a half since the death of Julius Caesar.

Chapter VIII

JOHN AND JESUS — ANTIPAS THE FOX

AUGUSTUS was dead: but the succession was assured. The emperor had realized the vital importance of leaving behind him a generally accepted heir, since, if there were any shadow of doubt, civil war might revisit the capital, Augustus' life-work be ruined, and Rome plunged back into the miseries from which he had rescued her. As explained in Chapter I, Augustus had no male heir of his body. His son-in-law, Agrippa, his stepson, Drusus, were dead, and so were his nephew, Marcellus, and his grandsons Gaius and Lucius. But in A.D. 4, ten years before his death, Augustus had adopted his other stepson, Tiberius, as associate and successor. The line was safe, but the steps by which it had become so were hardly such as to make Tiberius a devoted son or stepson. In order to marry Tiberius' mother, Livia, Augustus had divorced his own wife Scribonia, on the very day she gave birth to his only child, Julia, and had compelled Livia's husband similarly to divorce her, and to attend the second wedding. When Agrippa, who by another cruel divorce had been compelled to abandon his wife and marry Julia, died and left her a widow, Tiberius was made to marry her though she was already pregnant with Agrippa Postumus. In order to do so, he was made to divorce Vipsania, daughter of Agrippa, and grand-daughter of Atticus, Cicero's friend, to whom he was passionately devoted. Such was the brutal and shocking manner in which Augustus, in what he thought were the dynastic interests of his house, disposed of his relatives' happiness. It is hardly astonishing that in face of his own example his much-vaunted programme for the restoration of the sanctity of family life was a failure.

That Tiberius should show little affection either for Augustus or for his mother is not to be wondered at: but that he should have started his reign by the murder of Augustus' surviving grandson, and his own stepson, Postumus Agrippa, is an ugly symptom of the prevailing moral malady. The fact that certain of the legions had shown a preference for Germanicus, who had, however, remained inflexibly loyal to Tiberius, may have influenced him— and Livia, or Julia as she now was. Germanicus, too, was soon to die.

43

The character of Tiberius has been the subject of widely differing estimates. Modern historians generally dismiss the stories of the "orgies" that are supposed to have stained his declining years in the island of Capri. He was fifty-six when he succeeded. He was an experienced soldier, and had proved a successful general and administrator, in Armenia, in Pannonia, and especially in Germany, where on his second mission he had been Commander-in-Chief for seven years. He was well educated, and was fluent in both Greek and Latin. During his retirement at Rhodes, he had studied philosophy. One of his instructors there was Theodore of Gadara, the city of the Decapolis perched high above the south-east shore of the Sea of Galilee. It might well claim to be the "Athens of the East", for it had been the home of the poet Meleager, and of Philodamus the Epicurean, who had numbered Virgil among his pupils; and as late as the third century it would produce Apsines, who was to win fame in old Athens itself. From Theodore, Tiberius may well have heard about Palestine; but he would have been given a view of it favourable to the Greek colonists, rather than to the Jewish populace.

As we have seen, Augustus, during the last eight years of his reign, had sent three procurators to Judaea, each of whom held office for three years. Tiberius, during the next twenty-two, that is until his death, sent only two. It was a principle of his to appoint men for long terms. What his real motive was it is not now possible to say: when people tried to find out, he would quote the old fable of Aesop, about the fox and the flies; when a kind hedgehog offered to drive away the flies which had settled on the fox's wounds, the cunning old fox asked him not to, because the flies in possession had already had a good feast, while greedy newcomers, who would replace them, would plague him all over again. So it was, said the emperor, with officials: newcomers always felt bound to make a private fortune, so it was best that there be as few changes as possible. It was ironical therefore that, within two years of the arrival of his first appointees in Syria and Judaea, the inhabitants of both countries were petitioning for a reduction of taxes, with what result we do not know.

The new procurator of Judaea was Valerius Gratus (A.D. 15-26). Shortly after his appointment, Germanicus arrived in the East, invested by Tiberius with an overriding, extra-territorial authority. His task was to settle the affairs of the eastern marches, Armenia, Commagene and Cappadocia, and to consolidate relations with Parthia. He was brilliantly successful. The Arsacid king of Parthia, Artaban III, was granted a renewal of his alliance with Rome, his rival Vonones, unpopular among his people for his Romanizing ways, being banished to Cilicia, where he died the next year. As king of Armenia, Germanicus chose Zeno Artaxias, son of another client king, Polemon of Pontus. Commagene and Cappadocia, two other client kingdoms, were now reduced to the status of provinces, just as Judaea had been eleven years before. (Cappadocia had a personal link with Judaea, because Alexander, son of Herod the Great, had married Glaphyra, daughter of Archelaus, its last king [see page 22]. Tiberius disliked him because when he was at Rhodes, the king had shown him no attention. He was now retired and died within the year.) Germanicus' achievements, the result of moderation and insight, aroused the jealousy of the governor of Syria, Calpurnius Piso, who was a favourite of Tiberius and had been appointed to that coveted office for the express purpose of furthering Germanicus' career. Very foolishly, Germanicus now decided on a trip to Egypt, and went off there without seeking the permission of the emperor, which, as a man of consular rank, he was bound to do, in accordance with Augustus' regulation, made at the time when, after the defeat of Antony and Cleopatra, Egypt had become a Roman dominion. When he returned to Antioch, Germanicus found that Piso had done all he could to upset his dispositions. He remonstrated against this spiteful folly; but on the 10th October, A.D. 19, he died near Antioch, of poison contrived by Piso, it was generally believed. The death of Germanicus, the acknowledged heir to the principate, greatly afflicted the Roman people.

These events had no direct influence on Judaea, which, apart from the complaint about taxation, seems to have preserved its tranquillity. But it was an uneasy tranquillity, as we can see from the frequent change of High Priest. Valerius Gratus, almost as soon as he arrived, deposed Annas, and put in his place Ishmael Ben-Phabi, only to discard him in favour of Eleazar, son of Annas. In the year 17, Simon Ben-Qamhit held the office, but in the following year surrendered it to Joseph, surnamed Caiaphas, who retained it until the year 36 (see Table IV).

Such frequent changes are puzzling, until we remember what the status of the High Priest was. In the days of the Maccabees, he had been both spiritual head and secular ruler of the Jewish people. During the reign of Herod, he had been restricted to spiritual

functions, and, as we have seen, Herod did not scruple to depose
any pontiff who showed himself less than an ardent supporter of
his rule. Herod was, at least technically, a Jew, and so the
national enthusiasm could to some extent be divided between
Church and state. But, with the advent of the pagan Romans, the
status of the High Priest reverted to what it had been in the days
of the Seleucids, the Greek dynasty against which the Maccabees
had revolted: he was the focus of the national aspirations. Our
own age has produced more than one example of the authority
and prestige enjoyed by a mufti, an archbishop or a cardinal,
who for good or ill becomes a national leader in a régime where
national autonomy is denied, and of the clashes with the secular
authority that invariably result. The High Priest of the Lord
occupied a precisely analogous position. Moreover, the High
Priest presided over the Sanhedrin, the supreme legislative and
judicial tribunal of the Jews: and, now that the secular capital
had been moved to Caesarea, he had no rival to outrank him in
pomp and precedence, except when the procurator was visiting
the Holy City. By the time Jesus of Nazareth was arrested and
tried, Caiaphas had been High Priest for more than fifteen years:
and his father-in-law Annas was still alive. They and their party
constituted a national bloc that only a very strong and skilful
procurator could have overcome.

But in A.D. 19 Jewry was to be shaken by an incident which
took place not in Jerusalem, but in Rome.

There had been a Jewish community in Rome for more than a
century: as early as 139 B.C. we are told that they were expelled
from the city "for attempting to corrupt morals by the cult of
Jupiter Sabazios" (i.e. "the Lord God of Sabaoth"). Julius Caesar
had shown favour to the Jews; Herod the Great had used to the
full his great influence with Augustus and Agrippa to enhance
the security and honour of Jewish communities everywhere; and
we have seen the prominent part that Roman Jewry played in the
proceedings before Caesar relative to Herod's will (page 15).

It is not surprising that among the more sensitive spirits of
Rome there should be those who were attracted by the ethics of
Judaism, the moral rectitude of its Law, the devotional sublimity
of its Prophets. Among them were women. In the year 19, a noble
lady called Fulvia, a convert, fell into the hands of four Jewish
charlatans, who persuaded her to honour the Temple of the God
of Israel with a magnificent purple tapestry, and an offering of
gold, with both of which, of course, they made off. The matter was

reported to Tiberius by Fulvia's husband, Saturninus. It happened that a short time before Roman society had been scandalized by the corrupt hierophants of another foreign cult. The priests of Isis, in return for a large bribe, had persuaded a rich and gullible young matron, named Paulina, that the god Anubis had fallen in love with her and demanded her presence at a supper in the temple. She went; to fall into the arms not of Anubis, but of a long-baffled adulterer. The priests and the freedwoman who had acted as go-between were crucified, the temple destroyed and the statue of Isis thrown into the river. Tiberius was therefore in no mood for leniency when the adherents of a second oriental religion brought discredit upon a freeborn Roman. He now ordered the banishment of all Jews from Rome; and 4,000 men were sent as conscripts to Sardinia. Because military service necessarily involved work on the Sabbath and the partaking of forbidden foods, the Jews had always protested against it, and their exemption had often been re-affirmed. But now any pious recalcitrant was killed out of hand. The context of the story suggests that the 4,000 who were banished may have been, like the instigator of the plot, Jews from outside Italy resident in Rome. In A.D. 49 (see page 91) Claudius would renew the edict.

Meanwhile, Antipas, the tetrarch of Galilee and Trans-Jordan, had been doing his utmost to conciliate Tiberius, whose high favour he already enjoyed: not for nothing is he called "that fox" in the Gospel (Luke xiii, 32). He had already flattered the old empress, he would now adulate Tiberius. He decided to replace his capital city, Sepphoris, near Nazareth, with a new one, to be called by the emperor's own name. It should arise on the western shore of the Sea of Galilee. Sepphoris was cold in winter—his father had once captured it in a snow-storm—but "where the blue wave rolls nightly on deep Galilee" there is a perpetual summer: it lies 700 feet below the level of the Mediterranean Sea. Thus, near the famous hot springs of Amathus, Tiberias came into being. The presence of a cemetery on a part of the site made it a forbidden city for pious Jews for some time to come, and that is why there is but one mention of it in the Gospel story, so much of which took place in close proximity to the new capital. It was constructed on the usual Hellenistic plan, with a stadium, a forum and an acropolis on the slope above the springs, now called *Qasr Bint al-Malik*, "the Castle of the King's Daughter". There were also several synagogues, and the city was surrounded with a wall. The administration of the new capital was entrusted to a senate

600 strong, presided over by an *archon*, or ruler, a council of ten, assistant administrative officers, and a commissioner of lands. Antipas now put the word "Tiberias", surrounded with a crown of foliage, on the backs of his coins. To people his city he collected, sometimes by force, a crowd of Galileans of all sorts and conditions. The fox might well think that fortune was smiling on him, that he had a status and a prestige in some way comparable to that which he would have inherited, namely, the whole of the kingdom of his father Herod the Great, had not that monarch, in the very last week of his life, altered his will for the third time. It was true, but his pride was to go before a fall (see Plate 30).

Like most of his family, Antipas had strong links with Rome, and particularly with the court. On one of his visits to the capital he stayed with his half-brother, Herod-Philip, the son of Mariamme II, not to be confused with his other half-brother, Philip the tetrarch. While there, he fell in love with Herod-Philip's wife, Herodias. Herodias returned his passion. She was herself a granddaughter of Herod the Great, being the daughter of the ill-fated Aristobulus, and felt her ample spirit cabined by being the mate of a mere private citizen, whereas Antipas was already a tetrarch, and being so high in the favour of Tiberius, might well become a king. There were two obstacles to the marriage. The first was that Antipas was already married, to a daughter of Harith IV, the energetic and powerful king of Petra. This union had assured security on the eastern frontier not only of the tetrarchy but of the province of Judaea as well. The second obstacle was that for Antipas to obtain Herodias by divorce was a flagrant infraction of the Jewish law. But Antipas was determined to have Herodias. Herodias was equally determined to have Antipas, and had no intention of sharing him with a girl from Petra. She insisted that Antipas, too, should divorce his wife. The wife found out. She was clever: instead of making a scene, and before Antipas could suspect that she had wind of his intentions, she merely asked to be escorted to his hill-fortress of Machaerus, which dominates the Dead Sea from the east, just north of the great cleft of the Arnon which marked the frontier between the tetrarchy and the Nabataean kingdom. From there, thanks to the connivance of a Nabataean officer, she was able to escape to Petra. There was an ancient enmity between Harith and the Herodians; but the marriage of his daughter with Antipas had assuaged it. Now, this latest insult, combined with a boundary dispute in Gaulanitis, had rekindled it, implacably.

12. The British Museum coin from the first year of Caligula's principate, gives a more favourable portrait, of a young, if arrogant, aristocrat. A comparison of the two issues, particularly as regards the mouth, shews how quickly Caligula deteriorated.

In both coins, note the use of the patronymic Germanicus.

11. This coin shews a clever, but self-willed, young man, Caius Caesar Augustus Germanicus, known as Caligula. The name Caligula, which means "Little Boot", was conferred by the troops when Caius was a boy with his father Germanicus, a successful and popular general (page 45). Caligula hated the nickname, but it stuck.

THE HERODIAN FAMILY

AGRIPPA I

HEROD OF CHALCIS

[*Bibliothèque Nationale.*]

[*Bibliothèque Nationale.*]

13. The countenance is that of a lively, quick-witted man, an extrovert, interested in life and its vicissitudes: it bears a consciously "westernized" aspect.

14. More pensive and deliberate, less impulsive than his brother. Of his and Agrippa's grandparents, both of the maternal and one of the paternal were of Arab stock. Herod has a fine, firm, lean Arab head.

Even within Antipas' own dominions, and in Judaea itself, this
fatal marriage was to undermine his reputation and power. It
was consummated about A.D. 27, just when John the Baptist
was beginning his ministry. Not only the Gospels, but Josephus,
too, tells us of the success which attended John's preaching,
and the baptism which accompanied it, and of the great influence that John had upon the people. Antipas naturally
resented and feared this; John had opened his ministry at Beth-
abara, which means the "house of the ford", that is, at the ford
on the old highway which linked Jerusalem and Philadelphia,
just before the river reaches the Dead Sea. It had the double
advantage of being a very public and frequented place, and also a
spot where the converts could be washed with running water,
and yet remain on their feet. Later, since the left bank of the
river was in Antipas' jurisdiction, John moved up into Samaria,
and in John iii, 22, we find him baptizing near Salim, that is, in the
beautiful spring that gushes so unexpectedly from the northern
slope of the Wadi Fara', the valley that runs down from Shechem
to the Jordan. Here John was safe from Antipas, being in the
Roman province. In the end, he decided that he must have the
courage of his convictions. He braved the tetrarch in his own
territory, and denounced him for having taken his brother's wife.
Both Josephus and the Gospels tell us that Antipas put John to
death. Only the Gospels give us the dramatic details; but oddly
enough only Josephus tells us that Herodias' daughter was called
Salome. One of the best-known characters in the Bible is nowhere
named in it.

The year A.D. 27 saw the inauguration of a new régime in
Palestine, one of the most fateful in the history not only of that
country but of the world, for in that year Pontius Pilate succeeded
Valerius Gratus as procurator. In the previous year Tiberius
had retired to the island of Capri. He left Rome on the pretext
of dedicating some temples in Campania, but he never went
back alive. For the last ten years of his life he ruled the empire
from an island, his most trusted instruments being slaves. That
an old man of nearly seventy had left the world's capital to dedi-
cate his remaining days and nights to epicene orgies is not to be
credited. The real reasons were complex, fear for his life, combined with weariness of his glittering burden, among them.
One compelling motive was his mother. It comes as a shock to
realize that the old empress was still alive. She was, very much so;
and constantly harassed her son by her domineering presumption.

E

If she would not leave him, he was, at long last, determined to leave her. She died two years later.

The new procurator, who took over his charge on the eve of the ministries of John the Baptist and Jesus of Nazareth, had to reckon with the following factors.

First, the deep resentment of an eastern people, proud to the point of stubbornness, against the domination of a western people, of whom, until recently, they could claim that they were the allies, not the subjects.

Secondly, the intense religious fervour of the Jews, which came into constant collision with the pagan laxity of their overlords.

Thirdly, the internal stresses, as between the Sadducee conservatives and the Pharisee populists, with a Sanhedrin dominated by a powerful and *rusé* High Priest.

Fourthly, ruling in Galilee and in Trans-Jordan, an ambitious schemer, in the person of Antipas.

Finally, among the people in general, a strong current of Messianism, misunderstood as secular deliverance, this latter aspect being growingly enhanced by the sinister beginnings of Zealotism.

Such a conjunction of explosive elements, packed into the narrow receptacle of Palestine—it is about the size of Wales— clearly called for velvet-handed manipulation by a man of outstanding sympathy, foresight and resolution. Pilate was endowed with none of these qualities.

Not that he was a vicious or corrupt man. Pilate (of whose origins we know nothing) enjoys the unique distinction of having been execrated by Jews and Christians alike, but for wholly different reasons. The Alexandrine Jewish philosopher and publicist, Philo, has berated him for being violent and opinionated, insolent, greedy and savage, laying traps for the innocent, and of boundless cruelty. Every day, he says, Pilate used to condemn people to death without the vestige of a trial. This may be dismissed as just the sort of stuff that is traditional in a region where words have never been regarded as necessarily a reflection of fact, but are held to possess a being of their own, independent and free. The idea is as old as Homer; and to this day there are tribesmen in Arabia who will exhaust every gesture before uttering a word to a stranger, for fear he should take something living from them. To call Philo's rhapsody lying would be a mistake: he was merely conforming to a conception of language which is not that of the modern west.

The trouble with Pilate was not that he was wicked, but that he was weak.

Soon after his arrival, the time came to send the troops up from Caesarea to Jerusalem, to their winter quarters in the vast and commodious barracks attached to the palace, built by Herod the Great, now the palace of the procurator. These barracks were on the site of the present police barracks next to the Citadel. The ensigns of these troops bore the image of Caesar. Former procurators, Josephus tells us, had always been careful to see that the ensigns carried by the Jerusalem garrison bore no representation of the human form, because that, of course, would have insulted the Jews, as being a breach of the Second Commandment. If no Jewish ruler, king, ethnarch or tetrarch dare presume to put his effigy on his coins, how much less tolerable would be the image of the pagan and alien sovereign? This was perfectly well known, and Pilate must have been told about it. By no means all Roman regiments carried ensigns with human features on them (see Plate 8). Many displayed animals, and others the famous and familiar eagles. It might well have been possible therefore to choose troops whose ensigns would be less offensive. If none of these were available, then Pilate should have faced the issue squarely, and, unpopular as he knew it would make him with the army, he should have ordered them to leave their ensigns in Caesarea. He could not make up his mind to do that, and was no doubt afraid it would look as though he were insulting the colours. These were even more venerable then than they are now: Tacitus (*Ann.* II, 17), calls them "the particular gods of the legions", and Tertullian (*Apology XVI*) corroborates him. Moreover, to affront Caesar's standards was to slight Caesar himself. Pilate decided to compromise: the ensigns should go up to Jerusalem, but they should go up veiled, and by night. This expedient, far from conciliating the Jews, infuriated them. Pilate, they said, had tried to fool them as well as insult them. A multitude rushed down to Caesarea, to protest to Pilate against this shocking innovation. Pilate refused to hear them, from fear of being accounted disloyal to Caesar. But the crowd would not go away. After five days of this, Pilate summoned them to the stadium, where, seated on his judgment-seat, and supported by a strong detachment of soldiers with drawn swords in their hands, he called upon them, for the last time, to agree to the presence of Caesar's standards in Jerusalem. The only answer of the Jews was to stretch out their necks for execution. Overcome by such resolution, Pilate rescinded the order. The ensigns came back to Caesarea. The Jews had won; but how much had Pilate lost!

A little later Pilate, with all a weak man's obstinacy, made another attempt to honour Caesar in the Holy City without offending the Jews. He had placed in the palace there a number of gilded shields, which bore simply Caesar's name, and that of the giver, namely Pilate, without any representation of any living thing whatsoever. Far from being mollified, the opposition increased. It was the time of one of the major feasts, and Jerusalem had attracted all the nation's leaders. A deputation was chosen to intercede with Pilate. It consisted of the chief magistrates of the Sanhedrin, reinforced with the four sons of Herod the Great still living, namely Antipas and Philip, the two tetrarchs, with Herod-Philip son of the second Mariamme, and an obscure Herod, son of Cleopatra the Jerusalem Jewess. Seldom, before or after, can these four have acted in unison. Pilate was not to be persuaded. After all, neither Antipas nor Philip could claim to be pillars of orthodoxy. Besides, in Alexandria the very synagogues were decorated with votive shields dedicated to the emperors by the loyal Alexandrine Jews, and crowns of gold and *stelae* and much else beside. But the malignants were determined to humiliate Pilate yet again. They despatched to Tiberius a harassed but most respectful letter—they were seeking his sanction not to confer honour on him but to deny it to him—and back came the order to remove the offensive shields from Jerusalem and to hang them up in the temple of Augustus at Caesarea. No doubt the favour which Antipas enjoyed with Tiberius influenced the emperor's decision, which meant that Pilate must now count among his enemies not only the godly, but the Herodians as well. It is only fair to Pilate to say that Josephus omits this incident, and that Philo is our only authority for it. No doubt he shows Pilate in as bad a light as possible. Still, had Pilate been more prudent, he could have avoided the episode altogether.

In the eyes of the Jews, Pilate could now do no right. He tried to conciliate them by improving the water supply of Jerusalem. The city possesses only one spring, the Virgin's fountain, which, through the famous tunnel, supplies the Pool of Siloam. For the rest, the inhabitants depended on cisterns or open pools excavated from the rock and supplied by conduits which collected rain water. Since the days of the kings of Judah, this provision had been supplemented by an aqueduct which conveyed water from Solomon's pools, just south of Bethlehem. Winding its way along the contours

of the hills, and passing beneath Bethlehem in a tunnel, this
aqueduct takes fifteen miles to cover the distance of five and a
half as the crow flies. Herod the Great, when he built his great
fortress-palace of Herodium, had tapped this supply for it, and,
not wishing his capital to be deprived of water, especially at a time
when his sumptuous building programme called for an ever
larger supply, he constructed a further aqueduct fifteen miles
long, to bring water from the spring of 'Arroub, five miles further
south on the road to Hebron. He also added two more pools. It
was this aqueduct that now caused trouble. Ancient aqueducts
were in constant need of repair. Silt from a sudden torrential
rain, seismic shocks, above all, 'milking' by peasants en route,
all these necessitated constant care and maintenance. The
Jerusalem aqueduct, which remained in use right down to the
early years of the present century, shows many signs of repair.
Pilate undertook a major reconditioning of the supply. To pay
for it, he used the Temple treasure. He was entitled to do so,
because aqueducts are one of the objects specifically mentioned
in the tractate of the Mishnah *Shekalim*, which prescribes how
the treasure may be expended. Moreover, the aqueduct delivered
the water into the vast cisterns of the Temple. But the inhabitants
of Jersualem were no more grateful to Pilate for giving them
water than their successors were to be to the British who gave
them a far more copious supply 1,900 years later. In the Levant,
material benefit is as nothing when weighed against psychological
grievance. On this occasion, when the Jews accused him, yet
again, of sacrilege, Pilate immediately resorted to force. He
surrounded the demonstrators with soldiers armed with clubs.
Many of them were wounded, and some were killed. There was
no complaint to Caesar.

The yeast of Messianism was now at work. The Zealot followers
of Judas the Galilean, commonly called Galileans, were already
causing open tumult. As we learn from Luke xiii, 1, Pilate had
massacred a number of them while they were actually attending
a sacrificial service. They were the subjects of Antipas, who now
had an additional reason for disliking Pilate.

Such is the background against which Josephus mentions Jesus
of Nazareth, and such was the background against which Pilate
was called upon to preside at the most famous, most infamous trial
in history. He did all that he could to divest himself of the responsibility for what he knew was an unjust sentence. By law, it was
the Sanhedrin who found that a man was *worthy* of death, but it

was the procurator who must pronounce the sentence. Pilate
first of all tried to shuffle out of his predicament by sending Jesus to
Antipas: hearing that he was a Galilean, he delivered him to the
tetrarch of Galilee, who happened to be in Jerusalem for the
Feast, lodging in the old Hasmonaean palace down by the Temple.
Antipas was flattered by the attention, which beside gave him an
opportunity of seeing and insulting one about whom he would
have heard from his steward Chuza, whose wife Joanna was one
of Jesus' early adherents (Luke viii, 3); one, moreover, whom
he feared as being perhaps the re-incarnation of another prophet
whom he had already executed, John the Baptist. "And the same
day [Luke xxiii, 12] Pilate and Herod were made friends together:
for before they were at enmity between themselves." But Antipas
was far too clever to be tricked into doing Pilate's work for him.
He sent Jesus back. Pilate would still have liked to release him.
Caiaphas and his clique knew how to play on Pilate's weakness, on
his fear of being found disloyal to Caesar. "If you release this
man," they said, "you are no friend of Caesar." Pilate yielded,
after trying by a futile gesture to exonerate himself. But in his own
despite his name was forever to be linked with the death of Jesus.
"Christ," says Tacitus (*Annals* XV, 44), "suffered the penalty
when Tiberius was emperor through the procurator Pontius
Pilate."

It was the Samaritans who, in A.D. 36, caused Pilate's recall.
An impostor succeeded in persuading a number of them to
assemble on Mount Gerizim, the hill to the south of Nablus,
which was and still is the holy mountain of the Samaritans
(John iv, 20), promising to show them the sacred vessels "that
Moses had buried there". Rallying at the village of Tirathana,
they started to climb the mountain. Pilate's cavalry and foot set
upon them, cut down many and took a number of prisoners. The
Samaritans complained to Vitellius, the governor of Syria.
Vitellius sent down a friend of his called Marcellus to restore
peace in Judaea, and ordered Pilate to return home in disgrace to
report to the emperor. Before he reached Rome, Tiberius had
ceased to live (16th March, A.D. 37); but that did not absolve
Pilate from the vengeance of Tiberius' successor, Caligula, to
anticipate which, the Christian writers Eusebius and Orosius
tell us, the fallen procurator committed suicide, either in Rome
or, according to one version, in Vienne, whither, like Archelaus
thirty-one years earlier, he had been banished.

The Christian *Church*, far from reprobating Pilate, has held

him in high regard. The creeds do not blame him—the Armenian
version does not even mention him. Coptic tradition, following
Origen and Chrysostom, maintains that both Pilate and his wife
died Christians. The Greek Church commemorates them on the
27th October, the Ethiopian Church venerates Pilate on the 25th
June—a strange apotheosis indeed.

Dante, who in canto xxiii of the *Inferno* allots such harsh tor-
ment to Caiaphas and Annas, prescribes no punishment for Pilate.
He mentions him only obliquely, when in canto xx of the
Purgatorio he describes Philip IV of France, who in 1310 despoiled
the Templars, as "the new Pilate"; but it is clear from the context
that Dante has in mind, not the trial of Christ, but the earlier
episode of the ensigns.

Vitellius was an outstandingly good governor, who seems to
have been invested with the same general surveillance of the
provinces of the East as Germanicus had wielded sixteen years
before. His visit to Judaea for Passover, in the year A.D. 36, could
not have been more conciliatory. To start with he abolished the
sales-tax on agricultural produce. He then remitted to the Jews
the possession of the High Priestly vestments. It may seem strange
that such an indulgence should even have been called for. What
had happened is this: Herod the Great, as part of his policy of
maintaining control over a priesthood of which he himself, owing
to his not being born of priestly stock, could never be a member,
not only assumed the right of appointing the High Priest, but also
kept in his own custody the High Priest's sacred robes. These
robes, to which magical virtues were ascribed, were worn only
four times a year, at the feasts of Passover, Pentecost and Tabernacles, and on the Day of Atonement. It was the easier for Herod
to keep his hand on them, because the tower in which they had
been reposited in the days of the Hasmonaeans, the Bira, was the
very tower which he had transformed into his first fortress-palace,
Antonia, at the north-west corner of the Temple area. Archelaus
had continued Herod's practice. When the Romans took over,
they assumed possession of the robes. The vestments were very
reverently treated; but a period of seven days before each feast
was required for their purification, and they had to be returned
the day after the feast. Vitellius now placed them in the unfettered control of the priesthood. He also deposed Caiaphas, and
appointed Jonathan, a son of Annas, in his room. It was at the
end of this same year that he sent Pilate back to Rome.

The scene now changes yet again to Parthia. Owing largely to

Piso's jealous gaucherie, Germanicus' settlement of A.D. 19 had not lasted, and Artaban, the king of Parthia, was doing all he could, which in this vital area was much, to annoy and embarrass Rome. Tiberius decided that a new pact must be concluded—he was too good a general to risk a war. Vitellius was entrusted with the negotiations, and took Antipas with him. The reason for this was probably two-fold: first, that there was an ancient and influential Jewish community in Babylon, with whom he might be presumed to have influence, as his father certainly had done, and had settled colonies of Babylonian Jews in his dominions; and secondly that Antipas spoke Aramaic, the *lingua franca* of the whole region, and Vitellius did not (see Appendix II). The conference took place in the middle of a specially constructed bridge, spanning the Euphrates. Thanks, in part, to lavish bribery by Vitellius, it was a success. A new treaty was signed and hostages were handed over to Vitellius, among them a Jewish giant called Eleazar. Antipas entertained both sides to a magnificent banquet there on the bridge, in a specially erected pavilion. It was a typically Herodian touch, the sort of thing his father might have done. But his father would never have made the *gaffe* that Antipas now committed. He was so pleased with himself that he sat down and wrote a description of the whole affair to his friend Tiberius. This reached Rome before the official report of Vitellius, who, though naturally annoyed, prudently said nothing at the time.

It was in the year 33 or 34 that the blameless Philip the tetrarch died, and was buried in the monument he had prepared at Bethsaida-Julias. He left no children; so Tiberius attached his tetrarchy to Syria, but ordered that the revenues should accumulate in the tetrarchy itself. Had he in mind some further aggrandisement of Antipas? Salome married, as her second husband, her first cousin once removed, Aristobulus, who in the time of Nero was to become King of Lesser Armenia, and later of Chalcidice. They had three children (see Plates 15 and 16, and page 94).

Harith took advantage of the absence of Antipas and Vitellius on the Euphrates to pay off his old score of resentment against the tetrarch. Exploiting the pretext of the frontier dispute, he sent his army to attack Herod's troops, some of whom, formerly in the service of Philip, deserted to their Arab brethren. Antipas suffered a crushing defeat, which was popularly ascribed to God's anger at his execution of John the Baptist. For the last time Antipas appealed to Tiberius. The emperor sent a curt order to Vitellius to chastise Harith and to send him or his head to Rome.

As a client king he had no right to make war at all without the
emperor's permission. Vitellius soon arrived at Ptolemais (Acre)
with two legions and the necessary auxiliaries. Here he was met
by a deputation of Jews, who implored him not to pass through
Judaea with the standards uncovered. Vitellius, remembering
Pontius Pilate, at once agreed, sent his army through Lower
Galilee into Trans-Jordan and himself went up to Jerusalem with
Antipas to celebrate the Passover. It was the year 37. While in
Jerusalem, he made Theophilus, another son of Annas, High
Priest in the place of Jonathan. Vitellius had spent three days in
the Holy City, and was about to hurry away to the war when, on
the fourth, he received news that Tiberius was dead. With great
relief he recalled his army, and administered to the people the
oath of fidelity to the new emperor, Caius Caesar Augustus
Germanicus, generally known as Caligula. He was glad not to
have to fight on behalf of Antipas, whose star set with Tiberius'
death. Another Herod was now to be lord of the ascendant.

Chapter IX

AGRIPPA I: THE VAGABOND KING

IF Antipas is the least attractive of the Herods, Agrippa I is the most improbable. The story of his life, with its astonishing turns of fortune, reads like a tale from the *Thousand and One Nights*. One of the greatest living Jews has said that Agrippa might have been the original of the French caricaturist Caran D'Ache's "Haroun al Rothschild." Agrippa, certainly, far more than any other member of the family in four generations, came nearer to possessing the qualities which had made his grandfather, Herod the Great, the outstanding character he was. He had charm, he had political flair, he knew the secret of ingratiating himself with the Romans. He lacked Herod's solidity—he was flashy and superficial; but he also lacked the cruelty to his own kind, and the pathological suspicion that seared his grandfather's character. Above all, Agrippa, unlike Herod, was accepted by the Jews of Judaea, as well as by the Romans of Rome. This was a really important achievement. It is one of the tragedies of history that Agrippa died so young. Had he lived, the whole history of Jewry might have been different and happier.

Agrippa was born in the year 10 B.C., the year in which his grandfather, Herod the Great, dedicated his Temple. His father was Aristobulus, Herod's second son by his second wife, Mariamme. Mariamme, Aristobulus and Alexander, his brother, were all executed by Herod, the mother on a false charge of infidelity, the sons on charges of sedition, which, if not wholly false, were distorted and exaggerated. Alexander had also confessed to sodomy, which was by Jewish law a capital offence; but with Herod it was the suspicion of sedition that carried the weight, and it was for that that the two brothers were strangled. Despite this lamentable end, Herod took personal care of the education of his dead son's families, the reason being, in part, that, since Mariamme was of princely Jewish stock, it was on her issue that Herod chiefly depended for founding what he hoped would become a dynasty. Alexander, as we have seen (page 22), had married Glaphyra, daughter of King Archelaus of Cappadocia, and their issue were to rule as kings, but not in Judaea; it was in Armenia and Cilicia that they were given thrones. The offspring of Aristobulus were to reign in Jerusalem. He had been given as his wife his first cousin, Berenice, daughter of Salome the elder by the second of her three husbands, who was, like herself, an Idumaean. The family relationships of Herod's family are exceptionally confusing, both because they so often married their cousins or nieces, and because so many of them, in so many different generations, were called by the same names (see Tables I and II).

The names themselves may be divided into three categories. First come the pure Semitic names such as Salome, Mariamme, Phasael and Joseph. Next, Semitic names in a Greek guise, such as Kypros, which has no connection with the island of Cyprus, but is the Greek form of the Semitic *kufra*, the flower of the henna (*Lawsonia inermis*) so much prized for its scent, the "camphire" of the Song of Songs and known today as *chypre*. This was the name of the mother of Herod the Great, who came from Petra; and we find other similar names among the Arabs of Petra, for instance Aretas for Harith, and Malchus for Malik.

As the Herodian family became more and more at home in the Graeco-Roman world, they increasingly adopted names which were purely Greek or Roman. Thus names such as Archelaus or Philip became common. Agrippa I was called after the great minister of Augustus. He in his turn named one of his daughters Drusilla, after Caligula's favourite sister, the wife of Cassius Longinus, who after her death in 38 was consecrated, as Panthea— the first Roman woman ever to receive that honour. Drusilla, Agrippa's daughter, was born in 39, so that the bestowal of the name was a tactful piece of flattery.

The name Berenice had been borne by several princesses of the house of Ptolemy, of whom the most famous was the daughter of a king of Cyrene in the third century B.C. Her husband called a star "Berenice's locks" after her, and the Cyrenian poet Callimachus devoted a poem to the episode, which Catullus imitated (see Appendix III).

Agrippa I was one-quarter Jewish, and three-quarters Idumaean. He had two brothers and two sisters. Of the brothers, one called Herod was to be a king of Chalcis in Syria, the second, Aristobulus, was to marry the daughter of the king of Emesa (Homs) in Syria. Of the sisters, one was the notorious Herodias, the other Mariamme, of whom nothing is known (see Table I).

From their ancestry, we should imagine that this family would look predominantly Arab. And we should be right. Of the features of Herod the Great we have no direct record. No statues might be erected within Judaea, not even of its king. Outside the realm, we know that they were; but none of them has survived to our time. Nor did Herod dare to put his effigy on his coins, for even that would have been accounted a breach of the Second Commandment. His sons observed the same scruple. By the time of Agrippa, the Roman currency had become common, not only as the medium of the hated tribute, but through the ordinary dealings of commerce. Therefore, as Abel puts it (*Histoire*, Vol. I, p. 432), "Even the most pious Jew, who avoided looking at the profile of Caesar or the silhouette of a pagan deity, was not afraid to slip the coin into his wallet." Since images on foreign coins were now circulating freely, there seemed no point in excluding the features of the nation's own princes. Thus we possess coins of Agrippa, and of Herod of Chalcis, and of other members of the family. From those which appear in this book, now in the Cabinet des Médailles of the Bibliothèque Nationale in Paris, it will be seen that there is a remarkable family likeness, and that the general cast of features is aquiline, handsome and broad-browed. The set of the head is proud, almost arrogant, the chin determined, the mouth firm well nigh to the point of harshness. Of all of them, Agrippa is the most striking (see Plates 13-17).

As has already been explained, Herod the Great was not merely well known at Rome, he was the intimate of Augustus, and of Augustus' great minister Marcus Vipsanius Agrippa, after whom his grandson was called. Herod and his family were of the Julian clan; they could therefore claim, and exploit, familiar intercourse with the imperial house. Being clever, charming and rich, they enjoyed very high favour. Just as Salome the elder had cultivated the friendship of the empress Livia, so did her daughter that of the Lady Antonia, the child of Mark Antony and Octavia, Augustus' sister, who had married Drusus, Tiberius' brother. She was the mother of the future emperor Claudius. Antonia in her turn showed a special favour for Agrippa. Then, too, we must remember that Nicolaus of Damascus, the chancellor of Herod the Great, had settled down in the palace as Augustus' biographer. Agrippa therefore, who had been sent to Rome when he was about five years old, just before his grandfather's death, was brought up with the future emperor Tiberius' son, as though he were himself one of the princes.

The Roman court was not gay. Its members were generally

either vicious or dull, and not infrequently both. To gather from their recorded *bons mots*, the imperial family's standard of wit was that of a Victorian lower-schoolboy. In such an atmosphere, the sprightly eastern lad, lively, handsome and raffish, must have furnished relief and refreshment. He enjoyed his success, and set out to improve it. His sensible mother, while doing all she could to further young Agrippa's interests, nevertheless curbed his extravagance, for, although the family was very rich, she and her children represented only a cadet branch of it; but as soon as Berenice was dead (we do not know when she died), Agrippa, now fully in the public eye as the boon companion of the emperor's son, began to cut a dash. He lived sumptuously, entertained profusely, and bribed lavishly, the principal beneficiaries being the freedmen under whose direction the imperial government was increasingly falling. By the time he was about thirty-three he had exhausted his fortune. Drusus was dead, and Tiberius announced that he could not bear to see any of his deceased son's friends. Clearly, the Judaean prince could not remain in Rome. Agrippa's life in many ways resembles a game of "Snakes and Ladders". This was his first "snake".

There was only one place Agrippa could go to, and that was Idumaea, the home of his ancestors, the region in the south of Palestine, where the high, bleak hills of Judaea slowly descend, in tawny undulations, to the waterless desert of the Sinai peninsula. It is a bare, ungentle region, a savage contrast to the green felicity of Latium and Campania. The only dwelling Agrippa could find was an old watch-tower at a village called Malatha, near Beersheba. This, after the splendours of the Palatine, quite overthrew his spirit; and, like his grandfather in a similar state of depression, he contemplated suicide. It was his wife who saved him. She was a second cousin, the granddaughter both of Phasael, brother of Herod the Great, and, through her mother, of Herod the Great himself. Like her great-grandmother she was called Kypros. She had inherited all the enterprise of her forbears. She it was who wrote to his sister, Herodias, who was already living with Antipas, to ask for help. Antipas, who was now both uncle and brother-in-law of Agrippa, replied by inviting him to come to his new capital of Tiberias, where he was given a small government post, as inspector of markets. But it was not in Antipas to be generous, and he was at pains to make Agrippa, who was now over forty, realize that he was a pensioner and dependent. Matters came to a head one evening at Tyre, where the family was attending a feast.

Both Antipas and Agrippa drank too much, and started quarrelling. Finally, in front of the gentile company, whose guests they both were, Antipas told Agrippa that he was a pauper, who owed his very bread to Antipas' favour. Agrippa could stand no more. Fortunately, the governor of Syria, Pomponius Flaccus (A.D. 32-35), was an old friend of his from Roman days. Agrippa went to see him, and was very kindly received. Unfortunately, Flaccus already had staying with him Agrippa's brother Aristobulus, with whom Agrippa was not on good terms. Aristobulus soon had an opportunity of doing him down. Flaccus had to settle a boundary dispute between the cities of Tyre and Damascus. The Damascenes, knowing Agrippa's influence with the governor, offered him a large bribe to further their claims. Aristobulus got wind of the transaction, and reported it to Flaccus, who was justifiably angry at this abuse of his hospitality. He could no longer keep so embarrassing a guest.

Once again Agrippa was a wanderer. He went south to Ptolemais, and decided that he must go back to Italy. But how could he get there, with no money? He told his freedman, Marsyas, to see what he could do. Marsyas went to Peter, who had been his mother Berenice's freedman, and now, by the terms of her will, was in the service of Antonia, Agrippa's noble patroness. When Marsyas asked for a loan, Peter said that Agrippa had already cheated him once, and that if he gave him a new loan, he must deduct the outstanding debt from it. Marsyas had perforce to accept this arrangement and, having signed for a sum of about £1,000, received rather less than £900. With this Agrippa and Kypros now made arrangements to leave for Rome. Agrippa did not dare to show his face in a large port, such as Ptolemais or Caesarea, so he made his way to Anthedon, the little family property between Jaffa and Gaza. He was just about to slink off to sea, when a band of troops appeared and ordered him to stay. They had been sent by the steward of what was now the imperial estate at Jamnia, a few miles to the north, Herennius Capito, who said that Agrippa owed the imperial treasury £15,000 which he had borrowed from it when he was in Rome, and must consider himself under arrest. Agrippa pretended to acquiesce; but when night fell, he cut the cables of his ship, and so gave Herennius the slip. He made for Alexandria, intending to raise another loan from the rich Jewish community there. Their chief, Alexander, the *Alabarch* as he was called, was most reluctant to lend anything to this spendthrift vagrant, even if he was a Herod, but out of admiration for Kypros, he agreed to lend her £8,000. He was taking no risks—only £2,000 was paid in cash there in Alexandria, the rest being in the form of a draft payable at Puteoli, the port of Rome in the north-eastern recess of the Bay of Naples. Kypros had once again saved Agrippa. She now bade him farewell, and returned with the children to Judaea. Among them was a girl, called Berenice, who was later to marry Mark the son of Alexander, but it was not as his wife that she was to be known to after ages.

As soon as he reached Puteoli (Pozzuoli), Agrippa wrote to Tiberius, who was at Capri just across the bay, saying he had travelled all the way from Judaea to see him, and might he come and call? Tiberius wrote back very kindly, inviting him to come and stay, and when he arrived received him with all his old affection. Unfortunately, the very next day a letter arrived from Capito, giving details of the debt, and of Agrippa's flight. Tiberius, who could hardly be expected to give asylum to an absconded offender, told Agrippa that until the debt was paid he could not appear at court. Nothing daunted, Agrippa went straight off to Antonia, who found the money. Agrippa was back at Capri in no time. Yet another "snake" had been surmounted by yet another "ladder". These events had taken place during the period when Pontius Pilate was procurator of Judaea. It is hard, somehow, to think of them as having been contemporary with the ministry, trial and crucifixion of Jesus of Nazareth. And yet, so strangely compounded is the web of human life and destiny, they were.

Agrippa was now paramount at court, or nearly so. Tiberius, with his *status quo* mind, would not hear anything against Antipas; nevertheless he appointed Agrippa as tutor to his grandson, Tiberius Gemellus. Agrippa was looking ahead. Tiberius was an old man now, and could hardly be expected to last much longer: it would be better to make friends with the heir, Caius Caligula, and that should not be difficult, given his already firm standing with the young man's grandmother, Antonia. Caesar's friend found it easy, of course, to raise funds. He borrowed from a certain Thallus, a Samaritan, and one of Caesar's freedmen, the sum of £50,000. Of this, he used £15,000 to pay back his debt to Antonia, and sent the rest as a present to Caligula, and thus, as Josephus says, "became a person of great authority with him".

Agrippa now made a blunder which brought him to the very nadir of his fantastic career. He allowed his schemes for the future to run away with him. One day, as he was out driving with

Caligula, he said to him, in one of those confidential exchanges
which often take place between princes and their close friends
when they are out riding or driving together, beyond the range
(as they think) of eavesdroppers: "I wish to God Tiberius would
quit the stage, and leave the government to you, who are so much
more worthy of it." This imprudent remark was overheard by the
coachman, a freedman called Eutychus. He kept his counsel: he
would turn the speech to account some day. A little later,
Eutychus stole some of Agrippa's clothes, and Agrippa had him
arrested and examined by the prefect of the city, Piso. Instead
of blackmailing Agrippa on the spot (which might have led to his
immediate liquidation) Eutychus cunningly appealed to Tiberius,
on the ground that he had something to tell him that concerned
his safety. The damning inference was obvious. Piso had no
alternative but to send him off to Capri. Agrippa was on tenter-
hooks: what would Eutychus say? What would happen to Agrippa?
How he longed to know! The emperor's dilatory habits applied to
small matters no less than great, to prisoners no less than procurators; and it is in fact in connection with this event that
Josephus describes this trait at some length. Eutychus was simply
committed to prison and left there. At last, Agrippa could stand
the suspense no longer. Once again, he sought Antonia's help.
Antonia had great influence with Tiberius, who trusted her
completely, particularly after the rôle she had played in exposing
the plot of Sejanus, which had nearly cost Tiberius his life.
When Antonia asked the emperor to bring Eutychus to trial,
Tiberius, who had clearly already informed himself of what the
man was likely to say, begged her to leave well alone, and added
that Agrippa had better be careful or, in trying to secure punishment for Eutychus, he might bring it on his own head. Instead of
taking the hint, Agrippa was only the more insistent.

Tiberius had temporarily left Capri, and was at Tusculum,
near the modern Frascati, some thirteen miles south-east of
Rome, then, as now, the smiling setting for sumptuous villas.
Agrippa and Caligula, together with Antonia, had gone down
there to pay their respects. One day, after the midday meal,
the whole party were in the hippodrome, where the emperor
was taking the air, not on foot, because it was a very hot September day, and he was an old man, but in a litter with the
two men walking in front, and Antonia by his side. Once again,
she renewed her request. "God be my witness," answered
Tiberius, "that I am induced to do what I am going to do not

[Bibliothèque Nationale.

15. Son of Herod of Chalcis. His face closely resembles that of his father; but the shape of his head is closer to that of his uncle, Agrippa I. He became king of Lesser Armenia (see pages 56 and 94).

SALOME (DAUGHTER OF HERODIAS)

16. A markedly Arab type of countenance, with the firm chin of the Herods. She was the wife, first, of Philip the Tetrarch (see page 21) secondly of Aristobulus, above.

[Bibliothèque Nationale.

AGRIPPA II

[Staatliche Münzsammling, Munich.

17. A less forceful copy of his father, with a strong resemblance to his cousin Aristobulus (15 above). The other side of this coin shews two fish, a grateful reference to Nero's gift to him of Taricheae, the fishery centre on the Sea of Galilee (see page 95).

[*D. Brewster.*

18. The existing North Wall of Jerusalem, seen from outside Herod's Gate, looking east. The big building on the left is the Palestine Archaeological (Rockefeller) Museum; that on the horizon, the Kaiserin Augusta Victoria hospital. The wall in its present state is the work of Saladin, who rebuilt it after the fall of the Crusader Kingdom in 1188 (as commemorated by an inscription on the third, tall, bastion from the camera), and Suleiman the Magnificent, who repaired it in the middle of the sixteenth century.

The Third Wall of Agrippa ran along the same line, and traces of Herodian masonry underlie the existing structure. The Fosse has been largely filled in; but opposite the Museum (beyond the omnibus) the counterscarp can still be descried.

[*Henri Seyrig.*

BEIRUT

19. These two coins (of the reign of Elagabalus, A.D. 218-222) represent the Colony of Beirut. The first shews the monumental arch which probably gave access to the forum. On the forum stands the statue of Marsyas; above the arch, one of Eros riding a lion.

The second coin shews the nymph Beroë "surprised" by Poseidon, the god of the sea, as she is drawing water from a well—a charmingly "Victorian" composition (see page 80).

because I want to, but because you insist on it." He then told
Macro, the commandant of the Guards, to bring Eutychus
before him. He was produced at once. When Tiberius asked him
what accusation he had to make against the man who had given
him his freedom, Eutychus repeated what he had overheard, and
added that Agrippa on the same occasion had suggested that when
he became emperor, Caligula should murder young Tiberius,
the very lad who had been committed to Agrippa's charge. It is
true that Agrippa had neglected little Tiberius and had, despite
the emperor's wishes, paid his court to Caligula instead, and it is
also true that this had brought him into disfavour with the
emperor. But it is most unlikely that he had suggested the suppression of his ward. Still, Tiberius, who had certainly done all he
could to prevent the matter coming to an issue, now affected to
believe Eutychus. Turning to Macro, he said, "Arrest this man",
and moved on. Macro was bewildered, not knowing whom he was
to seize. When the litter had circled the hippodrome a second time
and came back to where they were standing, the emperor said:
"This, Macro, is the man I told you to arrest—I think I made
myself clear?" Macro still could not believe that he was to
arrest Agrippa. He asked point blank, "Which man?" "Agrippa,"
replied the emperor. Agrippa was dumbfounded. He tried en-
treaty, invoking his friendship with Drusus and Gemellus, but all
to no purpose. There and then he was loaded with chains, over his
imperial purple robes, and led off to gaol. What an ironical
catastrophe! If only he had not been such a good friend of Antonia,
if only Antonia had not possessed such an influence over Caesar,
this would not have happened.

Even in this crisis, Agrippa could show the nicer side of his
character. They had had little wine with their meal, and the heat
and the trial had made him very thirsty. He happened to catch
sight of one of Caligula's slaves, called Thaumastus, carrying a
pitcher of water. He begged for some of it to drink, which the
lad gave him. When he had finished drinking, he said: "My boy,
this will turn out to your advantage. If once I get rid of these
chains, I will secure your liberty from your master, because he
has looked after me in my distress, just as he did in my prosperity."

As he stood there in fetters before the prison, with a number of
others in like case, he sought the shade of a tree, and leaned
against the trunk. Soon after, an owl came and settled on the
tree, whereupon one of Agrippa's fellow-prisoners turned to the
soldier to whom he was chained, and enquired "who the man in

F

purple was". When the soldier told him, he asked to be led over to talk to him. Permission being given, the prisoner begged for an interpreter, because he was a German tribal chief, who knew but little Latin. He then asked that the following speech be translated. He realized, he said, that Agrippa would hardly believe him, but he predicted—and he well knew the risk he was running by making such a prediction—that Agrippa would soon be free, and advanced to the highest dignity and power. He was not saying this to curry favour, nor had he been bribed to say it; he only asked that when Agrippa was freed, he would try to free him as well. But let him take note: this same owl had been sent to him as a sign from God. The next time he saw the bird, he would have but five days to live.

This little story has a curiously circumstantial ring to it. From the point of view of folk-lore, it is of considerable interest. In the west, the owl, probably owing to its binocular vision, which is extremely rare in birds, has for ages past been a symbol of wisdom. To the Greeks it was the bird of Athene, and as such appeared on the coins of Athens. It was a bringer of good fortune. In the east, on the other hand, because of its ghost-like flight and sinister note, the owl is a bird of ill omen, and feared as the harbinger of doom. Here, in this tale, we have the western and eastern folk-lore combined.

Antonia, of course, was terribly upset by the whole affair; but, sensible woman that she was, saw that to say anything more to Tiberius would only make matters worse. She told Macro to see to it that Agrippa's imprisonment should be as tolerable as possible. As it turned out, the German was right. Agrippa had not long to wait—only six months, during which he was allowed his own food and bedding, and a daily visit to the bath. His friends were permitted to call on him, and the centurion in charge treated him with far-sighted lenity. One day, just as Agrippa was going out to the bath, the faithful Marsyas, who had been looking after him, rushed up to him, gave him a nod, and said, in Hebrew, "The lion is dead". Agrippa answered in the same tongue: "God bless you; I hope you are right." The centurion knew no Hebrew, but realized from Agrippa's face and tone of voice that something important had happened. Agrippa at first refused to say what it was, but in the end told him the good news. The centurion celebrated it by giving a jolly feast in Agrippa's honour. There was plenty to drink; but in the middle of the banquet, in came a messenger saying that Tiberius was not dead,

that he was in fact about to enter Rome. Back to the cells went
Agrippa, and he and his host spent a miserable night. But next
morning letters came from Caligula, both to the Senate and to
Piso, announcing the true and undoubted death of the old
emperor. Agrippa, said the new Caesar, was to be released from
prison, and to go back to his own house. He would have liked to
free him completely and at once. It was Antonia who prevented
him. That prudent lady realized that ostentatiously to conciliate
one who had been imprisoned for suspected treason would make
it appear that Caligula was glad that Tiberius was dead, which,
even if true, would be most unseemly. Nevertheless, a few days
after the funeral, Caligula sent for Agrippa, had him shaved, gave
him a new outfit, and a chain of gold of the same weight as the
iron chain he had so lately worn. He also appointed him king of
the region in which his uncle Philip had formerly been tetrarch,
promised to enlarge it, and placed a diadem on his head. The
diadem was a fillet of gold, which, rather like a close-fitting halo,
bound the brow and temples. It was the symbol of royalty. The
vagabond was king at last.

Chapter X

AGRIPPA I: THE TRIMMER

AS successor to Pontius Pilate (in whose place Vitellius had appointed Marcellus as a temporary measure), Caligula now sent out Marullus. It was the spring of the year 37. Agrippa was content to stay on in Rome. He was a rich man now, with the accumulated revenues of the tetrarchy at his disposal. The Senate invested him with the insignia of a praetor. He was in no hurry to return to a country which held such humiliating memories for him. But at the end of the year he changed his mind. With the political flair which was so strong in the abler members of the Herodian family throughout the five generations of their eminence, Agrippa saw that Caligula could not last long: he had already started on the career of folly, cruelty and madness that the mere mention of his name recalls. It would not do to be known as the intimate of such a man when the time came for a change. So, with the emperor's permission, Agrippa set out for Palestine. With him he took Thaumastus, the slave who had given him the drink of water after his arrest. He had obtained his freedom, as he said he would, and was now taking him out to be his chief steward of the family estates, a post he was to hold until his death in the days of Agrippa's children.

His arrival at Alexandria was the signal for ugly racial riots. Everyone was amazed by the turn of fortune, which had sent back the discredited and suppliant fugitive as a king, clad in purple, and attended by a bodyguard arrayed in gold and silver armour. The Jews, led by Alexander the Alabarch, were naturally jubilant at this elevation of one of their faith; the Greeks were equally jealous and resentful. They arranged a mock procession, in which with obscene and insulting symbols they derided Agrippa's reception. Violence and massacre followed, which the prefect of Egypt, Avillius Flaccus, openly encouraged. Even after Agrippa had left, the disorders continued, the rioters desecrating the synagogues, and placing statues of the emperor in them. Agrippa, with an eye on his interest with Caligula, could easily have remained inactive; but, like his grandfather Herod the Great, he was always zealous where the rights of Jewry were concerned, even where, as in this case, his own authority and reputation were not engaged; for, although he had family ties with the Alabarch, he had no jurisdiction whatever in Alexandria. He now complained to Caligula, who banished Flaccus to the island of Andros, and confiscated his art collection. Flaccus was executed in 39.

Agrippa's elevation proved Antipas' downfall. Herodias could not bear to think that her scapegrace brother should now be ruling as a king, a bare thirty miles away, up in Caesarea Philippi, while her husband, after forty-three years of service to Rome and to his people, was still only a tetrarch. Antipas, now in his sixties, was content with his lot; but Herodias was fatally determined that he should improve it. Antipas gave in, and in 39 the two of them set off for Rome, in the most magnificent style. Agrippa, who had of course been kept informed of the preparations, at first thought of going to Rome himself, but in the end decided to send ahead a confidential freedman, Fortunatus, with a letter instead. Fortunatus arrived hard on the heels of Antipas and Herodias, and was able to wait upon the emperor while Antipas was actually with him. This was at Baiae, the Brighton of ancient Rome, a thermal resort at the north-western extremity of the Bay of Naples, where many leading Roman families owned seaside villas. Caligula had received Antipas kindly, but, as soon as he was told that a letter had arrived from his dear Agrippa, he interrupted the audience to read it. Its contents were alarming. Agrippa accused Antipas, first, of having taken part in Sejanus' plot against Tiberius; secondly, of being at that very moment in league with Artaban, the king of Parthia, against Rome. As evidence of this last charge, Agrippa alleged that Antipas had in his armoury equipment for 70,000 men. Caligula asked him whether this was true. Antipas was unable to deny it.

There and then he was stripped of his tetrarchy, which together with all his fortune was given to Agrippa, and banished to *Lugdunum Convenarum*, which was not the modern Lyons, then an important mint and road centre, but Saint-Bertrand de Comminges, in Aquitaine, near the Spanish frontier.

Agrippa had now also arrived in Italy. When the emperor heard that Herodias was Agrippa's sister, he said she might keep her own property, and offered her exemption from the decree of banishment. Herodias replied that, having been the partner of her husband's prosperity, she did not intend to forsake him in his misfortune. Poor Herodias! For Antipas she had sacrificed her reputation; in an attempt to advance him she had ruined him, and had enriched the rival she had thought to humble. Nevertheless, she had been faithful to Antipas in her fashion, and preferred to remain so till the end. Of Herodias, as of Shakespeare's Cawdor, it may be said that "nothing in her life became her like the leaving it".

Agrippa's influence with Caligula was soon to be put to the test. Caligula had come to the conclusion that he was a god, a brother and partner of Jupiter himself. In Rome, his house was joined to the temple of Jupiter, so that the twin gods could share the same dwelling. It is true that Julius Caesar had been officially deified in 42 B.C., two years after his assassination, and that there was a temple to him in Rome. But it was also true that Augustus had always resisted any attempt to venerate himself as divine during his lifetime, though Horace does not scruple to describe him as the associate of gods on high, and even Virgil, in a famous line, describing the Roman peace, which Augustus had created, sings of it as the work of "some god". Augustus had been the recipient of many dedications, altars and temples and sacrifices, particularly in the east, where divinity had hedged kings from time immemorial. Herod the Great had indeed erected a temple to Rome and Augustus in Samaria. But this deification of the emperor, which grew gradually during his lifetime, and was crystallized, as it were, after his death, must be considered in the context of the age. To say that the gods of Rome enjoyed a status comparable to the saints, rather than to the Trinity, of the Christian Church, even that is to rate them rather high. They were symbols of nature, and of natural influences, of birth, fertility and death, of good fortune and ill. But they had no personal effect on morals or conduct. As will be shown later, by the middle of the first century almost any Roman who felt the need of a personal religion sought it in one of the eastern cults, of which Judaism was one, and Christianity was now spreading as another (see page 91). Divinity, as such, did not, to a Roman of Caligula's day, connote the ineffable sublimity of a supreme God. If an emperor claimed to be god, Rome might be disgusted; but it was not outraged.

The Jews were. For them, there was One God, and one only. Even to think of the possibility of any rival was blasphemy. God was sole, sublime and infinite. He could not be represented by any image made with hands. Nor (as we have seen: page 51) could any statue or representation of the human form be tolerated in Jewry, lest it became an object of veneration.

When Caligula proclaimed his divinity, sycophants throughout the empire vied with each other in erecting altars, statues and temples. Herennius Capito, the imperial steward of the Jamnia estate, instigated the Gentile inhabitants there to raise an unpretentious altar of brick to the new god. The Jews of the region at once overthrew it. Capito reported the insult to Caligula. After taking council with his chamberlain, an Egyptian called Helicon, and his favourite actor, Apella of Ascalon, neither of whom was likely to be a lover of Jewry, the emperor decided to punish these stiff-necked rebels by having a statue of himself, the new Jupiter, erected not merely in Judaea, but in the very Temple itself. It was to be more than life-size, and plated with gold. That would teach them.

The governor of Syria, Petronius, was ordered to see these commands carried out. Petronius was in a dilemma. He knew well that the Jews would never agree to such sacrilege; but he knew also that he would have to answer with his life for disregard of the imperial mandate. He decided to temporize. He immediately moved south with two legions and their auxiliaries to Ptolemais, the most southerly city of his province, on the verge of Judaea. Caligula commended him for his alacrity. But winter was now approaching, so that Petronius could legitimately suspend operations and claim that he would continue them in the spring. A deputation of Jews at once arrived to implore Petronius not to proceed with the proposal. They were very temperate, they merely stated the difficult truth: they would be killed rather than allow the erection of this blasphemous idol—for such of course in their eyes the projected statue was. Agrippa was still in Rome, and his brother Aristobulus was acting as his regent. Aristobulus had married Jotape, the daughter of Suheim, king of Emesa (Homs), within Petronius' jurisdiction. Aristobulus, therefore, together with a cousin called Helkias, went to see Petronius, and begged him to hold his hand. Petronius, to show that he had obeyed the emperor, had already ordered the statue to be made at Sidon. But how could he appease the Jews? They had proclaimed an agricultural strike, and if ploughing did not begin soon, the country would be ruined—the last crop had failed through drought as it was. There was only one way out: Petronius called a conference at Tiberias, and frankly told the Jews that, at the risk of his life, he was going to write to the emperor and ask him to countermand his orders. Hardly had he finished speaking, when down came the rain. It was hailed, says Josephus, as an "epiphany", a manifestation of God's power. Petronius, too, "was mightily surprised when he perceived that God evidently took care of the Jews". Nevertheless, Petronius regarded himself as a doomed man: he well knew what Caligula's rage would be, when he opened Petronius' despatch. Meanwhile, Agrippa had learned from Caligula himself of the fate which awaited the Jews for their disobedience. He was appalled. How could he save the situation? He set about it in a typically Herodian way. First of all, he sent the emperor a memorandum, in the drafting of which Philo, the Jewish divine from Alexandria, who was in Rome to rebut Apion's accusations concerning the riot of the year 38, lent a hand. He then invited Caligula to a banquet the like of which for sheer sumptuousness Rome had never seen. It was the sort of compliment that Caligula relished. He drank plentifully: when Agrippa had proposed his health, the emperor in his reply bade Agrippa ask a boon: "Everything that may contribute to thy happiness shall be at thy service, and that cheerfully." Agrippa, with just the sure psychological touch that his great-grandfather Antipater had shown when Julius Caesar had made him a similar offer, instead of disclosing his real intention, modestly said that he did hope the emperor would not think that he was out for any personal advantage: he was attached to Caligula for his own sake, as he had shewn when, contrary to Tiberius' wishes, he had consorted with him. Besides, the emperor had already loaded him with far more honour than he deserved. Caligula, as Agrippa intended, only reiterated his offer with more vehemence. Agrippa struck: he asked Caligula straight out not to have the statue erected. Caligula was caught: he could not go back on his word, given and confirmed in the presence of so many witnesses. He issued orders that if the statue had already been erected (he knew it had not, but it was a face-saving clause) it was to stay there, but if it had not been erected, the project was to lapse. It was a remarkable victory for Agrippa, who realized as well as anyone the risk he had taken. The Jews never forgot his valiant defence of their religion, at such danger to himself. Caligula, feeling that he had been tricked, was determined to find a victim. When he received Petronius' report, he wrote back ordering him to kill himself. It is pleasant to record that the ship bearing this missive was delayed by a storm, and that, before it reached Petronius, another post had arrived announcing that Caligula himself had been assassinated on January 24th, A.D. 41. Petronius, and the Jews, were saved.

Agrippa, too, must have been greatly relieved by the disappearance of his old friend. He had now become one of the most important men in Rome, and played a leading and, indeed, decisive part in the elevation of the new emperor, Claudius, or Tiberius Claudius Drusus Nero Germanicus, to give him his full name. He was an uncle of Caligula. He had been born at Lugdunum on the Rhone (Lyons) in the year 10 B.C., so that he was now in his fiftieth year. He had, of course, known Agrippa for many years. They were coevals, and had been brought up together; and it was Claudius' mother, Antonia, who had so favoured Agrippa. In the confusion that followed Caligula's assassination, Agrippa kept a cool head, and acted as a neutral and indispensable intermediary in the hurried and vital negotiations between Claudius, the Senate and the praetorian guard, which resulted in Claudius' being proclaimed emperor the very next day.

Agrippa's reward was golden. For him was to be reconstituted the entire kingdom of Herod the Great. This meant that, in addition to the northern regions which he already administered, he was to be given the whole of the procuratorial province of Judaea, including Jamnia and Azotus. The donation was made public by the usual means of an edict engraved on bronze and set up in the Capitol. Claudius also released Alexander the Alabarch, who was an old friend, and steward to his mother; he had been imprisoned by Caligula, as a result of the Alexandria riots three years before. His son Mark, who had married Agrippa's daughter Berenice, was dead, so Agrippa now gave her in marriage to his brother Herod, at the same time begging for him the region of Chalcis (the modern Anjar) in the Lebanon at the foot of Mount Hermon, with praetorian rank and the title of king. This meant that Berenice was now a queen.

Claudius was determined to liquidate the Alexandria affair once and for all. He sent to its citizens a rescript of which fortunately a copy has come down to us, preserved on papyrus in the British Museum. He ordered them to behave decently and humanely to the Jews, who had for so long inhabited the same city as they, not to interfere with their traditional religious rites, nor with their customs, as established at the time of the divine Augustus, and as he, Claudius, having heard both sides, had confirmed them. On the other hand, he strictly ordered the Jews not to try to enlarge their privileges, and never again to send an embassy to Rome as a rival to that of the citizens, as though the two parties inhabited two different cities. They were not to take part in the games (which were a purely Greek institution), but to attend to their own affairs. Finally, they were not to attempt to increase their numerical strength by attracting Jews from other parts of Egypt or from Syria. If they did, he would punish them in every possible way, as disturbers of world peace. It is a fair and statesmanlike document. Claudius was determined that the Jews should have justice; but he saw what widespread disturbances would be caused by any attempt to organize Jewish migration.

The re-establishment of the kingdom brought the Jews of Palestine to the zenith of their earthly felicity. Gone was the procurator, gone the legions, the eagles, the tax-gatherers. Judaea was Jewish once more. It seemed like a return to the days of Good Queen Alexandra, the Hasmonaean princess who had ruled in Israel just before the advent of Rome, from 76 to 67 B.C., that golden age when, it is said, the crops had been fabulous, and it had always rained at the right time. Agrippa behaved perfectly. If, in Rome, he did as the Romans did, in Jerusalem he was a devout Jew. On arrival in the Holy City, his first action was to give thanks to God, and to suspend in the Temple treasury the golden chain which Caligula had given him as a souvenir of his release from prison. He paid the fees for the shaving of the heads of Nazarites who had fulfilled their vows. "We are told," says Abel, citing the Talmud, "that he thought it not beneath his dignity himself to shoulder the basket bearing the first-fruits, and to carry it up the stairs of the courtyard, while the singers intoned the 30th psalm, which the king might well apply to himself: 'I will extol thee, O Lord; for thou hast lifted me up, and hast not made my foes to rejoice over me.'" At the Feast of Tabernacles in A.D. 41, as he was reading the passage in Deuteronomy xvii, 15, "thou mayest not set a stranger over thee, which is not thy brother", Agrippa burst into tears, whereupon the crowd cried out: "Be of good cheer, Agrippa! You are truly our brother", as, despite his Edomite ancestry, he certainly was, by the express provision of Deuteronomy xxiii, 7, 8. In order to maintain himself in a state of ritual purity, Agrippa habitually lived not at Caesarea, as the procurators had done, but in Jerusalem itself, which thus became once more the capital. As High Priest, he appointed Simon Kantheros, son of Boethus, to whom he was related, in place of Theophilus, son of Annas; but at the end of a year, offered to re-instal his brother Jonathan, who, however, declined the honour this time, in favour of yet a third brother, Matthaias.

On the material side, he conciliated his subjects by remitting

the house-tax. Indeed, Agrippa's policy was deliberately conciliatory, though, like his grandfather, he could be impetuous. As
Master of the Horse, Agrippa had appointed an old and tried
retainer, called Silas. The honour went to Silas' head, and he
was for ever harping on his past services, and saying how much
he had done for Agrippa, when he was a penniless fugitive.
Agrippa took this ill, "for the commemoration of times when men
have been under ignominy is by no means agreeable to them;
and he is a very silly man who is perpetually relating to a person
what kindness he has done him". Finally, Agrippa, unable to
tolerate Silas any more, dismissed him from his office, and sent
him back to his own part of the country under arrest. The king
soon repented, and when his next birthday came round, he invited Silas to the party. But Silas, who was a boor, sent back an
offensive refusal, and so stayed on in prison.

   Although he lived at Jerusalem, Agrippa did sometimes go
down to Caesarea, which was, after all, the second city of his
kingdom, even if its inhabitants were largely pagan. During one
of these absences, a fanatical lawyer, called Simon, got together a
number of the Jerusalem godly and accused Agrippa of impiety,
and even went so far as to propose that he be excluded from the
Temple, "since it belonged only to native Jews". Herod the Great
would have made short work of such a critic. Agrippa merely
summoned him to come and see him, and received him in the
theatre. As they sat there next each other, the king turned to
Simon and said, quietly and gently, "What is there here contrary
to the law?" Simon was overcome. He begged Agrippa's pardon.
The king granted it, and gave Simon a little present into the
bargain.

   One of the most attractive traits in the character of Herod the
Great had been his passion for building. The motive of much of
his construction may have been his love of grandeur; what he
built was, nevertheless, of enduring amenity, for Jew and Gentile
alike. Wherever Agrippa looked, the imposing memorials of his
grandfather's splendour met his eyes. In Jerusalem, the two great
palace-barracks, the theatre, the amphitheatre, the hippodrome,
the very walls of the city, nay, the great Temple of the Holy One,
shining like a mountain of snow on its great acropolis—all these
were Herod's work. Caesarea and Samaria were wholly his
creations. Beyond the frontiers of his dominions, Herod had to
many a city presented impressive and costly embellishments,
theatres, porticoes and gymnasiums. Agrippa decided to emulate

his ancestor. He began with Jerusalem. It was hard, here, to find anything that had not already been built or re-built. A certain amount of work was still going on to complete the vast artificial platform of the Temple: otherwise, the city needed nothing— except in one particular. Despite its recurring troubles, under Herodian and Roman rule, Jerusalem had prospered. As a result, a whole suburb, called *Bezetha,* or "New City," had arisen to the north of the Herodian ramparts. It was this region that Agrippa now determined to enclose.

From the time when its construction was undertaken by Agrippa in A.D. 41, down to the present day, the Third Wall (as it is called) has been a subject of controversy, never more so than during the last thirty years.

Since it will in any case be necessary to give some indications of the topography of Jerusalem when we come to the story of the siege of it by the Romans under Titus, it may be well to outline, very briefly, how the city had grown, and when, and for what purpose the *three walls* were built. The original Jebusite town was a little fortress erected on the rocky spur called Ophel that dominates the Virgin's Fountain, on the western side of the Valley of the Kedron. This is the only spring in the neighbourhood, and it therefore determined the site of the town. Its waters were con- veyed by King Hezekiah through the famous Siloam tunnel to the pool of the same name, in order that, even during a siege, the supply should be available to the defenders of the city and not to the attackers. In the days of the kings of Judah, the city spread to the west, as cities generally do, and the hill now called "Mount Zion" separated from Ophel by the Tyropoeon valley, and to-day crowned by the successor of Herod's palace known as the *Citadel,* was included within its limits. To the north, Solomon had built a temple on the obvious site, that is, the "high place" above Ophel. Like so many high places in Palestine, it was used as a threshing-floor, where the oxen could tread out the grain, and the west wind carry away the chaff (2 Samuel xxiv). The whole of this area was enclosed within a wall. On the east, south and west, the town was flanked by valleys. It was not therefore possible to expand in those directions. The wall, once built, remained on the same trace. It might be, and often was, breached or destroyed; but it was always rebuilt *in situ,* as we may read in the dramatic second chapter of Nehemiah. Only on the north side was growth possible, and, with prosperity, inevitable.

The northern boundary of the pre-Exilic city ran in a simple, straight line from the Citadel to the Temple. This is known, technically, as the *First Wall*. It was supplemented only by Antipater, the father of Herod the Great, in the year 44 B.C. The first wall had left half the west side, and the whole of the north side, of the Temple exposed. It had been pillaged ten years before by Crassus; and Antipater felt that the time had come to protect the sanctuary and treasury of the nation from a similar assault. He therefore built a zig-zag, diagonal wall, from the citadel to the north-west corner of the Temple, where his son Herod was to build his fortress of Antonia. This, comparatively short, rampart is called the *Second Wall*. The process of expansion to the north was greatly stimulated by the prosperity which attended the Herodian epoch, in the setting of the Roman peace: hence the New City or *Bezetha* which Agrippa now set about incorporating within the *enceinte* of the Walls.

The new rampart is known as the *Third Wall*. It was, Josephus tells us, a magnificent structure, fifteen feet wide and forty feet high. It was adorned with ninety square towers, furnished with cisterns and chambers, and protected by a fosse fifty feet broad and twenty feet deep. Tacitus also pays a grudging tribute to its grandeur, the height of its towers, which seemed to overcome all the inequalities of terrain and to be all of the same elevation, and to the skill with which the bays and bastions had been disposed, so that an attacker could always be taken on the flank by the defence. At the time when Josephus and Tacitus were writing in Rome, that is at the end of the century, this wall had achieved a bitter fame for the part it played in the great siege. It had in fact never been completed according to Agrippa's design, because he had died within two years of its inception, and, of course, no Roman procurator would finish such a work. Indeed, the Romans had good reason, in retrospect, to wish that it had never been started; and Tacitus (*Hist.*, V, 12) says that permission to build it was gained only by bribery, so that "in unbroken peace, they raised the walls as for a war". Josephus, on the other hand, both in the *War*, V, iv, and in the *Antiquities*, XIX, vii, says that the reason why the building of the wall was suspended was that it offended the Romans. Or had Agrippa, as so often, simply run out of money? We must remember that enormous sums were still being spent on the completion of the Temple. To start so grandiose a work as the Third Wall in order to please his Jewish subjects, and then to give as the reason for stopping it a pretext which implied complaisance to his Roman masters, would be wholly in keeping

with Agrippa's character. In reality, Agrippa had a perfect right
to build a city wall within his own kingdom, nor was Claudius, as
we know from Dio LX, 6, the man to be corrupted. Besides, he
himself undertook magnificent public works, and would have been
pleased rather than vexed if his old friend Agrippa did the same.
But Josephus, be it remembered, had become the pensioner of the
Romans, and was, moreover, writing for Agrippa's son, who
was, like himself, Caesar's client. It would hardly be tactful
therefore, to saddle Agrippa with the sole responsibility for a
work which, as finally finished, had caused so much damage to
Rome.

What exactly did this Third Wall enclose, and on what trace
was it built? This question has provoked one of the thorniest
archaeological controversies of the past century. In the age of
innocence, before the birth of scientific archaeology, it was
assumed that the Third Wall ran along the line of the present
north wall. But, in 1841, an American scholar, Edward Robinson,
published his *Biblical Researches in Palestine*, in which he advanced
a theory that the line of the Third Wall was to be found not
below the present wall, but in a breastwork of masonry, of which
traces were intermittently visible about a quarter of a mile to the
north of it. During the last thirty years, when building operations
have brought more and more sections of the breastwork to light,
the argument has become more and more acute. The northern
line has been championed by two eminent Jewish scholars,
Professor Leo Mayer and the late Dr Sukenik: the traditional line
has been defended by the renowned Dominican, Père Vincent,
the doyen of Jerusalem's resident archaeologists.

Where the protagonists are scholars, and scholars of such international eminence, it is not for an amateur to intervene. It will be
enough to say that thirty years' acquaintance with the topography of both lines, and study of the literature produced with
such gentlemanly persuasiveness by both sides, seem now to
lead to the conclusion that only on the trace of the present north
wall could a Third Wall of the proportions described by Josephus
have stood. The arguments in favour of this ascription are, very
briefly, as follows. They fall into two categories, the literary and
the archaeological. To take the literary first. Josephus tells us
(*War*, V, iv, 2) that the Third Wall, where it ran from west to
east, i.e. on its north face, (a) went past the tomb of Queen Helena
of Adiabene, which, as we know from *Antiquities*, XX, iv, 3, lay
about 700 yards north of the wall, and (b) 'past the sepulchral

caverns of the kings', or "Solomon's Quarries". Both these topographical indications fit the line of the present wall: neither fits the trace of the breastwork, which is less than 300 yards from the monument, and rather more than that from Solomon's Quarries. Secondly, in the same passage of the *War*, Josephus tells us that the masonry of the Third Wall was in no way inferior to that of the Temple itself, on which, be it remembered, masons were still at work, to the original Herodian design, at the time when the Third Wall was being built. During excavations made in 1937-8 by the Palestine Department of Antiquities at the foot of the towers which flank the existing Damascus Gate, enormous blocks of Herodian masonry were discovered, not merely re-used, as is so often the case, but *in situ*: they were beyond doubt relics of a Herodian-style construction. The masonry of the breastwork, on the other hand, is a hotch-potch of stones large and small. Some are Herodian, some are paving stones, some have been hastily fashioned, and often the joints are filled in with pebbles. Nothing could be further from the description which Josephus gives of the fine masonry of Agrippa's wall.

Turning now to the archaeological evidence, we come upon three important negative indications. The first is that, although the breastwork has been traced fairly continuously on the line running from west to east, i.e. where it faces north, not a single vestige has ever come to light of any construction running north and south on its two flanks which would have joined this north front to the previously existing walls: it is simply a detached bulwark, whereas Agrippa's wall was a continuous rampart. Secondly, between it and the existing wall no trace of habitation has ever come to light. Graves, yes; houses, no. And yet it was to protect the new suburbs that the Third Wall was built. Thirdly, of the tower Psephinus which stood at the western end of the Third Wall, a massive octagon, no trace has ever been found at the extremity of the breastwork; while beneath the north-west corner of the present wall, below the Collège des Frères, are the remains of a tower so massive that to this day it is called in Arabic the "Tower of Goliath".

It seems fair, therefore, to conclude, with the Dominican scholars, that the Third Wall was constructed on the line of the present wall, and that the breastwork, or Fourth Wall, as we must now call it (if only that so great a *savant* as Leo Mayer may have his own memorial), was hastily thrown together during the revolt of Bar Kozeba in 131, and was compounded for the most part of the débris of this very Third Wall, which had been overthrown by Titus sixty-one years before.

To return to Agrippa. He had made a continuous wall, from the Citadel to what is now the Collège des Frères at the north-west corner, down eastwards, past the monument of Queen Helena of Adiabene, over the famous Solomon's Quarries, to what was called the Tower of the Fuller, now the Storks' Tower, at the north-east corner, and then south to the north-east corner of the Temple. The whole circuit of the walls as thus completed by Agrippa was 33 stades, or three and three-quarter miles.

Having thus furnished Jerusalem with the one great work which his grandfather had left undone, Agrippa, like Herod the Great, turned to Gentile cities; because, strict Jew as he was within Jewry, he liked to play the cosmopolitan philanthropist outside it. The most international centre in the whole Levant was then, as now, Beirut. In the year 14 B.C. Beirut, *Beeroth*, or *Berytus* in its Graeco-Roman guise (the name means wells), had been refounded as a Roman colony, with the name of *Colonia Julia Augusta Felix Berytus*. Lying on the lip of that blue bay, with the snow-capped mountains of the Lebanon towering up to the east of the olive-clad plain, Beirut was for the Roman expatriate an almost Italian ambience. It was the ordained site for the little Rome from Rome which a colony was. Its appeal to Agrippa, who had lived so much of his life in Rome, must have been overpowering. He, like Herod the Great, embellished it with a theatre, an amphi-theatre, porticoes, baths—all the usual amenities of the Hellen-istic *polis*. He entertained its citizens with sumptuous shows, and held a musical festival. He also, alas! provided another enter-tainment: a gladiatorial contest in which no less than 1,400 con-demned men were made to fight each other to the death. As a Jew, Agrippa knew that this disgusting exhibition, wherever it might be held, was a breach of the commandment of God, "Thou shalt not kill" (see Plates 19, 27 and 28).

From Beirut, Agrippa went to Tiberias. The capital of his uncle Antipas, the town where he and Kypros had been so humiliated by the tetrarch and Herodias, it was now his; the city where he had worked as a junior official he entered now as king. He wanted everyone to know of his elevation, and so he invited five other kings to pay him a visit there. It was to be a brilliant durbar. First there was his brother and son-in-law, Herod of Chalcis; the others were Antiochus IV of Commagene, Cotys, king of Lesser Armenia, Polemon his brother, king of Pontus, and

20. The *atrium* or courtyard of the Tomb of Queen Helena of Adiabene in Jerusalem (see page 78) as it appears to-day. We associate the elaborate, architecturally-decorated, rock-cut tomb with Petra; but the art was also practised in Palestine. This is a particularly fine example of it. The tower of St George's Cathedral appears in the top left-hand corner—that is, to the west of the tomb.

[*Alinari.*

21. This statue of Isis (see pages 47 and 92), now in the Naples Museum, formerly stood in the *cella* of the Temple of Isis in Pompeii. As contemporary engravings shew, it was discovered *in situ* when the temple was excavated in the last quarter of the eighteenth century. Its authenticity is therefore unquestioned. The figure is interesting: Egyptian (note the *ankh* in the left hand) but acclimatized to Graeco-Roman taste. The worship of Isis had been introduced into Italy in the earlier part of the first century B.C.

"Sampsigeramus"—or *Shamash garama* "The Sun hath established" of Emesa (Homs). Agrippa no doubt assembled the party
just to show off; but the governor of Syria, Vibius Marsus, who
had been invited too, thought it a dangerous innovation. He did
not want to risk affronting Caesar's friend, but he slyly sent
messengers to each of the guests, to say that it would be prudent
if they went home. Agrippa was, of course, furious.

Caesarea, the magnificent city which his grandfather had
raised on the site of a little fishing village called Strato's Tower,
was Agrippa's chief port, and here, too, he could give rein to his
gentile tastes. He held games in honour of the emperor here, and
in the palace visitors could actually see statues of the three
daughters of the Jewish monarch, Drusilla, Mariamme and
Berenice. Agrippa's coins displayed the same assumption of
Jewish and gentile qualities. Those which were struck in Jerusalem
bore no effigy, whereas those which came from the mints of
Caesarea, Tiberias or Caesarea Philippi bore his own image or
that of the reigning Caesar. He and his family were members of
the Julian clan, and he liked to be called Friend of Rome and
Friend of Caesar in inscriptions.

It was at Caesarea that death came for Agrippa. It was the
spring of 44. His friend the emperor Claudius had returned to
Rome after a successful campaign in Britain. Agrippa went down
to Caesarea to preside over the thanksgiving celebrations. As we
know from Acts xii, he had also as his guests envoys from Tyre
and Sidon. Ever since Agrippa had taken the side of the Damascenes over the boundary dispute in the days of Flaccus, the citizens
of Tyre and Sidon had been at odds with him. More recently,
his annoyance with Marsus had induced Agrippa to place an
embargo on the export of provisions from Galilee and the Hauran
to the Phoenician cities. They had come to sue for peace. On the
second day of the games, Agrippa, when he entered the theatre
dressed in a glittering web of cloth of silver, was given a rapturous
reception. The populace, beside themselves with enthusiasm,
hailed him, as both Josephus and the Acts record, as a god.
Agrippa did nothing to rebuke this impiety: after all, his grandfather had built this city of Caesarea for his pagan subjects, and it
was they who were now honouring him after their custom. It
would be boorish to decline their ovation, only good manners to
accept it with relish. The king sat down on his throne, in high good
humour. As he leaned back on the cushions, his glance travelled
upwards. There, in the bright sunshine on one of the ropes of the

G

awning, sat an owl! Agrippa "immediately understood that this bird was the messenger of ill tidings, as it had once been the messenger of good tidings to him; and fell into the deepest sorrow. A severe pain also arose in his belly, and began in a most violent manner."

The king was carried back to the palace, where, his theatrical instinct alert to the end, he had himself conveyed into a lofty and conspicuous chamber, below which a multitude of his subjects assembled, as is the custom when a monarch is about to die, for everyone knew that he could not live long. It was the Jews who were the sincerest mourners. They brought their wives and families with them, they donned sackcloth, and sprinkled ashes on their heads. Their prayers and supplications were continually renewed. On the fifth day after his seizure, shortly after Passover of A.D. 44, Agrippa died. He was fifty-four.

Agrippa's sudden and early death, after ruling the re-united kingdom of his grandfather for only three years, was a disaster for Jewry. He had many faults. He was an intriguer, he was extravagant, he could be callous and even cruel. He was a sycophant, who did not scruple to win the Jews by tears, and the Romans by gold. Nevertheless, he had the great virtue, almost unknown in the Levant, of moderation, of being able to see that a question had two sides. He really did succeed in pleasing both Rome and the Jews. That was more even that his grandfather had done. If the methods by which he achieved this balance were sometimes questionable, it must be admitted that the result gave peace and comfort to his subjects, Jew and Gentile alike.

If only Agrippa had lived! It is one of the tragic "ifs" of history. Would he have continued to keep the balance? Could he have prevented the growth of Zealot intransigence, of Greek resentment, of Roman exasperation? We cannot tell; we only know that in his own brief day Agrippa had shown that it could be done.

But a new power, condemned alike by Jew, Greek and Roman, all of whose destinies it was mightily to influence, was already, during the days of Agrippa, coming to maturity. The little company of men and women who hailed Jesus as the true Messiah, and worshipped him as the Son of God made man, had already incurred the hostility of the court and the official pontificate. As early as the year 37, only four years after the Crucifixion, the Sanhedrin had taken advantage of the interregnum caused by Pilate's recall to take the law into their own hands, and to execute one of the most ardent followers of Jesus of Nazareth, by name

Stephen (cf. page 105). The defection of the Pharisee Saul was a disturbing event. He escaped to Arabia, but Damascus, although one of the cities of the Decapolis, proved no safe asylum. During the years 37 to 40, it was leased by Caligula to Harith IV, king of the Nabataeans. At the instance of the Jewish clergy, he sent orders to his ethnarch there to arrest Paul (2 Corinthians xi, 32), no doubt as a dangerous agitator. Paul was threatened in Jerusalem, and so returned to Cilicia, where, in 42 or 43, Barnabas came to take him to Antioch.

The original apostles had stayed on in Jerusalem. They, nevertheless, were beginning to attract followers, and were likely, as Abel points out, to rival the success of the Hellenists, and so become catalysts of national solidarity. In Samaria-Sebaste Peter had overcome his antagonist Simon; in Caesarea and in the plain of Sharon he had preached. But it was the success of the new faith in Antioch that brought matters to a head. There, the labours of Cypriot and Cyrenian missionaries had brought a number of Greeks into the fold. When this happened in the third city of the empire, it meant that it was no longer possible to regard those who walked in the new "way" as merely another, feeble, Jewish sect. They were now called Christians, from *Christos*, meaning Messiah.

This was disturbing news for Agrippa, no less than for the orthodox prelates of his capital. They had thought that this tiresome Messianic agitation, as of course it appeared to them, had been put an end to by Pilate when he executed Jesus of Nazareth eleven years before. The whole movement was subversive, they said, and might well lead to the overthrow of both secular and ecclesiastical authority. Clearly, the ringleaders must be punished. Agrippa started by executing James, son of Zebedee, one of those excitable Galileans who so often caused trouble. This gave great satisfaction to the godly. Agrippa decided to improve the occasion by executing another of the group, called Peter. Who were these people, anyway? They were ordinary fishermen, and had no right whatever to become leaders. Peter was seized. It was Passover, and as soon as possible after the Feast, he should be publicly executed. Unfortunately for Agrippa, Peter escaped, leaving behind him in Jerusalem a few little centres of the new faith, such as the house of Mary, mother of John Mark and aunt of Barnabas, and the upper room where James the brother of Jesus and the elders were wont to meet for prayer and fellowship. Such were the beginnings of the Church in Jerusalem.

Chapter XI

THE DISSOLVING PEACE

AGRIPPA'S death took everyone by surprise—everyone, that is, except the lawbreakers, who exploited it with an alacrity which must have seemed ominous, even in a country where tranquillity has never been accounted the *summum bonum*. The late king's brother, Herod of Chalcis, set a bad example: even before he made the official announcement of Agrippa's death, he and Helkias, who had succeeded Silas as Master of the Horse, sent a confidential servant called Aristo to kill that poor old warrior, as though it were by the order of Agrippa himself. It was an act of useless brutality. As soon as the obituary bulletin was published, trouble broke out in Caesarea itself. The Greeks, who had applauded Agrippa with simulated flattery while he lived, and had noticed with disgust the ostentatious lamentations of their Jewish fellow-citizens at his death, now gave full rein to their jealousy, rancour and ingratitude. Led by the soldiery, they broke into the Palace, carried off the statues of the late king's daughters, and set them up on the roofs of brothels where "they abused them to the utmost of their power, and did such things to them as are too indecent to be related". Then they gathered in the public places, and celebrated the day with feasting, wearing garlands, and pouring libations of gratitude to Charon, the ferryman of the river Styx, for joy that Agrippa was dead. There were similar demonstrations in Sebaste.

Claudius, when he heard how the memory of his friend had been insulted, was anxious to send out as his successor Agrippa's son, also called Agrippa, who was then living with him at Rome. But the lad was only seventeen, and the cabal of freedmen, led by Pallas, Narcissus and Felix, had no intention of allowing such a useful "place" to pass out of their gift if they could help it. They therefore persuaded the emperor that the situation in Palestine demanded firm handling, and that the country must once again become a Roman procuratorial province. So it was settled; and Cuspius Fadus was sent out as the first procurator of the new series. As a posthumous vindication of his friend, however, Claudius recalled Vibius Marsus, who as governor of Syria had

done so much to embarrass Agrippa, and sent in his place the
eminent jurisconsult Cassius Longinus, whose wife his niece
Drusilla had formerly been. He also sent orders to Cuspius that
the inhabitants of Sebaste and Caesarea were to be punished for
their contumely, and that the troops who had led the disturbances
were to be relegated to Pontus, and replaced by detachments from
the Syrian legions. Unfortunately, these orders were not carried
out. The soldiery sent ambassadors to Claudius "and mollified
him"—by what arguments we are not told. So they stayed on in
Judaea, where, as Josephus records, they "sowed the seeds of that
war which began under Florus". Only after the catastrophe did
Vespasian expel them from Palestine.

Cuspius Fadus had plenty of other troubles to occupy him,
without antagonizing the military and the Greeks; and it is at
least possible that he favoured this policy of condoning "loyalist"
aggression, disastrous as the consequences were eventually to be.
First there was a quarrel to be settled between the Greeks of
Philadelphia ('Amman) and the Jews of Peraea, concerning a
little village called Zia, to-day *Khirbet Zeiy*, in the fertile and fruit-
growing region just to the north of Es-Salt. The Jews had taken
up arms, instead of submitting the case to the arbitration of the
governor. Cuspius executed the ringleader, who had the curiously
un-Jewish name of Hannibal, and banished two others. Then
there was an arch-brigand, called Tholomy, who had terrorized
Idumaea, in southern Palestine, and even the region between
'Amman and Petra as well. He, too, was rounded up and executed.
Finally, there was an enthusiast called Theudas, who persuaded
a number of people to assemble at the Jordan, together with all
their belongings, telling them that he was a prophet, and that he
would divide the waters and allow them to cross dry-shod, as
their forbears had done in the days of Joshua. The fact that they
had brought their property with them argues that they intended
to set up some kind of society with Theudas as their chief. Be that
as it may, Cuspius was not going to tolerate any new "movements"
in a country already so unstable. He sent his cavalry to break up
the assembly. Many of them were killed, and others arrested.
Theudas was executed and his head taken to Jerusalem.

Having thus restored order, Cuspius decided to go a step
farther, and bring the High Priest's vestments once more into
Roman custody. As we have seen (page 55), the sacred insignia
had been handed over by Vitellius to the unfettered control
of the pontiffs; and it is a little difficult to see what Cuspius

thought he would gain by re-opening the question. That he did so, and that he claimed he was only carrying out Caesar's orders in so doing, does serve to show the national importance which now attached to the High Priesthood. Cassius Longinus, well knowing what troubles Cuspius' action might provoke, came down to Jerusalem with a large body of troops to hold an enquiry. Perhaps under the influence of the great jurist, both sides (for once) showed reason. The Jews forbore any rash revolt, the Romans any immediate enforcement. It was agreed that a Jewish deputation should go to Rome to place the whole matter before Caesar in person, leaving their sons with the Romans as pledges of good faith.

Agrippa the younger, who, as we have noticed, lived with the emperor in filial intimacy, prevailed upon him to grant the Jews' request. Claudius summoned the ambassadors, and tactfully telling them that they had Agrippa to thank for their good fortune, handed them a copy of an edict addressed to "the magistrates, senate, people and whole nation of the Jews" confirming and ratifying the *status quo*, as established by Vitellius. The document contained compliments not only to young Agrippa—who must have been highly gratified at being hailed thus early as the benefactor of his people—but to Herod of Chalcis as well; and it was to Herod that Claudius now confided the custody of the sacred vestments and tiara. He was also made treasurer of the Temple, with power to appoint the High Priests. This privilege attached to him and to his nephew Agrippa until the Temple itself ceased to be. Herod of Chalcis deposed Elion, son of Simon Kantheros, from the High Priesthood, and put in his place Joseph ben Qamhit. These frequent changes of High Priest, although, as we have seen, they were dictated partly by political expediency, consorted nevertheless with the tastes of the incumbents themselves. These prelates were drawn from the ranks of a worldly aristocracy, and, like certain prince bishops of a later age, must have found the ascetic demands of ritual purity hard to support. One year was generally the limit of their endurance. The refusal of Jonathan, son of Annas, to undertake the office for a second term is significant enough (see page 74, bottom).

After two years, in A.D. 46, Cuspius Fadus was succeeded by Tiberius Julius Alexander, a strange choice for a procurator of Judaea, because he was a renegade. Born one of the most prominent Jews of Alexandria, being the son of Alexander the Alabarch, and a nephew of the great Philo himself, he nevertheless fell away into paganism. The appointment may be explained by the fact that his brother Mark, now dead, had been the first husband of Berenice, sister of the younger Agrippa (see page 63), and that Alexander, despite his religious defection, and although Berenice was now married to Herod of Chalcis, was still regarded as one of the family. The new procurator showed himself a loyal instrument of Rome. He decided to come to terms with the Zealots. The movement was now directed by Jacob and Simon, two sons of Judas the Galilean who had started the disturbances against the Romans in the days of Quirinius (see page 39). Tiberius Alexander rounded them up and crucified them.

It was during Tiberius' term of office that the great famine took place which had been foretold by Agabus, one of the Christian prophets who had come down to Jerusalem from Antioch (Acts xi, 27-30). Help came from several quarters. The Christians of Syria collected what they could, and sent it to Jerusalem by the hands of Paul and Barnabas. There was also a certain queen, a tributary of the Parthians, called Helena. She ruled the little principality of Adiabene, between the Greater and Lesser Zab rivers, affluents of the Tigris, in what is now northern Iraq, the area of the great Kirkuk oilfield. Helena had been converted to Judaism by a Jewish merchant. Her son, 'Izzat, had also accepted the Jewish faith, and despite the intrigues of a portion of his subjects who affected to be scandalized by his conversion, had at the age of thirty-one safely acceded to the throne in place of his mother. He was to rule for twenty-four years. Helena found in the famine an occasion for a pilgrimage to Jerusalem. She sent agents ahead to buy corn in Alexandria, and she imported dried figs from Cyprus. 'Izzat sent his contribution in cash. Between them, these two kindly converts did much to relieve the distress of the Jews, who were grateful to them. When shortly afterwards 'Izzat died, at the age of fifty-five, Queen Helena, who had settled in Jerusalem, hurried back to Adiabene in great distress. She did not long survive him. His elder brother Monobazus, who was now king in his place, sent back the bones both of his mother and of his brother 'Izzat to Jerusalem, there to be buried in the splendid monument that the queen had already raised. This is the miscalled "Tombs of the Kings", north of the Old City and just behind St George's Cathedral. In its original form, three pyramids surmounted the sepulchral hypogeum. It is these pyramids which Josephus mentions as one of the landmarks by which the trace of the Third Wall could be fixed. The pyramids have long since been overthrown; but the great caverns are still there, the memorial of a generous woman, and an excellent example of first-century funerary architecture (see Plate 20).

Tiberius Alexander, like his predecessor Cuspius Fadus, was a successful administrator: "making no alterations of the ancient laws, he kept the nation in tranquillity", is Josephus' verdict. After a two-year tenure, he was succeeded in 48 by Ventidius Cumanus, who was to be by no means so fortunate. At the outset of his tour, his position was weakened by the death of Herod of Chalcis, who, like his brother Agrippa I, had shown himself a firm but sympathetic advocate of the policy of collaboration with Rome. His appointment as Guardian of the Vestments with authority to appoint the High Priests is clear evidence that he enjoyed the confidence of Roman and Jew alike. Almost his last act had been to install a new High Priest, Ananias Ben Nebedaios (in place of Joseph Ben Qamhit). In recording Herod of Chalcis' death, Josephus calls him "brother of Agrippa the great King". We know from an inscription in Beirut, reproduced in this book (Plate 27), that the title "great king" was given to Agrippa I by his family (perhaps by himself originally?), and Josephus was naturally careful to follow their lead. Claudius at once gave his little principality to Agrippa the younger, who may henceforth, therefore, be called Agrippa II.

Under Cumanus, says Josephus, "began troubles, and the Jews' ruin came on". It was the troops, whose relegation Claudius had weakly countermanded, that ignited the fatal train. They were locally recruited from the inhabitants of Caesarea and Sebaste, pagans who loathed their Jewish neighbours with the intensity that only propinquity can breed. It was asking for trouble to attempt to police Judaea with such levies. Trouble soon came.

It was Passover, and as usual the city and the Temple were thronged with pilgrims. Of recent years, the Roman garrison commander had taken the wise precaution of stationing troops on the roof of the Cloisters: the lesson which Sabinus disregarded had been learned. On the fourth day of the feast, "one of the soldiers pulled back his garment, and cowering down after an indecent manner, turned his breach to the Jews, and delivered such an utterance as you might expect from such a posture". Pandemonium inevitably followed this indecent blasphemy. Some of the outraged worshippers called upon Cumanus, who was present, probably on the gallery of the Antonia, to punish the shameless soldier, some even declared that it was Cumanus who had set him on, others, younger and rasher, started to pelt the troops with stones. Cumanus, fearing a general assault, sent orders to the upper palace for the whole garrison to turn out fully armed and come down to the Antonia. The flash and clatter of these troops, surging down the narrow city streets, dumbfounded the largely rural assembly. They tried to escape from the Temple, panic broke out, and thousands were crushed to death. "So great an affliction did the impudent obsceneness of a single soldier bring upon them": indeed, seldom can a single gesture, albeit a lewd one, have had such a tragic sequel.

The next calamity was again the work of a soldier. Near Beth-Horon (the name commemorates the Egyptian god Horus, and as *Beit Ur* survives to this day), on the main road from Jerusalem to Caesarea, a group of terrorists, inflamed by the Passover incident, held up a certain Stephen, one of Caesar's slaves, and robbed him of his entire baggage. Cumanus, of course, was bound to punish such brazen lawlessness with a strong hand. The crime committed in broad daylight on the main highway of the province can hardly have gone unobserved; but, as so often in later days, no one would say anything. Cumanus therefore gave orders that the neighbouring villages should be sacked, and the notables arrested. During this operation, one of the soldiers seized a copy of the Law, tore it to bits and threw them into the fire, to the accompaniment of gibes and insults. The equivalent of this outrage in a Catholic country would be the wanton desecration of the Host. Indeed, the Law is sheltered in the synagogue in a special repository, called *Arōn ha-Kodēsh*, which bears a striking analogy, in position and function, to the Tabernacle in a church. The Jews rushed to Caesarea to complain to Cumanus, and to ask for vengeance, not for themselves, but for their God. Cumanus acceded to their prayers. The offender was led away to a public execution.

Next it was the Samaritans' turn to cause trouble. To pass from Galilee to Jerusalem, a traveller must either make the détour by the Jordan Valley and Jericho, or pass through the country of the Samaritans. As we know from the Gospels, e.g. Mark x, 1; John iv, 4, our Lord and his disciples were familiar with both routes. The main road from Jerusalem to Galilee via Samaria ran, and still runs, through the beautiful little village of Jenin, the gateway from the plain of Esdraelon to the hills of Samaria. The name means *gardens*, from the copious fountains which water its groves. It is the "garden house" of 2 Kings ix, 27. It was the frontier post between Samaria and Lower Galilee. In it, the

Samaritans attacked a band of Galilean Jews who were bound to Jerusalem for a feast, possibly Tabernacles following the disastrous Passover, when the Jordan Valley route would still be intolerably hot, and killed a number of them. The Galileans complained to Cumanus, who, bribed, it was said, by the Samaritans, paid no heed to them. The feast was abandoned and tumults broke out yet again. The mob started marching north to Samaria, with a noted brigand, Eleazar son of Dineus, at their head. As soon as they reached the confines of Samaria, that is, the toparchy of 'Aqraba (the name is the same to-day), the Jews started to loot and to kill, deaf to the counsel of their lawful leaders. Cumanus came up from Caesarea with a troop of the *Sebaste* Horse, to restore peace. The notables of Jerusalem also implored the excited crowd to disperse, lest by angering the Romans they should bring war to their own gates. The main body dispersed; but the spirit of resentment and unrest had spread too deeply: the country was given over to robbery, assault and bloodshed.

As governor of Syria, Cassius Longinus had been succeeded in the year 50 by Ummidius Quadratus. To him the Samaritans now hurried off, closely followed, of course, by the Jews. The enquiry took place at Tyre, the ancient seaport whose proud palaces towered almost higher than those of Rome itself. Quadratus realized that merely to listen to charge and counter-charge would get him nowhere. Determined to investigate the rights and wrongs of the affair on the spot, he came down to Caesarea. There he ordered the crucifixion of all the Jews whom Cumanus had caught under arms. At Lydda, he heard the case of the specific attack near 'Aqraba, and ordered eighteen of the Jewish ringleaders to be beheaded. But a more permanent settlement he did not feel qualified to make. He therefore sent Ananias, the former High Priest, and Jonathan, his predecessor in 36, together with two other Jewish leaders, and the Samaritan notables, to Claudius. Cumanus, and his chief of staff, Celer, were also despatched to Rome. The removal of the ringleaders on either side had a pacifying effect. Ummidius went up to Jerusalem for the Passover of 52, found the city in tranquillity and returned to Antioch. Meanwhile in Rome the debate raged between Claudius' freedmen, who of course backed the procurator and the Samaritans, and young Agrippa II, who supported his brother Jews. Agrippa, who had inherited his father's and great-grandfather's flair for closet-warfare, enlisted the help of Agrippina, Claudius' iron-hearted empress. Agrippa won. Three of the leading

Samaritans were executed, Cumanus was banished, and Celer (who was no doubt held chiefly responsible for the behaviour of the troops), was sentenced to be sent back to Jerusalem, dragged publicly to the gibbet, and executed.

It was but natural that these disturbances in Palestine should cause unrest among the Jewish community in Rome. Claudius had received an embassy from the Jews of Alexandria, and had made a just and statesmanlike settlement of their claims (see page 73). He had, on his accession, restored to the Jews of Rome the privileges which Caligula had withdrawn but had nevertheless forbidden them to hold meetings. Now, in 49, we read both in the Acts (xviii, 2) and in Suetonius (*Claudius*, XXV, 4) that Claudius banished the Jews, "who [says Suetonius] at the instigation of Chrestus continually raised tumults". This seems to refer to the Christians, who were at first indistinguishable from the Jews to the pagan eye, and it is the earliest pagan testimony to the existence of the Roman Church in point of chronology, though Tacitus' reference to the Christians in connexion with the fire of Rome in 64 was presumably *written* earlier.

Why did Judaism, and now Christianity, excite the fear and suspicion of the Roman authorities? The answer is that Judaism, and, *a fortiori*, the new Faith, offered a challenge to the whole fading fabric of the old Roman dream. "If," says Streeter (*CAH*, XI, p. 279), "the Jew had too much law, the Gentile had too little; for the old local religions, and the moral sanctions associated with them, were collapsing in the cosmopolitan scepticism of the Graeco-Roman Empire." To fill this vacuum of the spirit, the west had nothing to offer. It was from the east that salvation was to come, and had come. As Carcopino (*Daily Life in Ancient Rome*, p. 126) puts it, "one great spiritual fact dominates the history of the empire: the advent of personal religion which followed on the conquest of Rome by the mysticism of the East". It is essential, if we are to understand the impact of Judaism and Christianity on Roman society, to grasp this fact, and to realize that these two religions were not solitary intruders, as it were. They were two of many: they attracted converts, and persecution, because they were the most potent, the most durable of the many. Of all the cults which flourished in Rome in the first century A.D., only Judaism and Christianity flourish to-day. The following is a brief catalogue of some of the more prominent eastern religions that had become acclimatized, as it were, in Rome. The Anatolian cult of Cybele had been brought to Rome in 205 B.C. Both it and the worship of Attis had been established by Claudius' decree reforming their liturgies. Tiberius had banished the Egyptian cults, but Caligula had publicly restored them to favour: and the Temple of Isis, which was to be destroyed by fire in A.D. 80, would be rebuilt by Domitian "with a luxury still testified to by the obelisks that remained standing in the Temple of Minerva, or nearby in front of the Pantheon, and by the colossal statues of the Nile and the Tiber which are now divided between the museums of the Louvre and the Vatican" (Carcopino, *op. cit.*, p. 134). Suetonius tells us that the Syrian Goddess, Atargatis, was the only deity whom Nero, denier of all other gods, deigned to recognize. More eastern gods and goddesses were continually arriving. Small wonder that the orthodox trembled with resentment; still less that they should concentrate their anger, bred of fear, on the two cults, Judaism and Christianity, which, from their point of view, were wreaking the worst havoc, among high and low alike.

For the crisis of 49 there was another reason. It was in that year that the Council of Jerusalem (Acts xv) had decided that Gentile converts to Christianity should not be required to accept circumcision and the full observance of the Mosaic Law. They were to abstain from fornication, from taking part in the ritual meals in pagan shrines and (a gesture to Judaism) from eating meat with blood in it. This meant that the new Faith was now divorced from its Jewish matrix, and could go forth to conquer in the name of Christ alone. The greater freedom which Christianity was thus able to offer to its adherents greatly enhanced its appeal. Conversions increased. So, inevitably, did the animosity of the Jews. It is to this state of affairs that the sentence "the Jews who at the instigation of Chrestus continually raised tumults" undoubtedly refers.

In the circumstances, it was all the more remarkable that Agrippa the Jew should prevail with Claudius. Agrippa was soon to enjoy another reward. He had been king of Chalcis for more than three years. But this modest principality was now to be exchanged for the former tetrarchy of Philip, his great-uncle, together with the fertile region of Abilene, north-west of Damascus, and the region of the Anti-Lebanon—the remnants of the little Ituraean state which, since 49, had been merged with the province of Syria. This new accession of territory brought Agrippa into neighbourly relationship with the king of Emesa (Homs) 'Aziz. To make the association sure and friendly, Agrippa offered his sister Drusilla to the king, on condition that he accept circumcision, which he did. Drusilla had already been once betrothed, to Epiphanes the son of King Antiochus of Commagene, but he, after promising to become a Jew, had gone back on his word. That was some years before, when her father was still living. Now it seemed that she had made a good match. But it was not to last. To succeed Cumanus, Claudius had appointed Antonius Felix, a freedman of Antonia, his mother (whence the *nomen* Antonius, instead of Claudius), and brother of his own freedman, Pallas. Tacitus (*Hist.*, V, 9) says of him that he exercised the authority of a king, with the mind of a slave, relying on his brother's influence at court. Suetonius also (*Claudius*, 28) tells us of the unheard-of rise to riches and power of this groundling, and says that he became the husband of three queens. The names of two of them are known to us. The first was a grand-daughter of Antony and Cleopatra, by which union Felix actually became related to the emperor himself. The second was Drusilla. She was a very beautiful woman, and Felix fell in love with her at sight. He sent a certain Cypriot Jew called Simon to persuade Drusilla to abandon her Syrian prince, and marry the Roman governor, and Caesar's friend into the bargain. Drusilla saw in the proposal a chance of getting even with her sister Berenice, who was again a widow, since Herod of Chalcis' death, and rankly jealous of her more beautiful sister. Disregarding the laws of her people, Drusilla deserted 'Aziz, and went off to live in adultery with Felix. They had a son, Antonius Agrippa, who perished in 79 during the eruption of Vesuvius which engulfed Herculaneum and Pompeii. 'Aziz died in 54.

Berenice, too, was behaving scandalously. During her second widowhood, it was only too commonly reported that she was living in incest with her brother, Agrippa II. To stifle the rumour, Polemo, king of Cilicia, was persuaded to accept circumcision, for Agrippa II, like his forbears, was a rigorously strict upholder of the Mosaic Law, and to marry Berenice, who had, in his eyes, the great attraction of being extremely rich. This third match did not last long. Berenice abandoned Polemo, and her religion. To what famous depths she was to sink will appear later in this narrative.

In the autumn of 54, Claudius died, poisoned, it was said, by his wife, Agrippina. This atrocious woman was a daughter of Germanicus Caesar, and a sister of Caligula. She was thus Claudius' niece. The marriage of an uncle and a niece, though in accordance with Jewish Law, was contrary to that of Rome, which accounted it incestuous. Agrippina was determined to be empress. Racine, in a famous scene (*Britannicus*, Act IV, Sc. 2) makes her describe the dilemma and its outcome:

> "*Mais ce lien de sang qui nous joignoit tous deux*
> *Écartoit Claudius d'un lit incestueux;*
> *Il n'osoit épouser la fille de son frère.*
> *Le Sénat fut séduit; une loi moins sevère*
> *Mit Claude dans mon lit, et Rome à mes genoux.*"

"But this same tie of blood which join'd us twain
Bade Claudius from th' incestuous bed abstain,
To wed his brother's daughter interdict.
The Senate was suborn'd: a law less strict,
Brought Claudius to my bed, Rome to my feet."

Yes, Rome was now her suppliant. She easily contrived that her son by her first husband, Domitius Ahenobarbus, should be adopted by Claudius, given the names Nero Claudius Caesar Drusus Germanicus, and accepted as heir to the purple in place of Britannicus, Claudius' own son by a former wife, Messalina, a woman who had proved herself more vicious, if that were possible, even than Agrippina, and had finally been compelled to end her own life. Within a year of Nero's accession, Britannicus in his turn had fallen a victim to Locusta, the fashionable poisoner who was said to have been employed to despatch his father. Such were the auguries of the new reign. Agrippina was, for the time being, paramount. She had herself proclaimed *Augusta*. The fact that Pallas was her lover naturally increased the confidence of his brother Felix, the procurator of Judaea. He was to hold office for eight years (cf. Acts xxiv, 10).

At the outset of his reign, Nero, like his predecessors, showed favour to the house of Herod. Aristobulus, son of Herod of Chalcis, was made king of Lesser Armenia, which meant that Salome the dancer was now a queen. That a Jew should rule in Armenia may seem strange; but there were in fact precedents for it. At the beginning of the century Augustus had appointed one of the sons of Alexander, son of Herod the Great, king of Armenia proper, under the title Tigranes, or Dhikran, IV. The experiment was not a success, and Dhikran was soon deposed and sent back to Rome, where he lived until A.D. 36, in which year he was executed. His nephew, known as Dhikran V, was to rule the

same kingdom in Nero's day (see page 117), so that it was not in-
appropriate that his second cousin should rule Lesser Armenia at
the same time. Suheim, who had succeeded his brother 'Aziz as
king of Emesa, was given the principality of Sophene, which
marched with Armenia proper on the eastern bank of the
Euphrates. Agrippa II obtained Tiberias—so prosperous now that
its citizens had their own chamber of commerce in Rome—and
Taricheae, the town, also on the Sea of Galilee, which was, as its
name denotes, the centre of the lucrative salted fish industry. He
also received Julias-Livias, the rich estate at the foot of Mt. Nebo,
with fourteen surrounding villages and Abila in Peraea. "This
donation," says Abel (Vol. I, p. 463), "emphasized the sporadic
character of the kingdom that the last king of the Herodian family,
Agrippa II, governed on behalf of the Romans. Except for a few
towns, and a piece of the Jaulan, this state, being located on the
periphery, eluded the grasp of the rebels, who, in 66, were masters
of a great part of procuratorial Judaea."

The appointment of Felix, who was to bring such calamity
upon Jewry, had been, ironically enough, the result of a request
made to Claudius by Jonathan, son of Annas, who had been
High Priest in 36-37, and was, together with his father (now the high
steward of the Temple), among those notables whom Cumanus
had sent in chains to Claudius. In making this request—strange
enough for a Jewish prelate—it is but natural to suppose that
Jonathan was acting at the instigation of Agrippa II, who wanted
to conciliate the powerful Pallas, and of Agrippina, who sought
advancement for the brother of her paramour. Certain it is that
Felix showed his gratitude to his patroness by frequently engrav-
ing her name on his coinage. The Jews, remembering her help
over the Cumanus affair, called one of the beacon stations, from
which they signalled the new moon to the *diaspora*, Agrippina. It
was probably Qala'at er-Rabad ('Ajlun).

Felix, sure of the imperial favour, at once set about the eradica-
tion of the brigands. He captured Eleazar, the son of Dineus, by
treachery. He promised him an amnesty, or at least his life, if he
would surrender. Eleazar did so, and was at once sent off to
Rome in chains. The rank and file were hunted down and sum-
marily crucified. It was becoming dangerous now to make daylight assaults. The terrorists evolved a new technique. They
adopted the short, curved knife, somewhat like a sickle, which
was used by the pirates of Illyria, the Latin name for which was
sica (sickle), whence those who used it were known as *sicarii*. As

early as 81 B.C. it had been necessary at Rome to legislate against them. The advantage of the *sica* was that it could be easily hidden in the clothes. One swift blow, and the victim was dead, while his assassin mixed with the appalled bystanders—a strikingly horrible precursor of the gunmen of a later age.

Felix had soon fallen out with Jonathan, "because," as Josephus drily puts it, "he frequently gave him admonitions about govern-ing the Jewish affairs better than he did." He decided to be rid of him, and it was to the very *sicarii* themselves that he turned to carry out his wish. He bribed Jonathan's best friend, Doras, to introduce a gang of the assassins into the congregation of worship-pers. Jonathan was struck down. His murderers escaped. The reign of terror had begun. No one felt safe. The assassins settled old scores, and ran up new ones. There was fear and murder on every side. And it was the procurator, the very man who should have championed public order and justice, who had unleashed them. The majority of the people were, as always, hunted not hunters. As always, the rebellion was the work of a small, professional, and single-minded minority, who cared nothing for the welfare of their fellows, and were prepared to use any number of good words, such as freedom and love of country, in order to advance their own bad ends.

Bogus thaumaturges exploited the general unrest. Pretending that they were divinely inspired, they lured multitudes into the desert, promising them signs and wonders of approaching liberty. The movement grew menacing, so Felix sent horse and foot to break it up. Many were arrested and others killed.

The most serious of these impostors was an Egyptian, the same who is mentioned in Acts xxi, 38. He proclaimed himself to be a prophet, and called upon the populace of Jerusalem to assemble on the Mount of Olives, to the east of the city. He announced that at his command the walls of Jerusalem would crumble, and that through the breach he would lead his followers into the citadel, overcome the garrison, and take possession of the city. Once again, Felix broke up the assembly, the inhabitants of Jerusalem giving him ready assistance: even a Roman procurator was better than an Egyptian dictator. Four hundred killed and 200 prisoners was the day's toll. The Egyptian escaped. That was why, when St Paul was arrested in the Temple, and rescued by the tribune of the cohort on duty, the officer asked him whether he was not that Egyptian who had led 4,000 *sicarii* into the desert.

Meanwhile, the terrorists were active up and down the country.

NERO

[Corpus Christi College, Cambridge.

23. This coin, an early issue, shews Nero as he was no doubt wished people to regard him: the far-sighted, sensitive artist. And yet, no amount of official tact can hide the degeneracy of the last of the Julio-Claudians (for such, through his mother, Nero was).

CLAUDIUS

[Corpus Christi College, Cambridge.

22. This beautiful coin is an excellent example of Roman imperial portraiture. It gives a wonderfully vivid representation of its subject, the elderly scholar, retiring and hesitant, now arrayed in the oak-leaves of empire. Even the mouth, somehow, suggests the hesitant speech, the stammer, with which Claudius was afflicted. Note the big ears.

[Alinari.

24. This bust of Nero in the National Museum at Naples is a portrait of self-indulgent depravity—one of the most repulsive that antiquity has bequeathed to us. Note, in the hair, the holes by which a golden garland was attached to the marble, and (for the last time) the ugly ears.

They plundered and burned the great estates, and murdered their owners. They said that submission to the established government was slavery; any village that refused to support the gangs was razed to the ground.

The growing chaos was aggravated by the Jews of Caesarea. This city, the capital of the Roman province, had been built by Herod the Great as a predominantly pagan city (see page 27). There were Jews living in it, as in other cities, and they lived there as of right, and not on sufferance. But they could not fairly claim preponderance in this new creation, built on the site of a small village in which, at the time of its expansion, there had not been a single Jew. Over the years, the Jews of Caesarea had become very rich; and now claimed that they should have the principal share in the municipal administration. They gave as their reason the fact that the founder of the city, Herod the Great, had been a Jew. This, in the context, was a specious sophistry. It is true that Herod was technically a Jew, and, in Judaea, a pious one; but the wholly Graeco-Roman city of Caesarea, embellished with the graven images so abhorred by Judaism, could hardly be accounted a Jewish creation. The Jews had the money, but the Syrians had the troops—it was from them that the regiments were recruited. One day, when the Jews, who besides being richer were also tougher than their Syrian fellow-citizens, had come off best in a street-fight, Felix intervened. Bloodshed and looting followed. Still the troubles continued. In the end, Felix adopted the standard solution. Notables of the two factions were packed off to argue the case before Nero in Rome. For the time being there was a lull; but, as sometimes happens in Palestine, an issue which seemed closed was in due course to provoke a far graver and more dangerous dispute.

H

Chapter XII

TOWARDS THE BRINK

IT was against this sombre and seething background that
the drama of St Paul's last appearance in the Holy Land and
his despatch to Rome was to be played out—a prologue, as it
were, to the tragedy which was so soon to engulf and ruin his
people.

omit

Ananias son of Nebedaios, a former High Priest, was one of
those who had been sent in chains to Claudius in the year 52,
accused of complicity in the Samaria riots (see page 90). He returned white as snow; and at once proceeded to exploit his
authority for his own greedy benefit. He was no longer the reigning
High Priest—Agrippa having, on Jonathan's refusal to accept a
second term, appointed Ishmael son of Phabi to the supreme office
—but so great was his prestige, so bare-faced his rapacity, that he
and his adherents were able to divert to their own use and disposal
the greater portion of the meat offered as sacrifices. Not content
with this, they sent their minions on to the very threshing-floors, to
carry off the tithes, which were due not to these opulent prelates,
but to the poor and humble members of the priesthood, many of
whom died of want in consequence.

Such was this man, Ananias, whom we find presiding (Acts
xxiii) over the deliberations of the Sanhedrin when it met to
consider the case of Paul, who had been arrested as he was being
expelled from the Temple by the mob.

Paul and his little company had arrived by way of Tyre and
Ptolemais (Acre), both of which had recently emphasized their
"Roman" quality. Tyre now called itself Claudiopolis, after the
late emperor; who in his last years had actually transformed
Ptolemais into a colony, *Colonia Claudia Felix Ptolemais*. It was
peopled by veterans of the four legions based on Syria, namely the
IIIrd, *Gallica* ("of Gaul"); the VIth, *Ferrata* ("iron-clad"); Xth,
Fretensis ("of the Straits", i.e. of Messina, where it was raised, or
perhaps had originally distinguished itself); and the XIIth *Ful-
minata* ("the thunderbolt"). Caesarea was the next port of call.
Paul had delayed for a week in Tyre, a day in Ptolemais, many
days in Caesarea. Finally, in Jerusalem, he lodged, not with his

own relations, some of whom lived there, but with a Cypriot called Mnason, one of the very first converts. With the apostle were Aristarchus, Trophimus, Timothy and four other Asian Greeks. What did this dilatory gentile itinerary, which Paul had deliberately chosen (Acts xxi, 4) instead of the direct overland route from Tyre to Jerusalem, and this gentile suite imply? They meant this: Paul was a Jew, and proud to be one; Paul was a Roman citizen, and proud of that, too. But, in his own eyes, he was now, principally and for ever, the apostle of the Lord Jesus to the Gentiles. Paul saw no incongruity in such a vocation; but both Jews and Romans were baffled by it, as the event was to show. Nevertheless, although he was dedicated to his gentile mission, Paul had no intention of overlooking the fact that it was from the Jews that the Church of Jerusalem had sprung, and that it was still chiefly composed of Jews who might well look askance, despite the resolution of the conference of 49, at his comprehensive concept of the Faith. Paul and his brethren had therefore brought a handsome present for them, a gift from the infant churches of Asia to the mother, Judaeo-Christian, church of Jerusalem. Even this did not wholly quell the apprehensions of the Jerusalem Christians. "Thou seest, brother, how many thousands of Jews there are which believe," they said to Paul, "and they are all zealous of the law." (Acts xxi, 20.) To quiet the fears of these godly men—for if they were, as we have deduced, predominantly of Essene origin, the Judaeo-Christians of the Holy City were amongst the most spiritually minded men of their age—the elders suggested that Paul make a public demonstration of his Jewishness. It was a wise proposal, and Paul, being wise, acceded to it. He chose the very method that Agrippa I had chosen when he first came to Jerusalem as king: he sponsored four of the brethren who were going to perform their vows as Nazarites, and paid their expenses. Paul accompanied them during the Temple ceremonies, he himself being in a state of ritual purification. It was only on the seventh and last day of the prescribed course that Paul was recognized by an Asian Jew, who stirred up the mob, and provoked the riot which led to Paul's preventive arrest.

Paul would now show that he was not only a Jew, but a Roman citizen. First, speaking from the head of one of the two staircases which joined the Antonia to the Temple area below, and by which the troops could have immediate access to the sacred precinct, he addressed the excited populace. The spot is indicated to-day by the minaret in the north-west corner of the

Haram esh-Sherif. It, too, has a staircase which gives access to the
Temple area, and from the top of it the prospect of the shrine and
its setting suggests in the most vivid and dramatic manner the
actual scene which confronted the apostle, as he stood there and
made his great apologia, to be answered by a frenzied outcry for
his death (see Plate 6).

The garrison commander, Claudius Lysias, was about to have
Paul flogged, as the first step in a judicial examination, when the
accused calmly asked his warder whether it was legal so to treat
an unconvicted Roman citizen. Roman citizen? Was this agitator
a Roman citizen? Consternation fell upon the centurion, who
hastened away to tell Lysias. As soon as he had satisfied himself
that Paul was telling the truth, Lysias tried to stop the proceedings. The next day, Paul appeared before the Sanhedrin,
because Lysias was anxious to know just what their accusation
against Paul was. Ananias, as soon as Paul began to speak,
ordered one of those present to strike him on the mouth. Paul
answered by telling Ananias that he was a whited wall, and that
God would smite him, who had dared to order that, contrary to
the law, an unconvicted man be struck. The court pretended to
be horrified at this "reviling of God's High Priest". Paul, with
calm irony, said he had not realized that it was a High Priest who
had thus violated the law. What would have been the result of
this unsatisfactory confrontation we do not know. Paul, knowing
that the Sanhedrin was composed not only of the high-priestly
clique of Sadducees, but also of a number of Pharisees, astutely
announced that he was a Pharisee, which was true, and that if he
was going to be called in question concerning the resurrection of
the dead. . . At once the court dissolved in chaos and dissension.
The Pharisees perforce rallied to Paul's defence, against the
Sadducees, who strenuously denied the resurrection, or the
existence of angels and spirits: they were a hard, materialist lot.
Hearing the uproar (for the Sanhedrin met within the Temple
precincts), Lysias sent down some soldiers to rescue Paul. The
next day forty fanatics bound themselves by an oath to take neither
meat nor drink until they had killed Paul. Paul's nephew got
wind of the conspiracy, and went straight to the Antonia, to tell
his uncle, who of course sent him to Lysias. Lysias acted with
promptness and resolution. That very night he sent Paul down to
Antipatris en route for Caesarea, with relays of mounts for his
comfort, and an escort of 400 foot and seventy horse for his protection. Lysias was taking no chances with a Roman citizen.

Lysias was a freed slave, who had, as he told Paul, bought his liberty, and not cheaply, either: his respect for the freeborn citizen was all the greater. Next day, the cavalcade reached Caesarea, where Paul was lodged in the basilica of Herod the Great. Thus did Paul come before Felix (Acts xxiii).

Lysias had sent Felix a hurriedly-written outline of the affair by the hand of the officer in charge of the escort. Felix, having determined that Paul was a citizen of Cilicia, decided to await the arrival of his accusers. They reached Caesarea five days later with an advocate called Tertullus. Tertullus' speech, as recorded by St Luke, might serve as a model for so many speeches made by so many Palestinian advocates in similar circumstances. It starts with nauseating flattery, proffered with mock humility, goes on to make wild accusations unsupported by evidence and but little related to the facts in question, takes care to denounce to the supreme authority the actions and motives of the subordinate on the spot (in this case Lysias), and ends with a confident appeal to justice. Paul contented himself with a recital of the facts. Felix thereupon decided to wait until Lysias himself arrived. Meanwhile, Paul was to be given all reasonable liberty, and his friends unimpeded access to him. A few days later, Felix and his Jewish wife, Drusilla, decided to hear Paul again. But Paul's earnest and eloquent exposition of the Faith was too much for Felix: when Paul spoke of justice, and of chastity, and of a judgment to come, Felix started to tremble. His conscience could not bear it. He temporized: he would hear Paul some other time, he said. He kept on seeing Paul, in the hope that a large bribe might be forthcoming as the price of his freedom. On the other hand, in order to please Ananias and his party, Felix did not scruple to keep under arrest a man who was innocent before the Roman law. This was in the year 58. For two years this captivity lasted, because Paul would not deign to compromise his innocence by paying to have it admitted. By an irony of history these two years were of incalculable value to the infant Church. They enabled Paul to establish close ties with the churches of Palestine and Syria; and they gave to St Luke an opportunity to acquaint himself at first hand with the acts and the memories of the first disciples of Jesus.

A disreputable intrigue of the corrupt Roman court had sent Felix to Palestine; it was his greed and his lack of principle which, as it turned out, benefited the Christian Faith. Of such strange strands is the fabric of history woven.

Towards the middle of the year 60, Porcius Festus came to

Judaea as procurator, in succession to Felix, who was recalled to Rome. Thither he was followed hot-foot by the leaders of the Caesarea Jews, who were determined to demand of the emperor the punishment of the outgoing governor. They might well have succeeded, had it not been for the intervention of Pallas, Felix's brother, who still had considerable influence with Nero.

Three days after arriving at Caesarea, Festus went up to Jerusalem. At once the disgruntled pontiffs, who had failed to secure Paul's destruction from Felix, set about his successor, in the hope that he might prove more pliable. They even suggested that the prisoner should be sent back to Jerusalem, having planned to have him murdered on the way, for it must be remembered that public security had almost ceased to exist before the activities of the *sicarii*, and one more highway murder could easily be added to the toll without anyone being called to account. Festus replied that, if they cared to come down to Caesarea, he would hear them there. Ten days later he went back to his capital. Once again the prelates followed, once again they made their unproven allegations against Paul. Festus was tired of this case: was it to drag on for another two years? He tried to compromise. Would Paul agree to be judged in Jerusalem, as his accusers wanted, provided that he, Festus, presided at the trial, thus safeguarding Paul's rights as a Roman citizen, and absolved him from any sentence save that of Festus himself? Paul refused this shabby makeshift. He was a Roman citizen, an innocent man; why should he be sacrificed to political expediency? He asked no more than justice. He appealed to Caesar, as he was entitled to do. Festus conferred with his council. Paul was within his rights, they said: Paul had appealed to Nero, and to Nero he must go.

A few days later, Agrippa arrived in Caesarea, having come down from his northern kingdom to pay his respects to the new procurator of Judaea. Agrippa had no territorial authority in Judaea, but his right of appointing the High Priests, and of guarding the sacred vestments, gave him an important influence on Judaean affairs. He also had a residence in Jerusalem. Already, as a young man in Rome, he had realized how important it was for the welfare of his people to be on good terms with the Romans. So now he had come to establish friendly contact with his Roman colleague at the outset of his term of office. With Agrippa was his sister Berenice, who, now that her hated sister Drusilla had gone off with Felix, was free to revisit her old home.

Festus saw an opportunity of turning to good advantage both

Agrippa's prestige as a Jewish king and his authority as one learned
in the Jewish law. If Paul was to go before Caesar, it was essential
that Festus should state a case, and in preparing it Agrippa could
be of great help, he said. Once again, Paul appeared, and once
again he delivered a defence of his life and faith. To the disgust
of the prelates, Agrippa openly expressed his admiration of Paul,
and advised Festus that, in his opinion, he had committed no
crime that called for death or even imprisonment. He might well
be released; but as he had appealed to Caesar, to Caesar he must
go (Acts xxvi, 32).

And so Paul set out upon the last stage of his life's voyage—
to Rome. It was the year 60.

The priesthood soon had an opportunity of getting their own
back on Agrippa. As has been said, he had a residence in
Jerusalem. This was the old Hasmonaean palace, which stood on
the site of the Akra, or citadel of the Seleucids, on the western
scarp of the Tyropoeon valley, which separated it from the Temple.
The palace was barely 600 feet distant from the Shrine itself, and
stood some forty feet higher (see Plates 26 and 33). Herod the
Great had abandoned this old palace, which he had acquired
when he married Mariamme, the Hasmonaean princess, first
for his new castle of Antonia, and later for his great palace on
the site of what is now the Citadel. Both of these were taken
over by the Romans; so that the Herodian family, since the
days of Antipas, had returned perforce to their first Jerusalem
home. It was old-fashioned and stuffy. Agrippa now decided
to erect on the roof a pent-house dining-room, from which
he would be able to keep an eye on all that went on in the
Temple, without rising from the table, that is, from the cushions
on which the diners reclined. After all, was not Agrippa, in a sense,
the supreme Temple authority? The priests were outraged: it was
profanation, they said, that the sacred mysteries should be quizzed
from a building dedicated to secular pleasures. So, without waiting
for permission either from Agrippa or from the procurator, they
built a wall on the western verge of the platform on which the
cella of the Temple stood, thus screening it not only from Agrippa's
new dining-room, but also from the western cloister of the
Enclosure, in which the Roman troops were customarily stationed
to maintain order during the great feasts. Festus was no less
annoyed than the king, and ordered the immediate demolition of
the wall. The sequel followed the now stereotyped pattern. The
offenders said they would rather die than remove one stone of the

Holy Place! Let the matter be submitted to the judgment of Caesar! Festus could but agree, and so ten notables, headed by Ishmael son of Phabi, the High Priest, and Helkias, the Temple treasurer, went off to Rome.

Agrippina was dead now. Her son, growing tired of her domination, and egged on by his mistress Poppaea, had got rid of her. She did not die easily. Nero's first idea had been to send her for a trip in a specially constructed yacht, which was to fall apart at a given signal, and drown her. The yacht collapsed according to plan, but Agrippina, undaunted, swam ashore. The freedman in charge, Aniketos, *the unconquered*, was determined to live up to his name. In the end, Agrippina had to be despatched by straightforward assassination in her own villa. Poppaea naturally could not be expected to show favour to Agrippina's *protégés*, Agrippa and his friends; but she was known to be favourable to Judaism, of which she may well have been a secret adherent. Josephus, who was himself to benefit at her hands, calls her *theosebes*, "god-fearing". The ten notables therefore returned to Jerusalem with permission to retain their wall. But Ishmael and Helkias were detained in Rome as hostages. Agrippa not unnaturally dismissed Ishmael from the High Priesthood (he later met his end by being beheaded at Cyrene), and replaced him by Joseph Kabi, son of the High Priest Simeon, yet another member of the Boethus family. The year 61 was now drawing to a close.

The Jews were soon to suffer a reverse at Nero's hands, which more than undid their recent victory. We must go back to the dispute between the two factions in Caesarea, described at the end of the last chapter. Two of the principal Syrians of the city won over Beryllus, Nero's Secretary for Greek affairs, by means of a large bribe; and Pallas naturally saw to it that he was included in the court which was to try a case in which his brother Felix was inculpated. Indeed, Abel concludes from a passage in Tacitus (*Annals*, XII, 54) that Felix himself appeared among the judges! The verdict was a blow to the Jews: far from being declared to have the pre-eminence over the Gentiles which they had claimed, they were now adjudged to have forfeited the status of equality which they had hitherto enjoyed. Abel comments (Vol. I, p. 470): "The difficulties which Jerusalem created for the Romans would certainly not encourage them to establish a second Jewish capital. Nero's rescript was promulgated in 62, the year that saw the death of Pallas and Festus. The Jews bitterly resented it, and

planned to reply to it by a war." Already, despite Festus' moderation, Judaea was in chaos. The *sicarii* and the brigands were more
active than ever. Once again, an impostor had rallied the credul-
ous in the desert, and once again it had needed the intervention of
the army to suppress him.

To make matters worse, Festus died while in office, which once
again, as after Pilate's recall, involved an interregnum. As ill luck
would have it, the High Priest of the year (for Agrippa had been
compelled to yield at least this to the extremists) was Ananus,
son of the High Priest Annas of the Gospels, four other of whose
sons had already attained the supreme pontificate. A rigid
Sadducee, to the accumulated pride of his family he added a
vindictive insolence of his own. As in 37, it was resolved to
exploit the interval during which no Roman procurator was in
effective control (cf. page 82, bottom). While Festus' successor
was still on his way, Ananus, quite illegally, arrested the elders of
the Christian community, including their chief, "the brother of
Jesus, who was called Christ, whose name was James". (This is not
the only mention of Jesus in Josephus, but it is nevertheless a very
significant one: *Ant.*, XX, ix, 1.) Paul, who had boasted of being a
Pharisee even before he had professed these new heretical ideas,
had escaped from the snare: Ananus would therefore punish those
who had harboured and encouraged him while he was in Jerusalem. For twenty years, ever since the execution of James son
of Zebedee by Agrippa, and the attempted killing of Peter,
the Church had lived unmolested. During all that time James the
brother of Jesus had been its Bishop. But in the eyes of the
Sadducees, his asceticism, his strict regard for the Law, his
saintly gentleness—these virtues could not compensate for the
fact that he was in communion with societies who admitted
converts without full compliance with the Law, that his life
was more holy than theirs, and finally that he was the recipient
of large sums of money which they could not lay hands on.
After trial before a packed Sanhedrin James was hustled away
to the south-east corner of the Temple, thrown down on to the
unconsecrated ground below, stoned, and given the *coup de grâce* by
the mallet of a fuller.

"The most equitable of the citizens," says Josephus, were disgusted by this illegal persecution and butchery. Messengers were
soon despatched north to Agrippa, and south to Albinus, who was
now on his way up from Alexandria. Albinus at once wrote to
Ananus threatening him with punishment. Agrippa, who was the

last man to suffer any infringement of Roman prerogative, and by his own nominee at that, deposed Ananus—he had been High Priest only three months—and appointed Jesus, son of Damnaios, in his place.

It was about this time, Abel reminds us, that there died the famous Rabbi Gamaliel the elder, grandson of the saintly Rabbi Hillel. It was "at the feet of Gamaliel" that Paul had sat as a youth. He had shown himself notably favourable to the apostles whom Ananus had illegally arrested, being a tolerant Pharisee. The Mishnah has preserved several of his legal *dicta* delivered on one of the steps of the Temple. "With his death," says the tractate *Sota*, IX, 16, "the glory of the Law was extinguished, and with it perished purity and Pharisaism."

It seems probable that Lucceius Albinus was in command of the garrison at Alexandria, this being a "knightly" appointment, when he received orders to succeed Festus as procurator of Judaea, where he arrived in the summer of 62.

He at once took strong measures against the terrorists, who replied—again the modern parallel holds—by the kidnapping of hostages. Their first victim was a clerk of Eleazar, son of Ananias, who was governor of the Temple. The *sicarii* offered to exchange him for ten of their own men held by Albinus. The new procurator had already been won over by Ananias, who was not only popular with the masses, but was also very rich. He gave way. The terrorists were not slow to exploit their victory: they launched a full-scale campaign of kidnapping, directed primarily against the adherents of Ananias, and so were able to recover large numbers of their own arrested followers.

Agrippa, meanwhile, was doing his utmost to keep in with the Romans, without proving false to his own people. In this delicate attempt he lacked the aplomb of his father. As early as the year 54 he had provided a contingent of troops for service against the Parthians: six years later he and Berenice had made haste to salute the newly-arrived procurator Porcius Festus (see page 102). He now enlarged his capital, Caesarea Philippi, and called it *Neronias*, a compliment he knew would please the emperor: the new name, and effigies of the emperor, appeared on Agrippa's coins. In Beirut, he built a grand new theatre, and presented sumptuous annual spectacles in it, at the same time making lavish donations of corn and oil to the inhabitants. The city was embellished with choice and valuable statues, many of them the works of old masters, and most of them requisitioned from collections in his own dominions, the owners of which were naturally resentful at being thus despoiled for the enrichment of an already opulent Roman colony. He liked to call himself "The great king Marcus Julius Agrippa, *philokaisar, pius, philoromaios*" ("Lover of Caesar, Dutiful, Lover of Rome"). Where his sister Berenice was associated with him in an inscription, her name precedes his, because, by her marriage with Herod of Chalcis, Agrippa's uncle, she had attained to royal status before Agrippa himself (see page 73 and Plate 27).

As High Priest, Jesus son of Damnaios was soon replaced by Jesus, son of Gamaliel, whose ambitious *fiancée*, Martha, of the family of Boethus, had not scrupled, it was said, to obtain the office for her betrothed by making a handsome present to Agrippa. Jesus was to be High Priest from 63 to 65. He carried on a feud with his predecessor which further widened the already deep rift between those who should have been united for peace. The Levites now obtained permission from Agrippa, who summoned the Sanhedrin to confirm the grant, that when they were officiating as choirmen in the Temple, they should be allowed to wear priestly vestments. This innovation was naturally resented by the priests. To add to the general discontents, and as though to make sure that no element of discord should be lacking, Albinus had shown himself ruinously venal. The only criminals who remained in prison, Josephus tells us, were those who could not afford to buy their way out. Even members of Agrippa's family joined in the general racketeering, blackmail and robbery: Costobar (the name originally borne by an Idumaean brother-in-law of Herod the Great) and Saul, by paying protection money to Albinus, were soon operating as prosperous gangsters. It was the year 63. In the midst of the growing turmoil, the great Temple of the Most High, begun more than eighty years before by Herod the Great, was at last brought to completion—only to be utterly destroyed seven years later, almost as though, like one of the offerings which loaded its great Altar, the Temple itself had been decked and made ready for sacrifice by fire.

Eighteen thousand labourers were thus thrown out of work, a figure which suggests that the final stages of the grand enterprise had consisted in the completion of the eastern rampart of the Enclosure. It is true that a portion of the *cella* itself had recently collapsed (Josephus, *Ant.*, XV, xi, 2); but it is equally true that, although Agrippa and the Temple authorities had intended to repair this damage—it consisted of a wall thirty feet high, which had crumbled owing to faulty foundations—they had not done so;

because the materials were still lying there during the siege, and were misappropriated by the defenders for warlike ends (*War*, V, i, 5). In any case, no repair of the shrine itself could possibly employ 18,000 men; whereas the construction of the rampart, which required not only enormous masses of masonry, but also prodigious earthworks, conceivably might. Moreover, as soon as the work was finished, the Temple authorities suggested to Agrippa, whose supreme authority over the sanctuary they thus recognized, that the eastern cloister should be rebuilt. This was called Solomon's porch. Originally designed, perhaps, by Solomon as part of his palace, it had been reconstructed by Herod the Great, who incorporated it in his splendid enclosure. A portion of it survives to-day in the "Golden Gate". The Temple authorities, fearing that, in the present disordered state of the city, 18,000 unemployed would create trouble, had been most careful to see that every workman was paid on the spot for his labour, and they had even thought of finding some sort of unemployment bonus from the Temple funds; only they feared that, if it were known that their treasure was being so disbursed, Albinus would find some excuse for helping himself to it. They were therefore all the more insistent that Agrippa should authorize the rebuilding of the cloisters.

Agrippa decided against the plan. It would be easy to demolish them; but, in such disjointed times, who could guarantee that they would ever be rebuilt? It would require a great deal of time and money, neither of which might be forthcoming. Instead, Agrippa put the men on to the provision of a much-needed public amenity, the repaving of the streets of Jerusalem, with white flag-stones. A remnant of this fine pavement may be seen to-day in the grounds of St Peter *in Gallicantu*, outside the Zion Gate (see Plate 29).

As High Priest Agrippa replaced Jesus by Matthias son of Theophilus "under whom the Jews' war with the Romans had its beginning".

Chapter XIII

JOSEPHUS

WE have now reached A.D. 65; and at this point we must interrupt the narrative to give some description of the man without whom it could not have been written, Flavius Josephus, who made his public *début* in the preceding year.

Josephus belongs to that small company of men who, having played a prominent part in great affairs, have later recorded them in books of abiding value and appeal. Thucydides was the first of them, St Luke another, Sir Winston Churchill the latest. Josephus was born in the year 37 or 38, the first of Caligula's reign, of a priestly father Matthias, and a mother who was "of royal blood", being descended from the Hasmonaeans. Josephus was brought up in Jerusalem with his brother, and, according to the testimony of his autobiography, was precociously intelligent, so that by the age of fourteen he was being consulted by the hierarchy on points of Jewish law. Two years later, Josephus decided to try for himself the three main religious orders, as they would now be called: Pharisees, Sadducees and Essenes. He was evidently greatly attracted to the Essenes, for he spent three whole years with a hermit called Bannus, possibly a disciple of John the Baptist, living a life of hardship and purity, depending (like John) upon nature for food and clothing, with frequent ablutions in cold water by day and by night.

Josephus was not by temperament an ascetic, nor a recluse: he was rather, as his life and writings abundantly prove, a sensitive extrovert, who sought the company of men, took a keen delight in observing and recording their conduct, and above all things sought their commendation. In this respect, though in no other, he closely resembles James Boswell of Auchinleck. It was only natural, therefore, that at the age of nineteen he should leave the desert for the capital, and become a member of the party of the Pharisees, who, he tells his Greek readers, are "of kin to the sect of the Stoics, as the Greeks call them".

At the age of twenty-six, Josephus entered public life. Certain priests of his acquaintance had been arrested by Felix on a trivial charge, and sent in chains to Rome, where they were compelled

to exist on figs and nuts, lest they infringe the dietary laws of their
Faith. Josephus, himself of priestly stock, knew these men, and
thought it would be an act of piety to secure their release. He set
out for Rome. Like St Paul four years earlier, he was shipwrecked,
and was one of the eighty survivors out of the complement of 600
who finally reached Puteoli, the port of Rome for arrivals from
the Levant. Here, says Josephus, "I became acquainted with
Aliturus, an actor of plays, and much beloved by Nero, but a
Jew by birth; and through his interest became known to Poppaea,
Caesar's wife; and took care, as soon as possible, to entreat her to
procure that the priests might be set at liberty; and when besides
this favour I had obtained many presents from Poppaea, I
returned home again." In this sentence is displayed all the
strength, all the weakness, of the Jewish position in Rome, as in
many another gentile community: the sure eye for the avenues of
influence, however shady they might be, and the disregard of
the jealousy which the use of such approaches must inevitably
arouse. (Poppaea had now been promoted from mistress to wife,
having contrived the suppression of her predecessor and rival,
Octavia.) It was on the night of the 18th July in the year 64 that
there broke out the great fire which in the course of the nine
succeeding days was to reduce the greater part of Rome to ashes.
Josephus may have witnessed the disaster. He would certainly
have observed its terrible legacy of devastation; and from his
co-religionists he would have heard full details of the manner
in which the new community of Christians had received their
first official recognition by being made the scapegoats for the
calamity, executed with every disgusting refinement of torture.
No doubt the general dislocation caused by the fire made it
necessary for him to prolong his stay in Rome to more than a
year.

By the time Josephus got back to Jerusalem, in the spring of 66,
the war had broken out. Josephus was in a painful dilemma. He
was staunchly faithful to the Law and the traditions of his fore-
fathers; he was proud of being a Jew. But for revolution he could
have no use. It was not only that he knew it would fail, that Rome
was unbeatable; he could not see that anything was to be gained
by it: Judaism was a *religio licita*, a permitted religion, and had
been for generations. Their legitimate rights, and additional
privileges, had been guaranteed to the Jews over and over again.
Political autonomy, in a world ruled by Rome, was an idle dream.
Josephus therefore rallied to the Pharisees and the clergy who

thought as he did but dared not and could not resist the reckless fervour of the extremists.

Josephus, as we shall see, played a prominent part in the war; but from the very nature of his upbringing and loyalties, it was an equivocal part. That he was of great service both to his country-men and to the Romans is, however, undeniable. He was for a time a soldier in the nationalist army; the forty-seven days of the siege of Jotapata marked his brief period of military fame. His own personal convictions led him to support the Roman government because it was the government. In his detailed description of the doctrine of the Essenes (*War*, II, viii, 7), Josephus notes that they "ever show fidelity to all men, and especially to those in authority", He himself observed this precept, which was carried over into Christianity. "Let every soul be subject unto the higher powers. For there is no power but of God: the powers that be are ordained of God", writes St Paul in his letter to the Romans, and goes on to elaborate the lesson in convincing detail (Romans xiii).

The sentiment was in fact widely diffused among Jewry, and the activities of the terrorists, and the appalling results which flowed from them, must not make us forget it. Thackeray (*Josephus the Man and the Historian*, by H. St John Thackeray, M.A., New York, 1929, Jewish Institute of Religion Press) quotes George Foote Moore's citation of Rabbi Hanina (*Judaism*, Vol. II, p. 116), in a dictum delivered most probably at the cessation of the daily sacrifice for Rome in 66, an action which made the war inevitable (see page 128): "Pray for the welfare of the govern-ment", said this pious Jew, "for if it were not for the fear of it, men would swallow one another up alive." The rabbi knew human nature, and was not afraid to say so.

Josephus reaped a rich reward from his Roman patrons. After thirty-three years, passed in Palestine as Pharisee, general and prisoner, he retired to the calm life of a man of letters in Rome, living as pensioner of the Caesars. How long he enjoyed this honourable existence we do not know, but the *Life* (65) mentions Agrippa II as being no longer alive, and we know from Photius, the Christian writer and bibliophile of the ninth century, that Agrippa died in A.D. 100. Josephus became a Roman citizen, whence his forename Flavius, that of the reigning house. Two grants of land in Palestine were made to him: the first, by Titus, was of an estate in the plain given him in exchange for a plot in the hills which had been expropriated as the site for a camp; the second, by Vespasian, of a large property in Judaea. These holdings were exempt from taxes. Josephus also received a pension, and lived in Vespasian's own house. Tertullian calls him "by far the most renowned Jew of his time". Eusebius, the great fourth-century Church historian, tells us in his *Ecclesiastical History*, III, 9, that a statue of Josephus was erected in Rome and that his books were placed in the public library. Josephus was married three times; his first wife deserted him, and he divorced the second. Three of his sons were alive at the turn of the century.

Such is the "success story" of Josephus. We must now consider his writings.

Four of his works are extant, to each of which reference has already been made: The *Jewish War*, the *Archaeology*, *Against Apion* and the *Life*.

The *Jewish War* is a brilliant piece of propaganda: it is written from the Roman point of view, as its name implies: it was hardly natural for a Jew to call an account of a war in which his people had been humbled by the Romans the *Jewish* war, which could only mean the war *against* the Jews. Its object was to show once and for all how foolish it was for anyone to suppose that they could possibly oppose the unconquerable might of Rome. The work was inspired by Titus and Agrippa II, to both of whom it was submitted before publication. Titus signed the order for publication with his own hand. Agrippa, Josephus says (*Life*, 65), wrote him no less than sixty-two letters on the subject-matter of the book. Josephus transcribes two—which give us rather a poor idea of Agrippa's Greek. Josephus also had access to Vespasian's memoirs, and to the official archives of the state. These were deposited in the Capitol, which, after escaping the Great Fire of 64, had been burned during the disturbances which followed Nero's death. To replace the originals, Vespasian had the entire empire ransacked for copies. The whole collection was engraved on 3,000 bronze tablets. The archives comprised all the acts of the Senate, texts of treaties, and grants of privileges to various persons and communities, including, of course, the Jews. That is why Josephus is able to quote so many official documents in the course of his works.

Within six years of the end of the campaign, one Aramaic and two Greek editions of the *War* had appeared. The Aramaic edition was intended, the author says, for those who lived in the east, particularly the Parthians, and Babylonians, not forgetting the Jews of those parts, who might be tempted to emulate the rebels of Palestine. The Greek editions were for circulation in the

[Alinari.

25. This statue is in the Naples Museum. The inhabitants of Naples, Pompeii and Herculaneum were very conscious of their propinquity to the court—from the days when Tiberius lived in Capri at the south end of their bay, to those of Nero, who enjoyed the amenities of Baiae in the northern arm of it. Their temples and public buildings, therefore, abounded in flattering statues and dedications. Note the hard, callous mouth, and the Julio-Claudian ears.

THE HASMONAEAN PALACE

[D. Brewster.

26. This photograph gives approximately the view from the Hasmonaean Palace, looking east over the Temple (pages 103 and 122). The palace itself was a little to the north of the road in the foreground. The Temple stood on the ground between the left-hand minaret and the Dome of the Rock, which marks the site of the Altar of Sacrifice. The open space, roughly quadrangular, below the modern road, was occupied by the *xystus* and the Tyropoeon Valley. The valley was spanned by two viaducts. The northern one, the arches of which still exist below the buildings at the foot of the left-hand minaret, marked

western lands of the empire, for even there, in the confusion which
followed the death of Nero, certain peoples—Josephus cites the
Gauls and the Celts—might be seduced into revolt. Josephus
could read Greek, but he could not write it accurately. He therefore employed assistants. The assistant who helped him in the
preparation of the *War* was a cultivated scholar, steeped in the
Greek classics, especially the dramatists. The result is a work of
art, nervous, concise and dramatic. Allowing for the defects
inherent in its purpose, and the equivocal rôle of its author in the
events with which it deals, to which reference has already been
made, it ranks among the great "war books" of the world. It
covers a period of nearly two and a half centuries, from Antiochus
Epiphanes (whom Josephus considered, rightly, to have sown,
by his attempted suppression of Judaism, the seeds of revolt in the
nation) to the end of the War. It is in seven books; and was first
published in A.D. 75.

The *Archaeology*, or *Antiquities*, as it is generally known in English,
would better be styled the *History*, for its aim is to tell, for Greek
readers, the whole story of the Jews, from the Creation until the
year A.D. 66. Josephus felt that such a work was necessary. The
Jewish war had quickened interest in the Jews: the famous
decorations of the Arch of Titus, which have survived to our own
day as one of the most poignant illustrations of Jewish history,
must have stimulated curiosity concerning the religion of this
strange race (see Plate 41). But neither the interest nor the curiosity was necessarily benign: on the contrary, the Jews, especially
since the war, were regarded with suspicion and dislike. Even
Josephus' patrons, Vespasian and Titus, had declined the honorific
Judaicus after their triumph, because of the stigma which attached
to the name. Josephus realized that much of the prejudice against
the Jews was founded, as prejudice generally is, on ignorance, on
the fear that springs from ignorance, and the hatred that is bred
of fear.

An example of this ignorance and its results is to be found in
Tacitus. The fifth book of his *History*, which dealt with the Jewish
War, and with the reigns of Vespasian, Titus and Domitian, is, to
our very great loss, incomplete: it takes us no further than the
beginning of the siege of Jerusalem. But this is preceded by a so-
called history of the Jews, a strange phantasmagoria of fact and
fancy, in which, among other fictions, they are said to be descended
from Egyptian lepers and to worship a donkey. This sort of gossip is
typical of the *incuria*, the mental lethargy of even the best Romans,

I

to which attention was drawn in Chapter I. Carcopino (*op. cit.*, p. 118) cites two other examples. "The Mauretanian state of Juba II, who had been brought up in the household of Octavia, was infested by troops of elephants. He preferred to trust the rubbish he had read about them and imaginatively vulgarize it further in his own writings, rather than go out and study these monstrous beasts with his own eyes. And fifty years later, when Caesar appointed Sallust governor of the new province of Africa, the historian took so little trouble to inform himself about towns not subject to his authority that in his *De Bello Iugurthino*, wishing to localize Cirta (the future Constantine) the ancient capital of Numidia, which had just been raised to the rank of an autonomous colony, he calmly placed it—'not far from the sea'."

If this sloppy indifference to facts was to be found in the pages of the leading authors of Rome, it is small wonder that accurate information about the Jews should be hard to come by. It was essential, Josephus felt, to supply it.

Vespasian and Titus were dead now. Domitian was emperor, and Domitian was no friend of literature. His only reading was the memoirs and despatches of the emperor Tiberius; otherwise, Suetonius tells us (*Domitian* 20), *nihil lectitabat*—"he never opened a book". His favourite recreation was spearing flies with a needle; but his fellow-creatures were by no means beyond the range of his loutish cruelty. It was safer not to be an author: Juvenal, Tacitus and Pliny all chose silence. Thus it came about that the *Antiquities* is a laboured work. It took nearly twenty years to write and was published in A.D. 93. The Greek assistant who worked on the earlier portion of it was the same as had helped with the *War*. Only for the last three books was Josephus in the hands of a rhetorical hack, one of the tribe of Thucydidean imitators on which Cicero and Lucian pour scorn. Jerome calls Josephus a second Livy; but he would have done better, Thackeray says, to call him a second Dionysius of Halicarnassus, for it is on Dionysius, who had produced his history in twenty books in 7 B.C., that Josephus models his, produced exactly a century later. His, too, must have twenty books, and that is why the nineteenth book, which covers a period of only three years and a half, is padded out with an irrelevant, detailed description of the death of Caligula and the elevation of Claudius. The work is dedicated to a certain Epaphroditus, probably a grammarian trained in Alexandria who lived in Rome. He had a library of 30,000 books, and was an authority on Homer and Greek mythology.

The book was intended for Romans, and so is written in a manner likely to please them, and at the same time to present Jewry
in as favourable a light as possible. For instance, the emperor
Tiberius is presented as a laudable character—this, of course, to
gratify Domitian. The miracles and wonders of the Old Testament story are given without comment—"relate and leave open"
was Josephus' rule, as it was Lucian's. Josephus was no enthusiast.
His knowledge of the Hebrew scriptures was profound, but he had
little interest in or concern with religion for its own sake. Realizing
that the story of the Golden Calf and the breaking of the first
tablets of the Law (Exodus xxxii) was a reflection on Jewish morals
and fidelity, Josephus simply omits it. But, unlike the Chronicler,
he saw no reason to miss out the story of David's sin and its sequel.
(2 Samuel, xi; 1 Chronicles xx; *Antiquities*, VII, vii): few Romans
would regard a successful adultery as a sin.

Josephus has given rise to but little controversy (so straightforward is his writing) except in one particular, and that is his
testimony to the life and ministry of Jesus of Nazareth. Until
the eighteenth century, few had thought to dispute its authenticity;
but it was then called in question by more than one of the sceptics
of the age. That Josephus had referred to John the Baptist and to
James the brother of the Lord was not denied, nor that, in a
passage quoted in the last chapter, James is described as "the
brother of Jesus, who was called Christ". This phrase is actually
quoted by Origen, in his commentary on St Matthew, about
A.D. 230, which is a very strong argument against the possibility of
its being an interpolation. That Josephus had knowledge of
Jesus, and of the events that preceded and followed his ministry,
is beyond doubt. Indeed, how could so comprehensive and accurate a chronicler have omitted to mention something which, as St
Luke puts it, "was not done in a corner"? (Acts xxvi, 26.) Even
the pagan Tacitus, writing but a little later, refers (*Annals*, XV,
44) to "Christ, who in the reign of Tiberius was brought to
punishment by Pontius Pilate the procurator". The passage which
has caused the controversy occurs in *Antiquities*, XVIII, iii, 3, and
is as follows: "Now there was about this time, Jesus a wise man,
if it be lawful to call him a man, for he was a doer of wonderful
works—a teacher of such men as receive the truth with pleasure.
He drew over to him many of the Jews and many of the Gentiles.
He was Christ; and when Pilate, at the suggestion of the principal
men amongst us, had condemned him to the cross, those who
loved him at first did not forsake him, for he appeared to them

alive again the third day, as the divine prophets had foretold these and ten thousand other wonderful things concerning him; and the tribe of Christians, so named from him, are not extinct at this day." The passage is quoted by Eusebius, about A.D. 324; and by Jerome, a stickler for textual accuracy, some seventy-five years later, but with the important variation: "He was believed to be Christ."

Thackeray submits the passage to a remarkable analysis, based on the occurrence or absence of idioms, words and turns of phrase peculiar to Josephus. His verdict is that, although the passage may have been retouched by Christian editors, it is, in essence, the undoubted work of Josephus.

Against Apion is really a misnomer. It is an exposition of the doctrine and practice of Judaism, and its venerable origins. It does contain in the second book a refutation of the slanders of Apion, the Alexandrine grammarian. It was written later than the *Antiquities*, and like them is dedicated to Epaphroditus.

The *Life* was intended as an appendix to the *Antiquities*, but was not written until after the death of Agrippa II, that is until after A.D. 100. Josephus' success, and the favour he enjoyed at court, had naturally exposed him to intrigue, jealousy and slander. In particular a certain Justus of Tiberias had accused Josephus of being responsible for the war. The *Life*, therefore, is chiefly— seventy-two chapters out of seventy-six—concerned to vindicate the author's behaviour during that crisis, for the satisfaction of Roman readers.

Such, in outline, was Josephus the man and the historian. Apart from a few references in Suetonius and the extant portion of the fifth book of Tacitus' *History*, he is the only authority for the events of the War. It is well indeed for us that, except where his own conduct is in question, he is such a comprehensive, well-informed, precise and conscientious narrator.

[*Beirut Museum.*]

27. This fine, though fragmentary and unfinished, inscription records (as restored) that "Queen Berenice daughter of the great King Agrippa and King Agrippa her brother adorned with marbles and columns the building which their ancestor King Herod (i.e. Herod the Great) had made, after it had fallen into decay through age". Berenice is mentioned before her brother Agrippa, because she was a queen before he was a king (cf. page 107). Her name is clearly visible in line one, and that of Herod in the line below it. The inscription came to light near the remains of a colonnade which was found on the site of the forum. This has now been reconstructed outside the Beirut Museum (see Plate 28); the inscription probably refers to it (see page 80).

[*R. Mouterde.*]

28. HERODIAN COLONNADE FROM BEIRUT FORUM

AGRIPPA II'S PAVEMENT

[D. Brewster.

29. Part of the stone pavement of the streets of Jerusalem which was undertaken on the initiative of Agrippa II when the Temple was finally finished (page 108). Before this time, the streets were unpaved, so a "pavement," such as that in the Antonia, is the Temple area (the Western Palace was a *new* emporium (cf. John xix. 13).

Chapter XIV

CATASTROPHE

BY the time Josephus returned to Palestine, in the spring of 66, the Jews were at war with Rome. In 64, Albinus had been succeeded by Gessius Florus, compared with whom in the recollection of the unhappy Jews, Albinus was a paragon, "for Albinus concealed his wickedness, and was careful that it might not be discovered to all men; but Gessius Florus, as though he had been sent on purpose to show his crimes to everybody, made a pompous ostentation of them to our nation, as never omitting any sort of violence, nor any unjust sort of punishment". Even Tacitus, no lover of the Jews, says in a famous sentence (*Hist.*, V, 10), "The patience of the Jews held out until the time of Gessius Florus: then the war broke out." Florus, the last of the procurators, was an upstart from Clazomenae, near Smyrna. He owed his position to a "job". His wife Cleopatra was one of Poppaea's cronies, and it was the empress who had contrived to have him appointed.

It is with this final change of procurators that we take leave of Josephus' *Antiquities*, which for the period from 168 B.C. up to A.D. 64 has been running parallel, though in a more expanded form, with the *War*, which starts with the former year: the *Antiquities* gives the period just three times as much space as the *War*, upon which, supplemented by some valuable information culled from the *Life*, we now rely.

Unfortunately, the governor of Syria, Cestius Gallus, was feeble and vacillating. He had probably been selected for those very qualities, for he had succeeded Gn. Domitius Corbulo, the greatest soldier of the age. It was Corbulo who, after a number of manœuvres rather than campaigns, had finally settled, on the best terms obtainable, the complicated and unrewarding Armenian problem. Tigranes V, the Herodian princeling, whom Corbulo had put on the throne, had fled the country (see page 94). A Roman army had capitulated. Finally, in the year 65, Corbulo had arranged that a Parthian prince should come to Rome to receive his diadem at the hands of Nero. "So ended," says the *Cambridge Ancient History* (X, 773), "ten years of marches and talk, punctuated by a disgraceful episode, which went by the name of war." It meant the virtual abandonment of Armenia to Parthia; but the reverse would have been far more radical had it not been for Corbulo. The reward he received from Nero was an order to commit suicide, which he did. His successor can hardly be blamed for preferring a quiet life.

The combination of the flaccid Gallus in Syria and the rapacious Florus in Judaea was utterly disastrous. Florus engaged in open rapine, and no man dare denounce him to Gallus. Like his predecessor, but on a more ostentatious scale, he went into partnership with the gangsters. Josephus comments (*War*, II, xiv, 4) that "the occasion of the war was by no means proportionable to those heavy calamities which it brought upon us". Of how many wars might that not be said? But it was never more truly said than of the war which Josephus was about to describe. When Gallus came to Jerusalem for the Passover of A.D. 66, the Jews implored him to restrain his colleague. Florus, who was standing by the Legate, simply laughed in their faces: he was Caesar's friend. Gallus made a few pacific promises, and then left for Antioch again. Florus went with him as far as his own capital, Caesarea, the city in which the first skirmishes of the war were now to take place. The Greek and Syrian inhabitants, elated by their unjust victory over the Jews—though it was the Jews who had first challenged the *status quo*—now deliberately provoked an "incident". The Jewish synagogue was in a Greek quarter of the town. The Jews, irked by the proximity of pagan neighbours, tried to buy out the nearest. He not only refused their offers, which were a good deal higher than market rates, but exploited his "nuisance value" by raising other buildings on his property, and then letting them as workshops. The synagogue was now more shut in than ever, and could be approached only by a narrow lane. Some young Jewish hotheads tried to stop the completion of the work by force. Florus arrested them. The Jewish elders went to him, and in desperation offered him a bribe of £4,000. Florus took it, promised redress, and at once went off to Sebaste, "leaving the sedition to take its full course, as if he had sold a licence to the Jews to fight it out". The very next day was a sabbath. Just when the Jews were assembling for the morning service, a Greek *provocateur* placed an upturned jar at the entrance to the synagogue, and proceeded thereon to sacrifice some birds—a travesty of the rites ordained in Leviticus xiv for the cleansing of a leper. At this affront, the two sides inevitably came to blows, despite all that the elders could do to restrain them. The army intervened, and the

Jews, salvaging their sacred books, retired to a little village called
Narbata, seven miles to the east of Caesarea. The notables hurried
off to see Florus, in Sebaste. They reminded him "with all
possible decency" of the £4,000. He imprisoned them: why had
they taken their books away from his capital? Were they afraid?
He felt insulted. And as for money, what need had he of their
stingy present? He would show them. He sent off to Jerusalem,
and ordered the Temple treasurer to hand over to him rather
more than double the amount of the bribe, £8,500, saying it was
wanted by Caesar. This theft appalled the Jews. In the old days
of the Greek dynasties, the robbing of temples was so frequent
that the Greeks had a word for it: *hierosylia*, which became of such
common currency that it survives in the Greek of to-day when
temples are no more, meaning, "a crime", "a pity", "too bad".
But under the *pax romana*, temples were no longer robbed;
Roman law and Roman justice guaranteed that. The last time
the Temple of Jerusalem had been pillaged was by Crassus in
54 B.C., more than a century ago; and what a terrible fate had
overtaken the robber. The Holy City was in an uproar. There
were demonstrations against Florus, and mock collections of
coppers for the poverty-stricken procurator, who, as soon as he
heard of it, neglecting altogether the outbreak in Caesarea, came
up to Jerusalem, bent on revenge. He sent a centurion ahead to
disperse by force a deputation of moderates who had come to bid
him welcome. He made for the Upper Palace, in front of which, on
the broad new pavement, he held his court. The clergy and secular
notables appeared. Florus demanded the delivery of the demonstrators. The elders answered that they could not identify them,
and that they had only done what they did because they were
young and foolish: the great majority of the people were law-
abiding citizens, etc., etc.—the usual speech on such occasions.
Florus replied by ordering his troops to loot the Upper Market,
which lay just to the east of the Palace, where the shops of David
and Christian streets are to-day, and to kill anyone they met.
Many innocent people were butchered in the narrow lanes.
Others were dragged before Florus, flogged and crucified, among
them Jews who were actually, like Florus himself, Roman citizens
and members of the equestrian order. The total casualties were
3,600.

It happened that Agrippa was on his way to Alexandria, to
congratulate Tiberius Julius Alexander, Berenice's ex-brother-in-
law, who had just been appointed governor of Egypt, *Praefectus* as

he was called, a position he was to fill with great credit. In going to visit him at this juncture, Agrippa showed that almost uncanny flair for dealing in political "futures" which distinguished his great-grandfather. In the ensuing war, both Agrippa and Tiberius were to be on the staff of the ultimate victor. But who could have foretold it now, and how important it was that the two men should be in firm agreement from the outset?

Berenice, who had accompanied her brother, stayed in Jerusalem to perform a Nazarite vow. She went bare-foot to Florus to intercede for the citizens (an action for which Juvenal was to pillory her). It was of no avail. Indeed the soldiers, who, being Caesareans, had no high regard for the woman whose own statue they had defiled, threatened her with violence, from which she only escaped by taking refuge in the Upper Palace, where she spent the night under guard. This happened on the 16th day of Ayar, or the 3rd June, A.D. 66. The next morning, there was a demonstration in the ruins of the Upper Market, which the prelates and notables were able to quell. Florus was not content with this. He had sent to Caesarea for reinforcements, and now required that a deputation go out to meet them. At the same time, he sent instructions that the greetings of the Jews were not to be returned, and that at the slightest suspicion of complaint or criticism arms were to be used.

Not all the citizens were in favour of so meek a policy, after the massacre of the previous day; but a procession of Temple dignitaries, bearing the sacred vestments and plate, followed by the choir, with their instruments, solemnly knelt before the assembled people, with dust on their heads, their garments rent, to beg them to show moderation and not to boycott the official welcome. They won over even the extremists, which was unfortunate; because when they had reluctantly gone out with the rest to greet the army, and the soldiers, in obedience to Florus' secret orders, had met their salutations with silent indifference, the hotheads started to cry out against him. This was the hoped-for signal: the troops fell on the unarmed procession. Panic ensued. Some were killed with clubs, some ridden down by the cavalry, and even more crushed to death as they struggled to re-enter the city through the two northern gates, corresponding to the Damascus and Herod's Gate of to-day. It was through the latter that the troops entered the walls, because they were making for the Antonia, on which Florus, too, was now moving with the soldiers from the Upper Palace, his intention being to occupy the whole circuit of the

Temple cloisters. Once again it was from the flat roofs of the
narrow lanes that the troops were successfully opposed: they were
forced to beat a retreat to the Palace. Meanwhile, the extremists
had isolated the Antonia from the Temple by breaking down the
cloisters and staircases that united it to the Temple. Florus had
failed. He summoned the chief priests and notables—who all
along, having a vested interest in the maintenance of the existing
order, had shown themselves ready to collaborate with the procurator, even so evil a procurator as Florus—and told them that
he was quitting Jerusalem, and would leave them such garrison
as they thought necessary to preserve the peace. They asked for
one cohort, stipulating that it should not be the one which had
committed the massacre. Florus humoured them, and went back
to Caesarea.

His rapacity was disappointed: he had been repulsed when the
treasures of the Temple were almost within his grasp. He was also
frightened; his credit with Caesar, even with a Nero, might well
dissolve before so scandalous a record as his now was. He therefore
sent off a prophylactic despatch to Gallus, laying all the blame on
the Jews. The Jewish notables, advised by Berenice, sent a counter-
blast, accusing Florus. Gallus, instead of moving on Jerusalem
with his legions, as Cassius Longinus had done in a far milder
crisis, temporized as usual, and sent down a member of his staff,
called Neapolitanus, on a "fact-finding commission". It happened
that Agrippa was now on his way back from Alexandria, and the
two men met at Jamnia, where a deputation of the moderate
leaders came to visit them. Agrippa, hiding his own anger at
the story of wanton brutality they had to tell, did his best to damp
down their indignation: his auditors acquiesced, "being desirous
of peace, because of the possessions they had". Agrippa and
Neapolitanus set out together for Jerusalem. When, at the top of
the Beth-Horon pass, they came on to the undulating plateau
across which lay the last eight miles of the highway, they were met
by a posse of howling women, the widows of those who had been
killed. These were followed by a great concourse, who called upon
Agrippa and Neapolitanus for justice. When they had entered
the City, the exalted visitors were taken to see the ruins of the
looted quarter, and Neapolitanus was told that, if he wanted
to see how pacific the mass of the people really were, he
could walk round the walls with one servant, even down to
Siloam, then, apparently, as now, a "tough" district. Neapolitanus
made the journey, and rounded if off by entering the Court of

the Gentiles of the Temple, and there congratulating the assembled people on their fidelity to Rome. For the sake of good measure, he then made his devotions—he could not of course enter the Inner Courts—and soon after departed to report to Gallus. The result of his visit, as of all such visits, was nothing whatever.

The Jews, who had seen through the manœuvre as the inhabitants of Palestine always do, turned in desperation to Agrippa. Should they not send a delegation to Nero direct, to prove that they were loyal subjects, and that it was only Florus they were opposed to? Agrippa, who knew the imperial court as few men did, thought that this would be a false step—Nero would be bound to back his favourite. On the other hand, he realized to what a violent and dangerous pitch the temper of the people had been wrought by recent events. He would make one last effort to avert the ever-approaching war. He therefore told the people to assemble, not in the Temple, where, particularly since the dining-room incident, he could not be wholly sure of his reception, but beneath the windows of his own Palace. This stood on the rocky crag to the west of the Tyropoeon valley (see Plate 26). To the north and to the south, the valley was spanned by the great viaducts (of which traces still remain) which gave access to the Temple from the Upper City. Immediately below was the *xystos*, or colonnaded gymnasium, which in the days of the Maccabees had given such offence to the Orthodox. The site made an ideal auditorium. When the audience had assembled, Agrippa came out on to the terrace of the palace, accompanied by Berenice, and proceeded to deliver one of the most famous speeches of which antiquity has record.

Among classical authors, it was a recognized rule of style that, in order to give the "commentary", or "background", as distinct from the narrative of events, an author should put into the mouth of one of his characters a general exposition which represented the author's views. The modern parallel is the leading article of a newspaper or review. Such speeches might take up a considerable part of a work; in *Acts*, for instance, they occupy over a quarter of the whole book. When an author was dealing with events which had occurred before his time, these discourses could often be little more than essays. On the other hand, where, as in *Acts*, the author was in close and prolonged contact with those of whom he writes, the speech will reflect the views, the recollected words, of the speakers themselves. Agrippa's speech comes into this second category. It would have taken about half an hour to deliver, in the version in which Josephus has preserved it, of which the draft was undoubtedly seen and revised by Agrippa himself.

He starts by saying that were he convinced that the whole nation was bent on war he certainly would not have ventured to advise them; but he knew that the majority were of a peaceable mind, and so he asked the rest to let him speak without interruption. First, why go to war on account of the procurators? It was not the procurators, but Caesar who was the ruler, and he had never done them any harm. Even if certain procurators had, "it is absurd to go to war with many for the sake of one".

Next, let them consider all the people who had succumbed to the might of Rome: the Athenians, who had once burnt their own city in the cause of freedom; the Spartans, heroes of Thermopylae and Plataea; the Macedonians, who still venerate the memory of Philip and Alexander; and a thousand others. Why should the Jews think it a disgrace to submit to the mistress of the world? And what sort of army did they rely on? Did they think they were going to fight the Egyptians or the Arabs? "Will you not carefully reflect upon the Roman empire," which stretches from the Euphrates to Cadiz, and from Libya to the Euphrates, "nay, they have sought for another habitable earth beyond the ocean, and carried their arms as far as such British islands as were never known before."

Agrippa then makes a brilliant verbal tour of the Roman empire. After emphasizing the ease with which Rome holds the frontiers with so comparatively few troops, he reviews the provinces of the empire itself. In the course of the survey he names the station of nearly every one of the twenty-eight legions of the then Roman army, omitting the four in Syria, which of course he did not have to mention, as his hearers knew all about them. Again, he draws comparisons to show the feebleness of the Jews. The Egyptians might be no good as fighters, but how rich they were! "They pay more tribute in one month than you do in a year." And those Britons: "Do you, who depend on the walls of Jerusalem, consider what a wall the Britons had: for the Romans sailed away to them, and subdued them although they were encompassed by the ocean." If they revolted, they could not expect aid from any quarter of the globe, for Rome ruled or controlled all. "What remains, therefore, is this, that you have recourse to divine assistance; but this is already on the side of the Romans: for it is impossible that so vast an empire should be settled without God's providence."

That clinched the matter. Agrippa ended by a graphic and chilling comparison of the horrors of war and the sweets of peace, exhorting his audience by their Sanctuary and the holy angels of God to accept his advice, and live in peace.

At the end of the speech, both Agrippa and Berenice—no doubt they had rehearsed it—burst into tears, which greatly affected a section of the crowd; but the hotheads still cried for vengeance on Florus. Agrippa replied that they had already taken it, by wrecking the cloisters, and withholding part of the tribute, and that this really amounted to a declaration of war. He then led a procession into the Temple area, where the repair of the cloisters was at once undertaken. The £20,000 deficiency in the tribute was soon collected from the defaulting villages.

Agrippa's great speech had scored an emotional success. Even at this distance of time, we are held by its scope, its fluency, its brilliance; but we have to admit that we are disgusted by its argument. It is in reality no more than a glorification of slavery. It demonstrates, more eloquently than any other passage of ancient literature, the great gulf that separates modern from ancient political ideas. The Roman world knew absolutely nothing of the idea of self-government, nor of the evolution of nationhood. That one people should rule another as a guardian, a trustee, whose proud aim it is to see the younger nation attain freedom and sovereignty, in whatever form of association with the elder it chooses to adopt—such an idea would have seemed folly to the Romans. They worked in precisely the opposite direction. The protectorates, or *client kingdoms*, as they were called, were only allowed to exist on sufferance, and generally only until such time as Rome was ready to absorb them as provinces under her direct rule. We have already noticed a number of such cases, including Judaea itself. Even the Nabataeans were to lose their independence in the first years of the next century. As Tacitus has it, Rome made even kings the instruments of servitude. Servitude: even for Romans, servitude was the only lot. No one in Rome dare talk of freedom any more. That was the basic fact of Roman life, and the basic fact of Roman decay. "So long as there is any subject which men may not freely discuss, they are timid upon all subjects. They wear an iron crown and talk in whispers. Such social conditions crush and maim the individual". The words which John Jay Chapman uses in his essay on Emerson of a crisis 1,800 years later apply with far more tragic force to the Roman world of Agrippa's day. In each case it was slavery, servitude, which

TIBERIAS

[*Rothenberg.*

30. The picture shews the Sea of Galilee, with the modern town of Tiberias in the centre, and the tomb of Meir Baal Hanes, a mediaeval rabbi, near the famous hot springs, in the foreground. Ancient Tiberias occupied the dark patch in between. The acropolis stood on the hill to the left, which is still called, in Arabic, the "Castle of the King's Daughter", i.e. Berenice. The Mountains of Upper Galilee close the horizon.

[*Rothenberg.*

31. Masada from the east. The Herodian barracks and dwellings were at the right-hand extremity.

[*Rothenberg.*

32. Masada from the west, shewing the ramp which the Romans constructed to gain access to it, and, on top of the hill, vestiges of the Herodian wall.

was the forbidden topic. Only in Rome was it the accepted condition of mankind. That is why the argument of Agrippa's speech,
brilliantly as it is presented, is, on reflection, so repugnant to a
modern reader.

Yet, in Agrippa's defence, it must be asked, what else could he
have advised? In a world where partnership, political equality,
of any kind, was unknown, what were the alternatives? War or
slavery? Was it possible to render unto Caesar the things which
were Caesar's and unto God the things that were God's?

Agrippa had no chance to find out. Exploiting the moderate
mood which, as he thought, his eloquence had produced, he now
urged submission to Florus, until the arrival of a new procurator.
The light which his eloquence had kindled in the minds of the
moderates was soon extinguished: the consuming flame of
fanaticism burned ever fiercer. The time for speeches had gone
by: only action could now express the dominant passion of the
Zealots. The tumult was renewed. Agrippa was insulted, even
stoned. He retired, perforce, to his kingdom. He could do no
more. The extremists had prevailed: they had passed the "point
of no return".

Chapter XV

JUDAEA CAPTA—ACT I

THE war which broke out between the Romans and the Jewish nationalists in A.D. 66, and was not concluded until seven years later, is one of the most famous in history, partly because of its consequences, which have lasted down to our own day, partly, too, because of the vivid detail in which Josephus has narrated it. His story of the seven years' fighting, as given in the *War*, runs, in the English version, to more than 65,000 words, or more than twice as many as he devotes in the same work to the preceding 234 years—and those he has by no means skimped. It is well, therefore, to bear in mind the purpose which Josephus had before him when writing, and also his need for presenting himself in a favourable, and where possible, prominent light. We may thus be able to preserve a balance between the events in which Josephus played a part and those in which he did not; lest the war, important as it was, usurp too large a share of the history as a whole, and the reader be distracted by irrelevancies.

The first engagements, as usually happens in nationalist rebellions, went in favour of the rebels. Despite the repeated warnings of growing dissatisfaction, despite the crimson signal of the recent bloodshed, neither Florus, nor Gallus, nor the commanders of the Judaean garrisons, realized, as Agrippa did, the fury with which the storm was about to break.

The first *coup* of the rebels was a successful surprise attack on Masada, the Gibraltar of the Dead Sea. This gaunt and desolate hill rises squarely above the lunar wilderness which bleaches the south-western confines of the lake. It dominates not only the sea itself, but also the caravan route which in antiquity ran across a causeway from the western shore of the sea to the *lisan*, or tongue, which juts out into it below Kerak, and so led to Petra and south Arabia. This road was the last link in the golden chain which bound Arabia Felix to Palestine, and so to the Mediterranean Sea and to Rome. The first to fortify Masada, says Josephus, was Jonathan, the brother of Judas the Maccabee; but his hold on southern Palestine was so sporadic and his military resources so slender that he can hardly have established a permanent fortress there. His nephew, John Hyrcanus, the conqueror of

Edom, or Idumaea, very well may have: we know he built one twenty-seven miles to the north. Be that as it may, it was Herod the Great who transformed Masada into an almost impregnable citadel. He surrounded the summit with a wall, built of dressed stone, seven furlongs in length, eighteen feet high and twelve feet broad. It was strengthened with thirty-eight towers which rose to seventy-five feet. Within the *enceinte*, which was shaped like a lozenge, with the long axis running north and south, there were barracks, magazines and a sumptuous palace, surmounted by four corner towers sixty feet high and embellished with monolithic columns whose mere conveyance to so lofty and remote a site was a triumph of skill and pertinacity. The enclosure also contained garden plots for the provision of fresh vegetables—a boon in that calcined desert—and vast cisterns to collect and store the rain water which falls but rarely in those regions. These reservoirs were so extensive that they furnished water not only for the gardens, but even for the elaborate baths with which the palace was equipped. This eyrie could be approached by two paths only: one, narrow, exposed and precipitous, from the shore of the Dead Sea, the other across the saddleback which forms the one bond between the isolated cone of Masada and the *massif* of the Judaean hills to the west. Even this approach was so tortuous that it was known as "the serpent". It was protected at its narrowest point by a tower.

Such was the famous Masada, of which considerable relics remain to this day. It was to be the scene both of the opening and of the closing scenes of the war (see Plates 31 and 32).

The greatest need of rebels at the beginning of a rebellion is arms; and the usual method of obtaining them, in our own century as in others, is a successful raid on a government armoury. That is what led Manahem to Masada in the summer of 66. He was a son of that Judas the Galilean who had rebelled in the days of Quirinius. He knew that Herod the Great had left there an arsenal containing arms for 10,000 men, besides large stores of food and munitions. Herod had put them there in the year 34 B.C. when he thought that he might have to fight Cleopatra, and the dry atmosphere had preserved them for a whole century.

Manahem surprised and killed the Roman garrison, helped himself to the arms, left a detachment of his own men in the citadel, and returned in triumph, "like a king", to Jerusalem, which he found in chaos. Eleazar, son of Ananias, of whom we have already heard in Chapter XII, when his clerk had been kidnapped by the terrorists, had by now gone over to them, despite his parentage, and announced, in his capacity as governor of the Temple, that no sacrifices were to be accepted from any foreigner whatsoever. This embargo applied to the sacrifice paid for by Caesar, and as such was an act of open defiance. The more prudent pontiffs, whose moderation was seconded by their own material interest, now assembled the people in front of the great bronze gate which gave access to the shrine on the east side of the court of the Gentiles, and besought them not to heed Eleazar: the Temple had always willingly received sacrifices from men and women of all nations, and did not the golden vessels presented by Augustus and Livia stand within its precincts?

The appeal fell in vain on ears attuned to more daring seductions. The prelates and their followers retired perforce to the upper city, leaving Eleazar and the rebels, who now included even some of the clergy, in possession of the Temple. The rupture with Rome was complete; and it is from this event—the interruption of the sacrifice for Caesar—that the beginning of the war may rightly be dated. It was the middle of August, 66.

The prelates, who feared being compromised by association, and so exposed to the repression which they knew would follow, sent messengers to Florus, headed by Simon, another son of Ananias, and to Agrippa, led by members of his own family, Saul, Costobar and Antipas. Florus did nothing. Agrippa, although he had no legal right to intervene by force in a province where his only authority was ecclesiastical, realized that it was now neck or nothing. He therefore sent down a wing of 2,000 cavalry, drawn from the Hauran and adjacent territories within his jurisdiction, commanded by his Master of the Horse, Darius, and Philip, one of Agrippa's most trusted provincial governors. It was his grandfather, a Babylonian Jew called Zamari, who had founded the military colony of horsemen in Batanaea, at the behest of Herod the Great. Philip the Tetrarch had found the colonists behaving as though they were independent, but his tact had won them back to allegiance. They now formed a body of troops, loyal to Agrippa, who had the additional advantage of being Jews. They were known as "the Royals". On arrival in Jerusalem, they occupied the upper city; and a week of skirmishes followed between them and the rebels. Then came the feast of the Woodgathering, when pious offerings of firewood—so rare and precious in Palestine—were brought from all sides to ensure that during the coming year the sacred flame on the great Altar of Sacrifice should never die. Eleazar excluded the peaceably-minded, but managed to introduce a large reinforcement of *sicarii*. He could now take the initiative. Under his orders, terrorists burned the palace of Agrippa and Berenice, the house of the High Priest Ananias, and then the public archives, in which were deposited all the loan contracts. This brought over to the rebels a large number of grateful, defaulting debtors. The leading priests and notables either went, literally, underground, hiding in vaults and conduits, or took refuge in the upper palace, whither Darius and Philip had withdrawn their troops.

A disaster of the first magnitude now befell the government forces: the Antonia was assaulted and, after only two days' resistance, collapsed to the rebels, who burned it and slaughtered the garrison. The Antonia was cut off from the upper palace, it is true; but that such a massive citadel, so strongly constructed, and nourished by such vast cisterns and storerooms, should have been carried after a resistance of only two days, by terrorists who had as yet no real military cohesion, is a startling revelation of the low ebb of discipline and efficiency to which Florus had allowed his troops to sink.

The terrorists, emboldened by this surprising success, now invested the upper palace. It was at this juncture that Manahem returned from Masada, with the welcome supplies of arms, and undertook the direction of the siege. Having no battering-rams, the attackers undermined one of the towers in the curtain-wall, only to find themselves, when it crumbled, confronted by another wall which the defenders had improvised. There was no heart in their defence, and they now asked Manahem for terms. Manahem was determined to destroy the hated Caesareans, as their comrades in the Antonia had been destroyed. He therefore offered quarter only to Agrippa's forces, and the other Jewish troops, who accordingly marched out. Had Philip, as his enemies later said, betrayed the garrison? It seems hardly likely; but Vespasian was later to send him to Nero to answer the charges of having done so. Fortunately for Philip, Nero was assassinated soon after his arrival in Rome, and he returned to his master unscathed. The regulars, who had been excluded from the first capitulation, now withdrew to the three great towers of the palace, Hippicus, Mariamme and Phasael, of which the relics still form the nucleus of the modern Citadel. The High Priest Ananias and his brother Hezekiah were dragged from their subterranean hiding place and killed. Manahem gave himself more princely airs than ever. Eleazar, who had started the revolt, became jealous and decided to

liquidate him and his party. Some of them escaped back to
Masada; Manahem was discovered hiding down in Ophel and,
together with his chief supporters, was tortured to death. Even in
those days, it had become the established rule among terrorists
that dog always eats dog.

Eleazar now turned his attention to the Caesareans trapped in
the great towers. He saw his way to settling an old score and did
not scruple to do it by treachery. He promised them their lives,
let them march out, waited until they had laid down their arms,
then slaughtered the lot, all except the commander, Metilius,
who was spared on condition that he embrace Judaism.

In little more than a month, the rebels had won control of
Jerusalem and Judaea. The moderates were aghast at the thought
of the retribution which must inevitably overtake the city, but
an ancient Jewish calendar, that of *Ta'anith* (the tractate of the
Mishnah which treats of Fasts), records as a feast-day the 17th
Elul (September), to celebrate "the disappearance of the Romans
from Judah and Jerusalem".

The massacre of the Caesarean cohort which had garrisoned
both the Antonia and the upper palace brought swift disaster to
the Jews of Caesarea, between whom and their gentile fellow-
citizens enmity had for so long existed. For those who live in a
society where there is no "Jewish question", no "Jewish quarters",
where the Jew is a citizen of the same loyalties, responsibilities
and privileges as his fellows, it is hard to understand that Jews
(or any other religious denomination) should be constrained to
accept any other status. But in antiquity things were very different.
The ordinary surroundings of a pagan city were obnoxious to
the Jews, who found that their ritual purity, and the liturgical
requirements of their Law, were constantly being compromised
by contact with the uncircumcised. They therefore tended to
segregate themselves, and to live together in quarters apart. It was
the Jews, not the Gentiles, who insisted on this separation. In
Alexandria, for instance, which housed one of the largest and
richest Jewish communities of the empire, Josephus tells us (*War*,
II, xviii, 7) that the Ptolemies, besides confirming the equal
citizenship of the Jews, "set apart for them a particular ward
[called *Delta*, i.e. *Fourth*] so that they might live without being
polluted by the Gentiles, and were thereby not so much inter-
mixed with foreigners as before". This seclusion suited the Jews:
but any society which regards as "foreigners" the free-born
citizens of the community into which they or their forbears have

immigrated, may well find themselves the object of a certain suspicion, even of dislike. Then, too, the religious exclusiveness of the Jew, the conviction that there was but one God, and that God the God of Israel, led him to express with more ardour than tact his disdain of the polytheism and paganism among which he lived, and to exalt into a virtue what should at most have been a necessity.

In ordinary times, the Jews got along well enough with their gentile neighbours. They were respected for their industry and their fair-dealing and for their contribution to the prosperity of those among whom they lived. But if ever it could be suspected that they were acting as Jews, not as citizens, that they were governed by a dual loyalty, or even a single, but alien one, then their position became precarious indeed. Above all, armed violence in Jerusalem itself, directed against Gentiles, was bound to bring disaster to Jews elsewhere. That is what happened now.

In Caesarea the entire community was destroyed. Twenty thousand were massacred in an hour. The few survivors were sent to the galleys. This, of course, infuriated the Jews in other parts of the country, who organized commandos to spread ruin and bloodshed in the Decapolis, the Jaulan (north-east of Gennesareth) and Galilee. Even the confines of Tyre were invaded, so were Ptolemais (Acre), Gaba and Caesarea itself. Sebaste, Gaza, Anthedon, Ascalon—all were sacked and burned. Hardly a Gentile city in Palestine or on its borders escaped. At Scytholopis (Beisan) the largest city of the Decapolis, the Jewish inhabitants helped their Greek brethren to repel the assailants. Nevertheless the Greeks, distrusting their real intentions, thrust them out of the town. The Jews found refuge in a sacred grove, where they thought they would at least be safe from molestation. The Greeks waited till night, then set on the Jews, murdered 13,000 and confiscated their goods.

The next link in this bloody chain reaction was forged, of course, by the Gentiles. Ascalon, Acre and Tyre either executed or imprisoned several thousand Jews; Hippos and Gadara contented themselves with taking off the potential ringleaders. Of the Decapolis, only Gerasa (Jerash) behaved with a humanity for which its citizens were later to pay dearly. They escorted to their frontiers those Jews who wished to depart and bade them go in peace. In the cities of Syria most distant from the area of disturbance, Antioch, Apamea and Sidon, the Jews were unscathed. Not so in the dominions of Agrippa. The king had gone up to Antioch, to urge Cestius Gallus to bestir himself and restore order. In Batanaea (the region that spans the main Damascus road north of

Dera'a), he had left in charge a certain Nuwwar, a relation of
Suheim of Homs. Nuwwar contrived the almost complete destruction of the military colony of Babylonian Jews, probably to spite
Philip, and massacred the Jews in Caesarea Philippi. Gamala
(rather surprisingly, for, though it was the capital of the Lower
Jaulan, it was also the home town of Eleazar) remained loyal,
thanks to the efforts of Philip himself. But not for long. It was soon
to become a rebel stronghold, whose reduction was to be one of
the most arduous feats of the campaign. In Peraea and Judaea the
last Roman strongholds were overthrown: Cypros, the great
fortress above Jericho, where the garrison was put to the sword
and the defences wrecked, and Machaerus, where John the
Baptist had been beheaded, of which the Roman garrison was
allowed to surrender.

Alexandria was the scene of violent fighting. Tiberius Alexander
did his utmost to calm Jewish passion, but to no avail. In the end he
had to call in the two Roman legions who were stationed in the city,
together with a contingent from Libya. The Jews were the sufferers.

Still Florus did nothing. Cestius Gallus was at last compelled to
act: after all, apart from the disturbances in Syria and in Egypt, a
whole province of the empire had passed out of Roman control.
Of the four legions under his command, the IIIrd, VIth, Xth and
XIIth, he chose the last, the "Thunderbolt", adding a mixed
contingent of 6,000 men drawn from the other three. Antiochus
of Commagene supplied 5,000 archers, of whom 2,000 were
mounted; Agrippa 3,000 foot and 1,000 cavalry, and Suheim
another 4,000, of whom a third were cavalry and the majority
archers. On the way from Antioch to Ptolemais, the army acquired a large number of auxiliaries, "who made up in their
alacrity and in their hatred to the Jews what they wanted in
skill". The total strength of the force must have been in the
neighbourhood of 30,000 men. Its first operation was to wreck the
neat little frontier township of Cabul, built in the Tyrian style
on the foothills above the bay of Acre. After reaching Caesarea,
Cestius Gallus sent one detachment to burn the city of Joppa,
where 8,000 of the inhabitants were killed; and another to deal
likewise with Narbata and its surrounding villages. The commanding officer of the XIIth legion was in charge of operations in
Galilee. Fortunately Sepphoris received him "with acclamations
of joy", which caused the rest of the district to do the same.
A few of the terrorists made off to the mountain of Asamon, or
Jebel al-Deidebeh, to the north-west of the Sahal-al-Battuf. The

cavalry rounded them up. Two thousand were killed, and only a very few escaped.

With Galilee thus unexpectedly pacified, and the whole of the coast in his hands, Gallus should have been able to press home his attack, and to have finished the whole campaign in a week or two. It was now October, and he could count on at least a month before the rains made the roads impassable. But the event was to be disastrously different. The army set out for the Holy City. From Antipatris a detachment was sent to Aphek, now Mejdel Yaba, and dispersed a concentration of Jews, while the main body moved to Lydda. The town was almost deserted, as its inhabitants had gone up to Jerusalem for the Feast of Tabernacles. It, too, was burned, and fifty stragglers put to the sword. The army started up the main road to Jerusalem, the road that to-day, as then, leaves the plain at Emwas (Nicopolis), and winds up through the hills by way of Beth-Horon (Beit Ur) and the citadel of Gibeon (Jib), whose inhabitants had been condemned of old to become hewers of wood and drawers of water. This village lies just over six miles north-west of Jerusalem. It should not be confused with Gibeah (Tel el Ful), a few miles to the south-east. Gallus had decided to camp at Gibeon, but he was not to be allowed to occupy it without molestation. Although the day was a sabbath, the Jews poured out of the city, led by princes of the royal house of Adiabene, who showed all the zeal of converts, by one Niger from Peraea, and Silas, a son of the Babylonian Jewish colony in Batanaea, who had deserted from Agrippa's army. They killed 400 footmen and 150 horsemen, while Simon Bar Gioras fell on the rearguard, as they were struggling up the defile from Beth-Horon, and carried off a number of laden baggage-animals. They then retired to Jerusalem.

For the last time, Agrippa tried to intercede, but of his two intermediaries, who were empowered to offer an amnesty to the rebels, one was killed and the other wounded. Gallus then advanced nearer to the city, and pitched his camp on what is to-day the municipal football ground and the level area between it and the War Cemetery. He was in no hurry to attack, thinking that the internal dissensions of the Jews would spare him the trouble. He dawdled for another three days, sending out foraging parties to seize the grain in the neighbouring villages. On the fourth day he did attack, and the rebels, abashed by the onslaught of the legionaries, whose disciplined might they were now experiencing for the first time, fell back not merely behind

Agrippa's wall, which was still unfinished, but behind the Second
Wall as well, thus leaving the whole of the new City at the mercy
of the Romans. This they burned, as was their custom, the timber-
market providing them with additional fuel, and, pressing on,
found themselves before the very walls of the upper palace, "and
had Gallus but at this very time attempted to get within the walls
by force, he had won the city presently, and the war had been put
an end to at once". Why did he hesitate? Had his officers really
been bribed, as Josephus suggests, by Florus, who wanted to see
the war prolonged? Even now, he was to be given a second chance:
the priestly party offered to open the gates of the city to him.
Gallus simply disregarded their offer, whereupon the rebels flung
the would-be collaborators down from the wall and stoned them.
After waiting, ignominious, feckless and irresolute, for five days,
Gallus launched an attack against the Antonia, or what was left
of it. Forming a *testudo* or "tortoise", by linking their shields over
their heads, as a protection against the missiles of the defenders, a
picked band of legionaries succeeded in undermining the wall,
and had everything ready for an assault on the Temple. For the
third time, Gallus had only to show some spark of initiative, and
the city would have been his. For the third time, he failed.
Gallus now decided to withdraw. It was the end of October.
The winter was approaching, during which the bleak highlands of
Judaea, 2,500 feet above the level of the Mediterranean, would be
lashed by chilling tempests, which no army encamped in the open
could hope to survive as a fighting force.

The retreat began. Gallus showed himself none the wiser for his
mauling on the way up the pass. He disregarded the first rule of
mountain warfare against guerrillas who know their country: he
failed to picket the hill-tops. As a result, the Jews played cat and
mouse with the doomed column, and the retreat became a rout.
Only nightfall saved the Romans, who sought refuge in Beth-
Horon. With the dawn, the Jews were ready for them again, and
kept up the pursuit as far as Antipatris. In his haste to escape,
Gallus abandoned his baggage and his siege-train, which fell
into the eager hands of the rebels. The human casualties amounted
to nearly 6,000, of whom all but 380 were foot soldiers.

The whole campaign had been a failure, its climax a calamity.
The first round of the war was over. It had ended in the complete
triumph of the rebels, who now controlled the whole of Jerusalem,
and a large part of Judaea, and even had a foothold (Machaerus)
in southern Peraea.

Chapter XVI

FIRST INTERLUDE—JOSEPHUS IN GALILEE

THE history of the Jewish war, like that of so many wars, is long and confusing: even the glowing pages of Josephus become tedious to the ordinary reader. Any fresh account of it—and the story has been told many a time by master artists—must be kept as succinct as possible. Fortunately, the whole drama falls into three clearly defined acts, of which the first has already been given. The second comprises Vespasian's first campaign, the third the siege and capture of Jerusalem. But between the first and second, and between the second and third, there occurred what may be called interludes, one played in Galilee, the other in Rome.

Josephus has given a disproportionate amount of space to events in Galilee, but this is understandable: they were "his war". Only here, only for seven short months, was Josephus the man of action, the dashing general, the resourceful leader. For the rest of the war he was a captive, honoured it is true, but still a captive, on the political staff of the Roman commander-in-chief. His narrative is confused: he had to justify his actions in the eyes of his compatriots, and to silence nationalist criticism, while at the same time pleasing the Romans and Agrippa, whom at one period he had openly opposed.

After the rout of Gallus, "many of the most eminent Jews swam away from the city, as from a ship when it was going to sink". The small Christian community, taught by their Master and his Apostles to render unto Caesar the things that are Caesar's, could have no part nor lot in a rebellion against that same Caesar. They too withdrew, as the Gospel bade them, when they saw Jerusalem surrounded by an army, crossed over the Jordan, and settled in Pella, now Tel el Fahl, in the fertile plain on the east bank of the Jordan, almost opposite to Beisan. Pella was a city of the Decapolis, that is to say it was predominantly Greek, but appears at this period to have formed part of Agrippa's dominions. At the head of the little Church was Symeon, the nephew of James the brother of the Lord: in the first days of Christianity a sort of caliphate was almost established.

Agrippa's relatives, Costobar and Saul, hastened after Gallus, who sent them at their own request to lay a full report on the state of affairs before Caesar, Nero, who was then in Greece winning ever-fresh laurels as singer, harpist and charioteer. They were to take care, said Gallus, to lay all the blame on Florus (who, according to Suetonius' account, was already dead) and not on himself.

At this juncture, the people of Damascus, knowing that they had little to fear from a Roman who had just been humiliated by the Jews, decided to get rid of their own Jewish citizens, despite the recorded fact that the wives of a large number of them had become proselytes; or perhaps that was why. They rounded up 10,500 in the gymnasium, and then cut their throats.

In Jerusalem, the victorious rebels set about the establishment of a regular government to replace the vanished Roman authority. The High Priest Ananus was appointed Supreme Commander, with Joseph Ben Gorion as his deputy. They at once set about repairing the walls of the city, against the siege which they knew to be inevitable. They struck their own coins of base silver, dated "the year one". The country was divided into six administrative districts, allotted as follows:

Idumaea	Jesus Ben Sapphias	
	Eleazar the son of Ananus who had started the revolt	
Jericho	Joseph Ben Simon	
Peraea	Manasses	
Thamna, Lydda, Emmaus, Joppa	} John the Essene	(The western region)
Gophna (Jifna) *'Aqraba*	} John, son of Matthias presumably the High Priest	(The central region)
Galilee	Josephus	

The foregoing list has a double interest. It shows that the administrative structure of the country, which Gabinius had imposed in 55 B.C., had proved a success. It has lasted in essence down to our own day. Secondly, there are scions of at least three priestly families among the ringleaders, and even one Essene, though they were a community of quietists. The alliance between popular religion and rebellion is the corollary, it seems, to that between orthodoxy and conservatism.

Josephus was thirty. He set about the organization of his district

A · B · C · D · E · F · G · H · I · J · K · L · M · N · O · P · Q ·

1 ·
2 ·
3 ·
4 ·
5 ·
6 ·
7 ·
8 ·
9 ·
10 ·
11 ·
12 ·

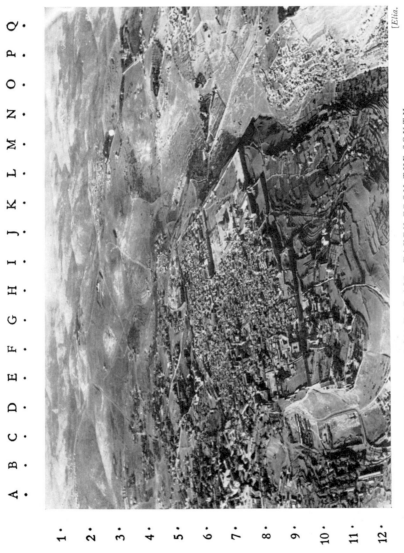

[*Elia.*

JERUSALEM FROM THE AIR. TAKEN FROM THE SOUTH

33. On the right is the Mount of Olives, with the camp of the Xth Legion at O 4. Below, N 6, the eastern, original, portion of the Garden of Gethsemane, with the Kedron Valley descending to Siloam, N 10, and houses on east side of valley. The Temple Area is conspicuous. The Antonia stood at I 6, the Hasmonaean Palace at J 8, Hippicus at E 8, Psephinus at B 7, the Tomb of Queen Helena of Adiabene at E 4, the camp of Cestius Gallus (see Plates 34 and 35) at C 4.

34. *From the North*
This view is taken from the spot where the troops of Cestius Gallus (page 133) and later two of Titus' legions (page 168) encamped on their first approach to Jerusalem.

In the first century there were no buildings outside the northern or Third Wall. From left to right, amid the modern dwellings, may be descried: (1) the camp of the Xth Legion, on the Mount of Olives (the point from which the view in Plate 35 was taken); (2) the octagonal white tower of the Palestine Archaeo-

1   2   3   4   5

35. *From the East*
This view is taken from the Mount of Olives, on the southern edge of what was the camp of the Xth Legion. From left to right, the following are visible: (1) Siloam, down in the valley; (2) the Temple Area, an extent of 35 acres, with the Garden of Gethsemane athwart the Kedron Valley below it (3) in front of the

[*D. Brewster.*

logical Museum (see Plate 18) which stands just north of the North East corner
of the Third Wall; (3) the Dome of the Rock, on the site of the Temple; (4) the
tower of St George's Cathedral, by the tomb of Queen Helena of Adiabene (see
Plate 20); (5) the spire of the church of St Saviour, a little to the west of which
stood the tower Psephinus.

If we can, in imagination, obliterate all the buildings in the foreground,
leaving only a line of wall from point (2) to point (5), we can form some idea of
how Jerusalem appeared to its Roman assailants.

      7   8   9

[*D. Brewster.*

left end of the King David Hotel, the Citadel; (4) the two domes (the bigger,
dark, behind the lesser, white) of the church of the Holy Sepulchre; (5) St Saviour's
spire; (6) just below the horizon, a barrack-like pile, the hospice of Notre Dame
de France; (7) the Palestine Archaeological Museum; (8) St George's Cathedral
tower; (9) the point from which the view in Plate 34 was taken.

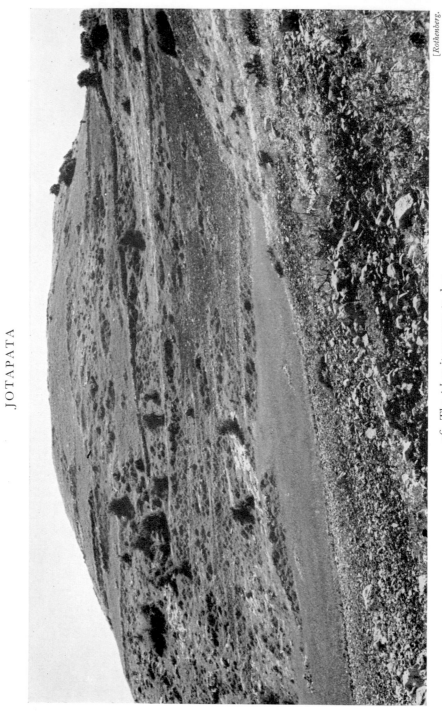

JOTAPATA

36. The *tel* as it appears to-day.

[*Rothenberg.*

with energy and enthusiasm. His first act, he says, was to conciliate the inhabitants by allowing them to manage their own affairs. In every town a council of seventy, and a bench of seven, were appointed. Next came protection. Josephus rebuilt the walls of Mount Tabor, Tiberias and Taricheae, refortified the grottoes in the Wadi Hamman, above the Sea of Galilee, and furnished with walls five smaller towns in Lower Galilee, four in Upper Galilee and three in the Jaulan, across the Sea of Galilee and the Upper Jordan. Josephus says he "allowed" the people of Sepphoris (who were really at heart on the Roman side) to build their walls at their own expense. He then raised a levy of 100,000 youths, and armed them with old weapons he had somehow collected. From this militia, he formed a regular army of 60,000 infantry with a cavalry wing. These were embodied, trained and disciplined on the Roman model, for Josephus knew that it was Romans they would have to fight.

These measures, which had made young Josephus of Jerusalem the most prominent man in Galilee, naturally aroused local jealousy, which became personified in a man called John, son of Levi, from Gischala to the north of Safad, a wild man from a wild country, a gangster and a racketeer. He tried to undermine Josephus' authority, by saying that he was preparing to hand the country over to the Romans; then from the Jerusalem junta he acquired not only the contract for re-fortifying his native town, and a grain monopoly, by both of which he did extremely well, but even a concession to supply "kosher" olive oil to the Jews of Caesarea Philippi, on which he made a profit of 800 per cent. His gang consisted of 400 roughs, mostly wanted criminals from the confines of Tyre, who terrorized the hill villages.

Even Josephus' own army thought itself entitled to loot. The road joining Agrippa's kingdom with the south ran beneath Mount Tabor through a village called Dabaritta, now Dabburiya. It is an ideal place for an ambush, because any approaching caravan is visible for miles, as it plods across the Plain of Esdraelon, or up from the Sea of Galilee, and at the village itself the road runs through the pass that separates Mount Tabor from the Nazareth hills. One day, the garrison of Dabaritta fell upon a rich convoy which was under the charge of the steward of Agrippa and Berenice, a Jew called Ptolemy, and looted it of silver plate, gold coin and rich textiles. The soldiers took their booty to Taricheae, where they proudly laid it at the feet of Josephus. They were naturally disgusted when, instead of "dividing the spoil", Josephus arranged for it to be sent back entire to its owners. Before this could be done, John exploited the anger of the soldiers, raised the cry of "collaboration", and egged on a mob to collect in the hippodrome of Taricheae demanding Josephus' death. Josephus only extricated himself from John's toils by promising that the loot should be employed on strengthening the walls of Taricheae, which he said was what he had all along intended it for. He then got even with the ringleaders by summoning them to a private conference and having them whipped to the bone.

Josephus had other enemies, besides John. One of them was his colleague Jesus Ben Sapphias, who had been appointed by the rebels as one of the governors of Idumaea (see page 136). He appears not to have taken up the post (and the deep south of Judaea can have had little attraction for so restless and intriguing a spirit), but to have gone north to Galilee, where he now appears not only as the leader of a gang of rogues, but as one of the notables of Tiberias. Josephus was himself responsible for their first open clash. It must be remembered that Josephus at thirty was by no means the suave collaborator, the friend of Rome and the Romans, of Agrippa and of Berenice that he afterwards became. He was still an ardent young Pharisee. The palace which Antipas had built in Tiberias offended him, with its sculptured friezes in which, contrary to the second commandment, animals were represented. The people of Tiberias had no love for Agrippa, to whom the palace now belonged. They were jealous of the primacy which Sepphoris had acquired as capital of Galilee, and charged Agrippa with having usurped their traditional right of levying their own taxes. Nevertheless, they saw no reason why the palace should be wantonly destroyed. The rebels insisted. At this juncture, Jesus Ben Sapphias, with an eye to a little personal enrichment, got in ahead of Josephus. He set fire to the palace, and collected the molten gold as it rained down from the rich ceilings. He also looted some Corinthian bronze candelabra, finely wrought tables, and a quantity of uncoined silver. These Josephus recovered. The rebels, urged on by Justus son of Pistus, a prominent intellectual of Tiberias, who was later to be one of Josephus' most virulent calumniators, massacred the Greeks of Tiberias, and crossed over the lake to burn villages belonging to Gadara and Hippos on its south-eastern shore.

John of Gischala now determined to rid himself of Josephus. He pretended to be ill, and said he wanted to come and take a cure at the famous hot baths of Tiberias. Josephus gave orders that he was to be shown every attention, and John duly arrived to put his plan into execution. The assassination was to take place in the stadium, where Josephus was haranguing the people. Just in time he was warned of the presence of the would-be killers, ran from the stadium, was carried to the beach on the back of one of his men, jumped into a boat and made for the middle of the lake. From there he conducted negotiations with the people of Tiberias, who were angry with John for having used their city as a means of furthering a private vendetta. Josephus went safely back to Taricheae, while John had to retire to his own Gischala, and stay there.

The people of Tiberias, in fact, were growing weary of their nationalist liberators, as sometimes happens in such cases. They now showed a disposition to return to the allegiance of Agrippa. They requested his return, and a herald was sent round, announcing the banishment of the governor of Galilee, i.e. Josephus. He had only a small bodyguard of seven men with him, so he decided to get the better of his adversaries by a ruse. He collected 230 boats (the presence of so many is evidence of the flourishing state of the lake's fisheries), and put four men on the prow of each. The citizens of Tiberias, when they saw this flotilla, with what looked like a formidable army on board, approaching their shores, decided to capitulate. Josephus, leaving his fleet at a discreet distance, where its true complement would not be detected by those on land, and accompanied only by his seven stalwarts, bristling with arms, made for the quay. The inhabitants rushed upon the ramparts, waving branches to signify submission, and implored him to spare the town. Josephus, instead of landing, bade them send off to him a delegation to negotiate. First came ten notables, then another fifty, and then more and more, all no doubt anxious to be in on the discussions. Josephus had them taken back to Taricheae and put in prison. The citizens, fearing the worst, now told Josephus that the revolt was entirely the work of one man, Clitus. Josephus, who had no desire, he says, to kill anyone, ordered a guard, called Levi, to go ashore and cut off Clitus' hands. Levi was afraid to land; so Josephus summoned Clitus, and pretended that he was himself coming to execute his own sentence. Thereupon Clitus begged that one of his hands be spared. Josephus agreed, provided that Clitus himself cut off the other. Clitus drew his sword, and with his right hand cut off his left. The story ends with Josephus setting free all the prisoners, and having Pistus and Justus to supper, in order to explain to them that he was really on the side of the Romans, and to advise them, like him, to wait for an opportunity of showing their true allegiance, and meanwhile to put up with Josephus as their governor.

This story, with its hairbreadth escapes, improvised stratagems and sudden reversals of fortune might, like that of Agrippa I, have come from the pages of the *Thousand and One Nights*. Yet Josephus published it as a "true narration": he gives it not only in the *War*, but in the *Life* as well; and, indeed, it may well have happened, for in the Levant life is far more *staccato* than in the cold north.

John of Gischala now tried to get rid of Josephus by denouncing him to the rebel junta in Jerusalem. He knew that Josephus had enemies in the Sanhedrin, who were of course jealous of his success in the north, and John thought that by a little well-placed bribery he could persuade them to depose his rival. He was right: a commission of three Pharisees and one Sadducee, well supplied with money and armed men, set out for Galilee. Josephus was at Cabul, fighting Placidus, the lieutenant of Cestius Gallus. One night, while he was at dinner, a soldier was announced. He brought a letter, he said, which demanded an immediate reply. From the man's insolent demeanour, and his refusal to join the party, Josephus knew quite well what the contents of the letter would be: a summons to appear before the commission. Besides, his father, who had been informed of the plot, had written to him from Jerusalem to put him on his guard. Josephus went on with dinner. Several hours later, when the guests had gone home, all except four of his intimates, Josephus, after a covert glance at the letter, called for the soldier, and gave him twenty drachmae. Noting the alacrity with which the man pocketed it, Josephus immediately added: "If only you will sit and drink with us, you shall have a drachma for every glass you down." The soldier was soon quite drunk, and came out with the whole story of the plot. Not content with deposing Josephus, the commissioners intended to kill him. Josephus wrote back very politely saying he was sorry he could not come to meet them: he was too busy fighting the enemy. It was an impeccable alibi.

The energetic governor got to work at once. The commission was met at every turn by deputations of peasants declaring their affection for Josephus, who, meanwhile, kept well clear of his enemies' wiles. He sent messengers, Galileans, to Jerusalem to inform the Sanhedrin of the true state of affairs, and of their loyalty to Josephus. The hostile four were ordered to come back to Jerusalem. Once again, Josephus had beaten John. He marched on Tiberias, at the head of 10,000 men, and rounded up the chief malignants. John found his own followers reduced to the men of his own village and 1,500 Tyrian thugs. Sepphoris had appealed to Cestius Gallus, and the Galileans, now once more loyal rebels, looted it. Its rival, Tiberias, would have suffered the same fate for having asked Agrippa to return, but Josephus, by ordering his soldiers to burn one house on the outskirts, so terrified the inhabitants, that they submitted to him, and so saved their own city.

Josephus had demonstrated that it was he who held sway in Tiberias. "Thus," says Abel (Vol. I, p. 494), "he was involved in open hostilities against Agrippa II, the ally of the Romans, which gives the semblance of truth to the accusation brought by Justus of Tiberias against his fellow-historian, of having been the cause of the revolt of Galilee against Rome and the king. In fact, Taricheae, Tiberias and Gamala had not waited for the arrival of Josephus to throw off Agrippa's authority, any more than Justus himself had to go and ravage the territory of the Decapolis. Not being a bitter extremist of the stamp of John of Gischala, the governor from Jerusalem kept himself within the decent limits of a service performed without much enthusiasm."

It is nevertheless true that Josephus had made war on Agrippa. Having raised an army, he had to feed it, preferably at the enemy's expense. To this end, he raided the grain stores at Besara (Sheikh Abreik) at the western end of the Plain of Esdraelon, where Berenice had collected the wheat of the surrounding villages. It was a daring foray, which had succeeded despite the endeavours of the Roman area-commander to thwart it. Josephus now tried to carry Sepphoris, but was repulsed. As if to make matters even, the Roman commander, Arquus Modius, failed to recover Gamala for Agrippa, despite a siege of seven months. For the rest, it was a campaign of skirmishes, of marches and counter-marches. In one of these engagements, near the Upper Jordan, Josephus was thrown from his horse in a quagmire. He sprained his wrist, and was carried to Capernaum in a fever, and so back to Taricheae.

Meanwhile, during this winter of 66-7, the rest of the country was as disturbed as Galilee. In Jerusalem, under the direction of Ananus, feverish preparations were being made to defend the city. The walls were perfected, the artillery, if such it can be called, captured from Cestius Gallus, was assembled and mounted, weapons and armour were forged, and the youth spent their time in martial exercises. Up in 'Aqraba, Simon son of Gioras acted as an independent war-lord. He looted, tortured and killed, until Ananus and the junta sent troops to suppress him. He escaped to Masada, whence he terrorized Idumaea, whose rulers had to garrison the villages to protect them.

Of the cities in Palestine, that which for the Jews above all others epitomized gentile arrogance was Ascalon, the immemorial stronghold of their Philistine adversaries. It alone had never been subject even to Herod the Great. It had remained "free", and was a bastion of Hellenism and "Romanizing". The rebels, puffed up by their success against Gallus, decided to humble this unclean city. Niger of Peraea, Silas the Babylonian and John the Essene, led a great host down from Jerusalem, bent upon revenge. Ascalon was held by only one cohort of infantry and a few hundred horsemen. But they made up for their small numbers by their discipline and experience. They cut the confident Jews to pieces—fighting on the level plain, where cavalry could manoeuvre, was a very different matter from the hill-skirmishes, to which alone the Jews were used. They left 10,000 corpses on the field, including those of John and Silas. Niger and the survivors escaped to a neighbouring village. Undaunted by their losses, the Jews, before their wounds were healed, before even their dead were buried, launched another onslaught against the city. Once again, Antonius, the Roman commander, routed them, killing another 8,000. The remainder fled to Mejdel, between Ascalon and Gaza, shutting themselves up in the fort, to which the Romans set fire. Niger jumped down from the walls, and escaped by hiding in a cave, to the joy of his men, who, despite these reverses, still regarded their leader as inspired, and their cause as sacred. Their blind confidence was soon to be put to the test, for up in the north the second act of the drama was about to begin.

Chapter XVII

JUDAEA CAPTA—ACT II

IN the winter of 66-7 Nero, now rising thirty, was engaged in a tour of Greece. He had decided to "liberate" Hellas (which meant that it would be exempted from the tribute), to construct the Corinth Canal, of which, like modern royalty, he ceremonially cut the first turf with a golden spade, and to appear as actor, singer and charioteer in the four great national Games, which, for his convenience, were all celebrated in the same year. Amid these artistic triumphs—for Nero, of course, won all the first prizes—the emperor was reminded of the more sordid cares of sovereignty by the arrival of bad news from the East. Whether (as Suetonius affirms) the Jewish rebels had killed Florus, and captured an eagle, or not, the defeat of Cestius Gallus was in itself disastrous enough. But suppose the disaffection should spread? The Armenians, the Parthians themselves might take the opportunity to turn their arms once more against Rome. Nero put a brave face on it, but inwardly he was deeply alarmed. Clearly, a major campaign lay ahead: it was essential for the very life of Rome that the East should be secure.

Who was to be the commander-in-chief? Corbulo was dead. Everything pointed to a general called Vespasian. Flavius Vespasian, now fifty-eight years of age, came of an obscure family. His father, an undistinguished knight, had ended his days as a money-lender in what is now Switzerland. His two sons entered the Senate, the elder becoming Prefect of the City, the younger, Vespasian, taking to the army. For his part in Claudius' invasion of Britain, where he captured the Isle of Wight and Maiden Castle, he was awarded the insignia of a Triumph. After his consulship, in 51, he retired into private life, through fear of Agrippina, who disliked him as a protégé of Narcissus. Later, he became governor of the province of Africa, from which he returned a poor man, and, after mortgaging all his estates to his brother, was forced to become a horse-coper, whence he acquired the nickname "Mulio" or muleteer. Nevertheless, he secured a place in Nero's suite for the Grecian tour; but once again fortune frowned on him. The old soldier did not appreciate Nero's singing, and showed his indifference either by absence or sleep. He was advised to leave the court. But he was a capable soldier, and besides he had the great advantage in Nero's eyes of being a man of no origin, who could never possibly be a competitor for the supreme power.

So in February 67 Vespasian was appointed, with the rank of Legatus, to subdue Judaea and to be its governor, in succession to the procurators. He started out at once, making for Antioch by the overland route, via the Hellespont and Turkey. Here, he picked up two legions, the Vth *Macedonica* and Xth *Fretensis*, and marched down to Ptolemais. At Tyre the inhabitants presented their complaints against Agrippa, who accompanied Vespasian, and it was on this occasion that the king adroitly extricated himself from a delicate situation by sending his general, Philip, to Rome to justify himself. At Acre, delegations from the Decapolis having accused Justus of Tiberias of burning their villages, Vespasian handed him over to Agrippa, who put him in prison. No doubt this episode increased his venom against Agrippa's future friend, Josephus. Sepphoris had already been garrisoned by Roman troops, but Vespasian willingly granted the request of the inhabitants for a reinforcement to protect them from the Galilean bandits. Sepphoris was a vital headquarters for the coming campaign. Vespasian brought the garrison up to 6,000 men.

Titus, Vespasian's elder son, now appears on the scene. He was twenty-seven. Despite his humble birth, he had been brought up, no doubt through Narcissus' interest, as the intimate of Britannicus, whose death by poison he almost shared, and whose life he later commemorated by two statues, one of gold and the other of ivory. Titus was remarkably gifted. Although short and rather stout, he had a noble and handsome countenance. He was a splendid athlete, a finished horseman. He was fluent in both Latin and Greek, composed poetry and sang. He was also an accomplished stenographer, and liked to boast that he would have been a first-rate forger. He was in fact an "all rounder" well-endowed to be what Suetonius calls him: "the world's darling". He had already seen military service in Germany and Britain, and had appeared in the courts as an advocate, for the sake of reputation rather than gain. He had made a good marriage with the daughter of a former commander of the Praetorian Guard. Upon her death, he married a second wife, from whom he was now divorced. He had served as quaestor, and was with Nero in Greece when his father was appointed to Judaea. Vespasian had sent him to Alexandria, to assume command of the XVth legion, *Apollinaris*, at whose head he now reported at Ptolemais.

The client kings furnished contingents: it was one of the terms on which they were allowed to rule. Agrippa, Suheim of Emesa and Antiochus of Commagene each sent 2,000 foot-archers and 1,000 horsemen, Malik II of Petra 1,000 cavalry, and 5,000 infantry, of whom the majority were archers. Without counting the serving men, most of whom could fight as well, the total strength of the army was not far short of 60,000, made up as follows:

3 legions, of 6,120 men each	18,360
10 cohorts, of 1,000	10,000
13 cohorts, of 720	9,360
6 wings, of 1,000	6,000
Auxiliaries of Syrian kings (3×3,000)	9,000
Nabataean auxiliaries	6,000
	58,720

At this point in his narrative, Josephus introduces a detailed description of the Roman army, its arms, armour, discipline, order of battle and camps. It was intended, of course, for those in such countries as Babylonia and Parthia who had never seen a Roman soldier. Even to-day, the picture is so vivid, so dramatic, that it strikes the reader with something of the horror and helplessness, of admiration and despair that must have chilled the hearts of those who first beheld those glittering and invincible warriors. The awful pageant was now to be displayed in Galilee and in Judaea.

Vespasian had never been a brilliant commander, but he was a prudent one. His experience in southern England had taught him that every wood or thicket might shelter an ambush. He was not going to place his forces in situations where they would be at the mercy of guerrillas, or expose them to hill-skirmishes, of which they had no experience. The whole army was to be kept together, to proceed with all caution, and to attack only one objective at a time. These tactics, the only ones possible in the face of the fanatical determination of the rebels, lengthened the campaign, but were justified by results.

The tribune Placidus, with 1,000 horsemen and the garrison of Sepphoris, was striking back against the bandits, and sacking the villages, whose inhabitants found refuge within the towns that Josephus had had the foresight to provide with walls. Thinking to disrupt the defence, Placidus made for the strongest of these, Jotapata or Yodpat (now Jefat), nine miles north of Sepphoris, but having no siege engines he was repulsed and broke off the engagement. When Vespasian advanced with his formidable host, courage began to desert the soldiers of Josephus, who was encamped at Garis, the modern Reineh, some three miles from Sepphoris, on the road to Tiberias, whither Josephus now withdrew his remaining followers. Vespasian's first target was the village of Garaba, probably 'Arrabet el-Battuf, five miles distant from Jotapata. The position was carried at the first assault, and, like the neighbouring villages, was subjected to the horrors of fire and massacre. The Romans wanted to avenge the disgrace of Cestius Gallus, who was now dead, the victim (Tacitus suggests) of humiliation and remorse. There were but few survivors, for the Romans spared neither youth nor age.

Jotapata must now be reduced. Josephus, feeling in duty bound to direct its defence, came up from Tiberias, much to the satisfaction of Vespasian, who reckoned that the capture of the leader would make the reduction of the province all the easier. The siege lasted for forty-seven days, in the height of summer, which even in the hills of Galilee can be distressingly hot. It was the last military action in which Josephus was destined to have an active share. In later years, the Roman citizen, Caesar's friend, writing at peace in Rome, no doubt looked back upon these stirring times in Galilee as his finest hour; nor can he be blamed for giving us an almost day-by-day account of the siege, which was contested on both sides with great resource and resolution.

The first thing the Romans did was to construct a broad road across the rocky approaches. The pioneers finished it in four days. The Romans established their camp to the north of the town, for like Jerusalem it could be attacked only on that side, all the others being protected by deep valleys.

For five days the Romans assaulted the wall; but the furious sorties of the defenders prevented them from securing any foothold, and it became clear to Vespasian that he would have to form a regular siege, using all the resources at his command.

Roman siegecraft of this period relied on six different devices, most of which had been in use for many centuries.

The first, the mine, has already been mentioned. The object of the mine was to sap the foundations of a defensive system.

Beneath the enemy ramparts a tunnel was driven, of which the roof was generally secured with what in a commercial mine would be called pit-props. Very often combustibles were then introduced and the timber set on fire. The collapse of the supports often brought down the wall above, unless that is, the defenders had already outwitted the attackers by countermining.

Next came the battering-ram. This, to quote Josephus' specification, "is a vast beam of wood like the mast of a ship; its forepart is armed with a thick piece of iron at the head of it, which is so carved as to be like the head of a ram, whence its name is taken. This ram is slung in the air by ropes passing over its middle, and is hung like the balance in a pair of scales from another beam, and braced by strong beams that pass on both sides of it in the nature of a cross. When this ram is pulled backward by a great number of men with united force, and then thrust forward by the same men with a mighty noise, it batters the walls with that iron part which is so prominent; nor is there any tower so strong, or walls so broad, that can resist any more than its first batteries, but all are forced to yield to it at last."

The third device was the tower. This was a pagoda-like structure, which was dragged towards the wall on wheels, or rollers. It might have five or six storeys and be fifty, or even ninety feet high, depending on the height of the wall it was designed to overlook. It was plated with iron or hides to protect it from the defenders' shafts; and some towers were even equipped with a primitive fire-fighting device, whereby water was forced by syringes through pipes of animal-gut to the upper storeys.

Neither the battering-ram nor the tower could produce any effect unless they were in physical contact with the defences. It was to prevent such contact that fortresses were provided with fosses. These were never intended to be filled with water, as in later northern fortifications, but merely to provide the ancient equivalent of a "tank-trap". Very often, therefore, one of the first tasks of a besieging army was to try to fill up the fosse, so that the engines could be brought right up to the wall.

The fourth device consisted of earthworks. Apart from the filling-in of the fosse just mentioned, there were two major uses of earthworks. The first was the construction of ramps, inclined planes which served the same general purpose as the towers. They were more solid and secure, but lacked the mobility of the tower. The two, as we shall see, could be used in conjunction. The second use of the earthwork was in circumvallation, that is the throwing-up of a continuous dyke round a walled city, to deny to the defenders any access or egress, and so starve them into surrender.

Fifth came the "artillery", which consisted of catapults, of various weights and sizes. In the heaviest model the base of a beam, like an inverted metronome, would be fitted into a great loop of resilient cords, generally long, thick strands made from the hair of horses or women. The beam was then swung back into an almost horizontal position, and in a cup at its summit were placed stones or iron-shod missiles. The strands were twisted by means of windlasses, until they were taut. The beam was then released and the missiles sped towards the enemy. The machine sounds primitive, but it was apparently very effective. Josephus says that the projectiles, which might weigh as much as a hundredweight, would break up whole formations of troops (as chain-shot was later to do), carry away pinnacles of the wall and damage the towers. He says he himself was standing by when one of his men was hit on the head by a stone from a catapult, and his skull carried away to a distance of 600 yards.

The sixth, and final, component of the siege-train was the scaling-ladders, to the placing of which, often supported by the *testudo*, in readiness for the actual assault, all the other devices had led up.

In his siege of Jotapata, Vespasian used all these weapons, with the exception of the mine, of which the site hardly allowed. He first of all ordered the construction of a ramp; but the defenders contrived to raise the height of their wall *pari passu* with the progress of the earthwork, which, in numerous sorties, they succeeded in piercing. Despite all their efforts, the battering-ram was finally brought up, while 160 catapults, seconded by archers and slingers, sent a rain of missiles against the Jews on the ramparts. The wall began to crumble, when Josephus thought of an expedient to minimize the damage: he lowered sacks filled with chaff, to deaden the strokes of the ram, just as in a later century the inhabitants of Bradford were to hang woolsacks on the walls of their church to protect it from the artillery of the Royalists.

The Romans, aided by the sun, were winning. There is no spring at Jotapata, and the water was running low. Josephus rationed it, and even spread damp cloths on the ramparts to persuade the besiegers that there was no shortage within. The construction of the ramps proceeded relentlessly, and the day came when they were finished, three of them, and atop of each stood a great armoured tower, fifty feet high. The first assault was a failure. The defenders defeated the *testudo* by the use of boiling oil, which penetrated the carapace of shields, and then found its way through the joints of the attackers' armour, inflicting agonizing burns.

Meanwhile, Yafa, the pretty village south-west of Nazareth, on the hill-terrace above the Plain of Esdraelon, heartened by the defence of Jotapata, declared for the rebels. Vespasian despatched 1,000 horse and 2,000 foot to reduce it, under the command of Trajan, the commanding officer of the Xth, and the father of the future emperor. The defences consisted of two ramparts, of which the outer was easily taken. Trajan wanted to reserve the honour of taking the inner wall for Vespasian, who sent Titus in his place, with 500 horse and 1,000 foot. Titus led the storming-party, which, having carried the second wall, took six hours to clear the streets. The usual massacre followed, the dead numbering 15,000. The prisoners, mostly women and children, amounted to 2,130. This happened on the 13th July, A.D. 67. Two days later, Sextus Cerialis Vettulenus, commanding the Vth, slaughtered 11,600 Samaritans, who had assembled on their holy mountain of Gerizim in a defiant mood, they too having been emboldened by the defence of Jotapata. Only those who refused to lay down their arms were killed; many others surrendered. The fact that Vespasian could thus detach on punitive raids the commanding officers of two of his three legions argues that he was relying on hunger and thirst to weaken the defences of Jotapata, before making another assault upon the town.

This he did a fortnight later. A deserter had come over to the Romans with the story that the town was now in the last straits and could easily be entered. At first Vespasian was not disposed to trust him, knowing how faithful to one another the Jews were, and how staunchly they withstood torture; "this last, because one of the people of Jotapata had undergone all sorts of torments . . ., yet would he inform them nothing of the affairs within the city, and, as he was crucified, smiled at them". But the man's tale sounded probable, and Vespasian was prepared to risk it. He decided to attack just before dawn, at which hour, the deserter said, the exhausted guards snatched a little sleep. Titus, accompanied only by a tribune of the XVth and a handful of soldiers, crept silently into the citadel, helped by a thick morning mist, cut the throats of the sleeping guards, and opened the gates to their comrades. It was the 29th July. The siege was over: it had lasted forty-seven days. The defenders suffered 40,000 casualties from first to last. Only 1,200 were taken prisoner. The fortifications were razed, the town burned.

Josephus, with forty notables, sought refuge in a cave. After two days a woman gave away their hiding-place, and Vespasian sent two officers to offer him his life if he would surrender. At first Josephus refused, but when a third officer, Nicanor, a friend of his, was sent to reinforce the offer, he accepted it. His compatriots at once accused him of ratting: how could he prefer slavery to death? they asked, and drew their swords. Josephus, who, he says, "was not destitute of his usual sagacity", tried to dissuade them from suicide, but finding them determined suggested that the most satisfactory arrangement would be to draw lots, as to who should kill whom, and in what order. By a remarkable chance, "or by the providence of God", Josephus drew the last lot, and so, with the other survivor, came out of the cave alive.

Vespasian, when Josephus was brought before him, ordered that he was to be kept under strict guard, as he intended to send him to Nero. "Vespasian!" replied Josephus. "I am no ordinary captive: I come to you as a messenger of higher things. Do you send me to Nero? It is you, Vespasian, who are and shall be Caesar and emperor, you and your son. You shall be lord not only over me, but over land and sea and all mankind."

On this remarkable prediction the *Cambridge Ancient History* (X, 859 *n.*) comments: "The fact that Talmudic tradition credits Johanan Ben Zakkai with the same prophecy does not lessen the trustworthiness of Josephus' statement, backed as it is by Suetonius, *Vesp.* 5 and Dio LXVI, i, 4, and so probably contained in the Memoirs of Vespasian."

Josephus remained a prisoner; but he was kindly treated by Vespasian, much to the satisfaction of Titus, who was much the same age as Josephus and had already taken a liking to him.

The Roman army, particularly the metropolitan troops, needed a rest after the rigours of a campaign conducted in the height of summer. The Vth and Xth legions were withdrawn to Caesarea, the XVth to the less salubrious Scythopolis (Beisan). The inhabitants of Caesarea gave the victors an enthusiastic welcome, loudly demanded the death of Josephus, and complained that Jewish refugees had settled in the ruins of Joppa and were using that port as a base for piracy up and down the coast of the Levant. Vespasian disregarded the clamour against Josephus, but sent a force against Joppa. At its approach, the pirates took refuge on board their vessels, which, caught by one of those sudden storms to which the port is notoriously exposed, were smashed on the rocks, with the loss of 4,200 lives. The Romans established a camp on the ruins of the citadel of Joppa and subjected the neighbouring villages to their usual "scorched earth" policy. Meanwhile, in Jerusalem, the news that Josephus was still alive, and being given preferential treatment, caused disgust all the more vehement because for a whole month the Zealots had gone to the trouble and expense of having him publicly mourned.

Like his soldiers, Vespasian needed a little relaxation, so Agrippa suggested a visit to Caesarea Philippi. There, soothed by the rills and cascades of the infant Jordan river, refreshed by the snow-cooled breezes which even in July fan the southern slopes of Mount Hermon, with the scene of his recent triumphs spread out before his eyes, the Roman general spent three weeks as Agrippa's guest. He was fêted by the king, and publicly returned thanks to God for the success of the imperial arms. This idyll was rudely ended by the intelligence that, barely thirty miles away to the south, the towns of Tiberias and Taricheae, both portions of Agrippa's dominions, were once again the victims of sedition. Vespasian at once ordered Titus to go down to Caesarea on the coast, bring up the Vth and Xth, and meet him at Scythopolis, where the XVth was already quartered. At the head of the three legions, Vespasian marched north to the Sea of Galilee, camping at Sennabris, to-day *Sinn en-Nabra*, or Kinneret, some four miles south of Tiberias. Neither Vespasian nor Agrippa had any desire to cause further damage or bloodshed to the town, the majority of whose citizens they knew to be well-disposed. To parley with them a junior officer was sent forward with fifty horsemen, who, as a sign of their pacific intention, dismounted and approached the walls on foot. Immediately, a gang of rebels, led by Jesus son of Sapphias, rushed upon them, scattered them and carried off their horses. Vespasian restrained his natural desire to punish this treacherous assault, particularly as the city belonged to Agrippa. The elders and notables soon came to throw themselves at his feet, and to implore forgiveness. Jesus and his bandits had made off to Taricheae. On the following day, Vespasian made his formal entry into Tiberias, whose inhabitants, demolishing a section of their walls as a symbol of submission, hailed him as their saviour and benefactor. This delivery of Tiberias is one of the few happy incidents in a brutal war; and it is pleasant to think that it was due

to the hold which Agrippa had already established on the friendship of the future emperor.

Taricheae was now the chief focus of the malignants.
Vespasian moved south along the western shore of the lake, and
established a new camp, some way short of Taricheae, which
stood at the extreme south of the plain of Gennesareth. Archers
stationed on the neighbouring hill of Arbela had the town at their
mercy; Titus' cavalry broke up the sorties of the defenders. The
young general decided on a bold stroke. The city being situated
on the shore of the lake was protected on its eastern side only by
the water, through which Titus now led a troop of horse, thus
turning the fortifications and entering the town. Vespasian was
delighted at his son's prowess and resource, and hastened to join
him. Meanwhile the terrified inhabitants had taken to their
ships; so on the following morning Vespasian ordered the construction of heavy rafts, which he filled with soldiers and despatched in pursuit of the fugitives, who soon succumbed to the
superior armament of the Romans. This unusual naval victory,
together perhaps with the success of Joppa, accounts for the
inscription *Victoria Navalis* on the coins of Vespasian and his
sons.

The prisoners had now to be disposed of. Of those who were not
citizens of Taricheae, but had taken refuge in it, the old and useless, 1,200 in number, were slaughtered out of hand in the stadium.
Of the younger ones 6,000 were sent off to Nero, to work on his
abortive Corinth Canal, while those who were Jews from
Agrippa's kingdom the king sold as slaves. The remainder,
30,400 altogether, were auctioned by the Romans. It was the
26th September of the year 67.

The stench of the corpses rotting beneath the autumn sun, with
fresh ones continually being washed up on the beach, made the
locality intolerable. Vespasian moved north again, and enjoyed
a short respite at the hot baths of Amathus, before tackling the
last stage of this northern campaign. The fall of Taricheae had
brought about the submission of the whole of Galilee, except for
Gischala and Mount Tabor. In the Jaulan, Gamala, about twelve
miles to the east of the lake, still defied Agrippa. This town, of
which the silhouette, as its name implies, resembled that of a
kneeling camel, was even stronger by nature than Jotapata, and
possessed, besides, a spring and a citadel newly built by Josephus.
Once again, the ramps were constructed and the battering-ram
brought up. A breach was effected, and the Romans entered the

city, only to be ignominiously thrown out by the defenders, leaving a number of dead behind. Agrippa was wounded. Vespasian himself was hard pressed, and had a narrow escape. Titus had been away, on a mission to Mucianus, the governor of Syria. On his return, indignant at this humiliating reverse, he decided to redeem it in person. On the 10th November, at the head of 200 picked horsemen, he succeeded in entering the citadel, and annihilating its remaining defenders, of whom 4,000 died by the sword and 5,000 by throwing themselves into the abyss below the town.

Meanwhile, the tribune Placidus had occupied Mount Tabor. Once again the rebels had attempted treachery: coming down from the top of the mountain with the avowed object of making their submission, they attacked the Romans by surprise. Placidus, who had been contemplating a little treachery himself, pretended to flee, lured the Jews across the plain, then turned and scattered them. Some escaped, and made for Jerusalem. The rest agreed to surrender the mountain fortress, of which the cisterns were exhausted. Only Gischala now remained to the rebels in all Galilee. Titus, dismissing the three legions to their quarters in Caesarea and Scythopolis, rode up to the stronghold with 1,000 horsemen. He was tired of bloodshed, and the majority of the population, peaceful *fellahin*, wanted only to live in peace. But John had no intention of falling into the hands of the Romans if he could help it. He pretended to be ready to come to terms, but said that as it was the sabbath he must postpone the formalities until the morrow. Titus, as a pledge of his own good faith, withdrew to Kadesh Naphthali, over the Tyrian border. When night fell, John, dragging with him a multitude of helpless men, women and children whom he later callously discarded, made off in the direction of Jerusalem. Next morning, when Titus discovered how he had been tricked, he sent a troop of horse in pursuit. Six thousand of John's wretched dupes were slaughtered, and the women and children brought back. Gischala opened its gates to the victor. The whole of Galilee was now at peace—lulled in the hush of the *Pax Romana*.

As soon as he arrived in Jerusalem, John started to build himself up as a "patriot"—a figure familiar enough to students of the Levant. On the older and more level-headed section of the populace he made no impression: they knew him for what he was, an unscrupulous, calculating egotist, who had already been beaten by the Romans. But the young, for whom in that region a whiff of "patriotism" can induce dreams as fantastic and alluring as any more material narcotic, flocked to his support. The Holy City was soon rent with discord, its population sundered into implacable factions, its streets stained with familiar blood. By a cruel irony, it was its sacred character that increased the sacrilege; for by tradition its gates must stand open to any child of Israel who chose to resort to it. Brigands and bandits from all over the country converged on the sanctuary. There was now no garrison in Jerusalem, no watchmen on the walls of the palace, no guards in the Antonia. These unwelcome pilgrims were therefore able to inaugurate their own reign of terror. They seized several notables, including a certain Antipas, a member of the Herodian family, and the City Treasurer. After being kept for a time in prison, they were murdered, their butchers giving out that these men had intended to hand the city over to the Romans. Next, they decided that they must "purge" the hierarchy, who were known to be on the side of law and peace. The Jewish priesthood was hereditary in the "sons of Aaron". If a man was so descended, he was a priest, and had only to undergo the rite of consecration to belong to the Temple clergy. If he were not so descended, nothing could ever make a priest of him. "The Priesthood," in Schürer's words, "was therefore a fraternity fenced round with irremovable barriers, for they had been fixed for ever by natural descent." There were, of course, many persons qualified by birth to be priests, who never sought consecration. Josephus himself was one. The rebels now sent for the most obscure of the pontifical clans, that of Eniahin, and, by an impious travesty of ancient custom, cast lots as to who should be High Priest. The lot fell on a village stone-mason, Phannias Ben Samuel. He was carried off to the city, arrayed in the sacred vestments, and schooled in the sacerdotal functions, of which of course he was wholly ignorant. By such a blasphemous imposture was appointed the man who, as it turned out, was to be the very last of the High Priests. It seemed almost as if the Holy One, Blessed be He!, were thus warning his servants of the doom which was to come upon them and upon the Sanctuary which they had defiled.

The gangsters, who now had things all their own way, called themselves Zealots (it is here that Josephus first uses the word), "for that was the name they went by, as if they were zealous in good undertakings, and were not rather zealous in the worst actions, and extravagant in them beyond the example of others." They installed themselves in the Temple, with Eleazar Ben

Simon and Zachariah son of Amphicalles, both of priestly families, as their leaders.

The population of Jerusalem, shocked out of their inertia by these murders and profanations, now rallied to Ananus. The Zealots were attacked, and driven from the outer court of the Temple into the shrine itself, where a posse of 6,000 armed men of Ananus' party held them confined.

John of Gischala, betraying the confidence of Ananus, disclosed the plans of the Sanhedrin to the Zealots, and suggested to them that the only way in which to defeat them was to call in the Idumaeans. The rumour was accordingly spread that Ananus was preparing to surrender Jerusalem to the Romans, whereupon 20,000 Idumaeans, their natural ferocity seconded by their convert ardour, surged up the Hebron road to Jerusalem, "making haste to a battle as if it were a feast". Ananus had ordered the gates to be shut, whereupon one of the Idumaean leaders taunted him with excluding genuine Jews, at the very time when he was preparing to welcome the Romans.

One night there was a violent storm. The imprisoned Zealots, profiting by the noise of the tempest and the thunder which accompanied it, fetched saws from the Temple workshops, and sawed through the bars of the gates. They then made their way to the city gate opposite to the Idumaean camp, opened that in the same way, and admitted their allies. The Zealots and Idumaeans now combined to terrorize the city. They spared nobody. The men on guard in the Temple were slaughtered; the blood from 8,500 bodies stained the pavement of its courts. Ananus and Jesus son of Gamala were murdered, and left unburied. The young nobles were hunted from house to house and killed. At last the bloodlust of the Idumaeans was slaked. They saw that no attack by the Romans was imminent, and so withdrew to their own country. Their last act was to release from prison 2,000 men, who at once went off to join Simon Bar Giora.

The Zealots could now carry out their programme, which was to level out society. They posed as "democrats" and "lovers of liberty", but anyone of any distinction, whether of birth, or service, rank or office was doomed. Vespasian, who meanwhile had reduced Jamnia and Azotus, was reluctant to attack Jerusalem, both in order to spare his men, and also because he reckoned the Zealots were doing his work for him. John of Gischala, active and ambitious, tried to unite the warring factions. He failed, before the jealousy of his fellows. Yet a third party now made head, namely, the *sicarii*, who, under Simon Bar Giora, had made Masada their headquarters.

They celebrated the Passover of the year 68 by raiding Engeddi, the little oasis on the shore of the Dead Sea some ten miles to the north. The men ran away, but the *sicarii* had the satisfaction of massacring the women and children and burning the village. Vespasian was now engaged in securing Peraea, on his eastern flank. At the invitation of the inhabitants, he made his headquarters at a place called Gadora (not to be confused with Gadara) now Tel Jadour, above a spring of the same name, near the modern town of Es-Salt. A number of rebels had left the town on the approach of the Romans. Vespasian left Placidus to deal with them, with 500 horse and 3,000 foot. He followed the fugitives down the Wadi Shaib and overtook them just where the valley debouches on to the plain, above the Jordan. Very few escaped. News of the disaster started a train of refugees, all moving down to the Jordan, with their families and flocks, hoping to ford the river and take refuge in Jericho. At that time of year the Jordan is not fordable (Joshua iii, 15). Those who escaped the Romans were drowned in the river. A few reached the Dead Sea, where Placidus sent men after them in boats to kill them. Peraea, as far as Machaerus, was now, like Galilee, at peace. Machaerus remained in rebel hands.

Vespasian at last saw the way clear for an attack on Jerusalem. He established an advance headquarters at Antipatris, the staging post between Caesarea and Jerusalem, and a camp for the Vth at Emmaus. The Idumaeans were soon chastened. Begabris (Beit Jebrin) and Caphartoba (et-Taiebeh) were taken, and 10,000 men were slain. Vespasian returned to Emmaus, went up to Shechem, where a "new city", *Neapolis*, or Nablus, was soon to be founded, down the Wadi Fara', under the Alexandrium, and so to Jericho, where those inhabitants who had run away were killed. Vespasian visited the Dead Sea, and satisfied himself that it was really as buoyant as men said by having some prisoners who could not swim thrown into it with their hands tied behind their backs. They all floated. Some of his soldiers occupied the Essene "monastery" of Qumrān, nearby, leaving there for twentieth-century archaeologists coins newly-minted in Caesarea, their base. Vespasian was now rejoined by the victorious troops from Peraea. He already had with him Trajan, commanding the Xth. The fortifications above Jericho, which the rebels had destroyed, were repaired, so as to safeguard the eastern approaches to

Jerusalem, just as Emmaus, and Hadida, near Lydda, guarded the access from the west.

The people of Jerash, who, alone of the cities of the Decapolis, had spared their Jewish citizens during the massacres two years earlier, were now to be punished for their clemency. Vespasian had learned that Simon Bar Giora came from Jerash, and that his first exploit had been to cut up Cestius Gallus' rearguard near Beth-Horon, and capture some of his baggage-animals. One day, Simon would grace Vespasian's triumph, before being strangled amid the plaudits of the Roman people. Meanwhile, Jerash felt the heavy hand of Rome. A thousand of its youth were killed and the beautiful city was looted.

Vespasian was anxious to finish the war as soon as he could, for already rumours of revolt in the west had reached him. He had shown the utmost prudence, he had taken no risks. Step by step, he had crushed rebellion in Galilee, in Peraea, in Judaea itself. Only Jerusalem now remained. He was about to attack it, when news was brought to him that on the 9th of June the emperor Nero, to escape his would-be assassins, had committed suicide, and that the Senate had proclaimed Galba emperor.

Vespasian suspended his campaign: he could not proceed without orders from the new Caesar.

Chapter XVIII

SECOND INTERLUDE—
THE FOUR EMPERORS

NERO'S death ended not merely a reign but an epoch. Ever since the battle of Actium, all but a century ago, though there had been warfare on and beyond the frontiers, the Empire had enjoyed internal peace, the peace first forged for it by Augustus, and perpetuated by emperors of the Julio-Claudian line. In theory, the principate lapsed with the death of each *princeps*, but in practice it had become hereditary; and the ruling house had acquired a prestige so great that it could even support—for a time—the shameful burden of a Caligula or a Nero. The dynastic fabric, to be sure, had been shaky. In no case had a son succeeded a father, and, of the five emperors of the line, only the first had died a natural death; but somehow, by adoption, or relationship, the line had been continued. Augustus was succeeded by a stepson, Tiberius by a great-nephew, Caligula by an uncle, Claudius by a great-nephew and step-son.

Besides this tacit acceptance of the hereditary principle, another, more sinister, clause had found its unwritten way into the Roman constitution: the empire depended on the army. Augustus had secured his primacy by force of arms. Tiberius was a proven and successful general by the time he became emperor. Even Claudius had taken part in the invasion of Britain. Nero's victories had been won by generals like Corbulo, whose death, at the command of his master, combined with Nero's degrading exhibitions as actor and charioteer, had strained the loyalty of the legions to breaking-point. It was the Senate which, by declaring Nero a public enemy, had driven him to end his life; nevertheless, the future of the empire lay not with the Senate, but with the army. And the army was dispersed all over the empire.

As Tacitus puts it (*History*, I, 4), with Nero's death "the secret of empire was now disclosed—that an emperor could be made elsewhere than at Rome".

This is the crucial factor in the "year of the Four Emperors", and in the final elevation of Vespasian. An astrologer had foretold that Nero was to be lord of Jerusalem. The astrologer was wrong:

it was the man whom he had despised, the obscure man, the aging soldier—he it was who would become lord of Jerusalem, and of Rome, too. The instruments of his success were the soldiers of Rome, aided by a strange and unearthly ally (see page 161).

That would be the outcome of the contest; but first the eliminating rounds, if such a term may be permitted of so cruel a competition, must be played off. The Senate, when they proclaimed Nero an outlaw, had accepted as his successor a provincial governor called Galba, who, supported by another governor and part of the army, had already shaken off his allegiance. In truth, Galba had little to commend him except his noble birth, and it must be remembered that the true Roman aristocracy had almost ceased to exist. The senatorial families were constantly dying out, to be replaced by freedmen; "In the reign of Nerva," says Carcopino (p. 68), "there survived in Rome only one half of the senatorial families which had been counted in A.D. 65, thirty-five years before; and thirty years later only one remained of the forty-five patrician families restored one hundred and sixty-five years before by Julius Caesar." Galba could trace his descent from several of the leading nobles of the republic. He had been a consul under Tiberius, and as long ago as 41, when Caligula was assassinated, had been considered as a possible candidate for the purple. He had governed Upper Germany, and since 60 he had been in Nearer Spain, where his administration had recently shown signs of weakness. And no wonder: Galba was now seventy-three.

He could not last long. He hastened his own end by surrounding himself with men of no reputation, delaying his arrival in Rome until the autumn, allowing himself to be drawn into a fracas as he was entering the city, and then starting an "economy campaign", which (as sometimes happens) produced more discontent than revenue. Finally, he adopted as his successor a person of no merit, called Piso, who was destined to be heir apparent for five days only. One of his staff, called Otho, a former husband of Poppaea, who had been drawn to Galba by his natural hatred for Nero, had expected to be named Galba's successor, and to be given the hand of Galba's daughter. He now determined to supplant him. On the 15th January of the year 69, Otho, having attended Galba for the morning sacrifice, and being greeted as usual with a kiss, hurried away to the camp of the Praetorian Guard, where he had already bribed his way into favour. He was now saluted as emperor. Before the day was ended, Galba had been butchered in the very Forum itself, and Piso in the Temple of Vesta, where he had sought sanctuary.

It was of Galba that Tacitus uttered his famous epigram (*Hist.*, I, 49): "*omnium consensu capax imperii nisi imperasset*"— "everyone agreed that he was the man to be emperor, if only he had not been!"

Otho, at the age of thirty-seven, was now emperor. But already another rival had appeared. This was Aulus Vitellius, son of the Vitellius who had been governor of Syria under Tiberius.

Even before Galba's death, Vitellius had been hailed as emperor by the troops of both Upper and Lower Germany, and they had already started to move on Italy. For several weeks, Otho did nothing. Then he sent an army northwards, later following himself. The two rivals met at Bedriacum, near Cremona. Vitellius won, and Otho committed suicide. At the end of May Vitellius reached Cremona, and proceeded south with his *farouche* and brutalized legions. These rough men from the north treated Italy as though it were hostile territory. They looted, raped and killed, while their boorish general guzzled. Once again, men looked for another and better leader. It was to Vespasian that they looked.

Vespasian had delayed six months before resolving formally to recognize Galba. It was only in December of 68, and despite the hazards of winter navigation, that he decided to send Titus to salute him. Agrippa went as well. While they were sailing up the coast of Greece, they heard the news of Galba's death. Titus, realizing that the succession of Otho quite altered the military outlook, at once returned to his father. Agrippa, scenting political intrigue of the first order, went on to Rome.

Back in Caesarea, Vespasian learned of Otho's defeat, and of Vitellius' glutton's progress towards Rome, which he took six months to reach. News had been brought to him from Syria and Judaea that the East had taken the oath of fidelity to him, whereupon both general and army, feeling themselves secure, abandoned themselves "to every excess of foreign morals".

Vespasian was sixty. He had two sons, the younger a mere boy. Could he put all to the touch, in a civil war? He well knew how brave those German legions were, what victories they had won. On the other hand, Rome was disgraced and polluted by Vitellius, the memory of Augustus was outraged. The representatives sent to Syria by Vitellius were arrogant and uncouth. Discontent increased and it was well known that the army of the Danube

VESPASIAN

[Corpus Christi College, Cambridge.

37. Vespasian as emperor, successful, benign and confident. He bears a resemblance to another soldier who rose to supreme civil authority, Dwight D. Eisenhower.

TITUS

38. This coin shews Titus as emperor. The "World's Darling" has grown rather fat, but there is no mistaking the air of alert authority.

[Corpus Christi College, Cambridge.

JUDAEA CAPTA

39. Instead of the usual soldier standing over a weeping woman beneath a palm-tree, this coin shews a trophy of arms, the symbol of victory, dominating a seated woman, the emblem of defeat: it has a curiously modern look. The legend IUDAEA makes quite clear what event the coin commemorates.

[Corpus Christi College, Cambridge.

[*Alinari.*

40. Titus inherited his father's robust, bluff habit. This bust, in the
Naples Museum, shews an intelligent athlete, with a gentle, sensitive mouth.

would welcome a change of masters. Tiberius Alexander in Egypt
was of the same mind. Thus, should Vespasian enter the field, it
seemed probable that he would have at his back fourteen legions,
half of the whole Roman army, besides his auxiliary forces.

His mind was finally made up by Mucianus, the governor of
Syria. At first, he had not been on good terms with Vespasian, but
he had been captivated by Titus—he had no children of his own—
and that had led to a *rapprochement*. Mucianus overcame Vespasian's last scruples by pointing out that Vitellius would certainly
treat him as Nero had treated Corbulo, if he were given the
chance. But if Vespasian bid for supreme power, would the army,
would public opinion, sustain him? Signs were not lacking that
they would, and, by an extraordinary irony, one of the strangest
of which history has record, it was Jewish prophecy, Jewish
Messianic prophecy, which was to convince men's minds that the
sovereignty over the Roman world should be committed to the
man who was destined to conquer the Jews, and in so doing, compel them to put their trust yet again in God only.

Both Tacitus (*Hist.*, V, 13) and Suetonius (*Vespasian*, 4) tell
us that, in the latter's words, "there had been spread throughout
all the East an opinion of old, and the same settled in men's
heads and constantly believed, that by the appointment of the
destinies about such a time there should come out of Judaea those
who were to be lords of the whole world". Both authors add that
this prophecy clearly foretold the elevation of Vespasian and
Titus. Josephus, remarkably enough (*War*, VI, v, 4), is equally
emphatic. After quoting the prediction, he says: "The Jews took
this prediction to belong to themselves in particular; and many of
the wise men were thereby deceived in their determination. Now
this oracle certainly denoted the government of Vespasian who
was appointed emperor, while he was in Judaea."

This prophecy was seconded by 'the god Carmel', that is, the
shrine of the god Baal, on Mount Carmel, that very god whose
prophets Elijah had discomfited in the days of Ahab and Jezebel
(1 Kings, xviii), that very mountain which was later to become
one of the most famous shrines of Our Lady; for it is a rule in the
Levant that, when once a place has been hallowed, it will remain
holy, whatever priests may serve its sanctuary. Mount Carmel belonged not to Judaea, but to the staunchly pagan Ptolemais across
the bay. Its god, like all the mountain gods of Phoenicia, was a god
of tempest and thunder, a form of *Baalshamin*, the great *baal* of the
heavens. Baal of Carmel, as a recently discovered inscription

M

attests, was still flourishing in the third century A.D., having by that time become assimilated to Jupiter of Baalbek-Heliopolis, the city of the Sun. (To this day, a certain village in the Lebanon is called Baalshamiya.) Thanks to the colonists of Beirut, this god became extremely fashionable. Even the legionaries of the East had learned to inaugurate their day's work by "saluting the rising sun" (Tacitus, *Hist.*, II, 24). An oracle from this god, therefore, would carry enormous weight with civilians and soldiers alike. When Vespasian went to consult it, he found still in existence the primitive "high place" of olden times, with no statue, no shrine. He duly sacrificed, and stood wrapped in his own meditations. The priest, after a diligent examination of the entrails, told Vespasian that in any enterprise he might undertake, he was assured of triumphant success. "This mysterious prediction," Tacitus continues, "was forthwith spread abroad, and now received an interpretation. Nor was there any more frequent topic of discourse among the populace: still more frequent were the conversations upon it in the presence of Vespasian himself, in proportion as more things are said to those who entertain hopes."

Vespasian could now go forward in confidence. In response to a personal appeal, Tiberius Alexander, the governor of Egypt, became the first to declare openly for him, on the first of July, 69, which was henceforth regarded as the first day of his reign. Two days later, the army of Judaea saluted him as Caesar. By the 15th the Syrian legions had followed suit, Mucianus having spread a rumour that Vitellius intended to transfer them to Germany. Antioch was won over, and very soon the whole of the Orient. Agrippa, having been informed of what was afoot by his own intelligence agents, left Rome for Beirut, before Vitellius had wind of the East's defection. For Agrippa, it was a wonderful turn of fortune. Once again, with the family flair, he had backed a winner. His sister Berenice, who, at the age of forty, was still, so Tacitus tells us, a very beautiful woman, lavished her wiles, and her wealth, on Vespasian, "notwithstanding his great age". Suheim of Edessa and Antiochus were there, too. Asia Minor and Achaia soon declared for Vespasian, who was now at Beirut.

The Beirut conference decided (1) that Mucianus should lead the army into Italy against Vitellius; (2) that Titus should continue the war in Judaea, and (3) that Vespasian should establish himself in Egypt, from which he could if necessary starve Rome into submission. The king of Parthia promised not merely neutrality, but a force of 40,000 mounted archers. Vespasian now

recalled that, even while Nero was still alive, Josephus had foretold his sovereignty. At the instance of Titus, he ordered that the
prisoner should be set at liberty, and his chains cut in pieces, as a
demonstration of his innocence. Josephus "received this testimony
of his integrity for a reward, and was moreover esteemed a person
of credit as to futurities also".

Without awaiting the arrival of Mucianus, the seven legions of the
Danube crushed Vitellius' army near Cremona at the end of October. They swept on to Rome, which once again saw the horrors of
civil war. The Capitol was burnt, Vespasian's elder brother was
killed. Domitian only escaped by donning the robe of a priest of
Isis. Vitellius was slaughtered and dismembered. He was fifty-
seven, had reigned less than a year, and died eight months after
Otho.

Thus, by the end of the year 69, Vespasian was the undisputed
master of Rome and the empire. From east and west alike flocked
delegations of congratulation. It was not until the beginning of
the summer of 70 that he set out for Rome: he knew he was
secure, now. He sailed in a passenger vessel to Rhodes, where he
transferred to a warship. He reached Rome in October.

Such, in brief, is the story of the Four Emperors, and of
Vespasian's triumph. We must now return to Judaea, and to the
interrupted story of the war.

Chapter XIX

JUDAEA CAPTA—ACT III

THE rebels had, of course, exploited the enforced inactivity of the Romans. While the imperial kaleidoscope was forming and dissolving the transient images of Galba, Otho and Vitellius, Simon Bar Giora made himself master of Idumaea. Masada, ideal as a refuge, was too remote to serve as a base for offensive operations. He moved into the bleak hill country between Jerusalem and Hebron, and sent out heralds to announce that the slaves were to be free, and the free rich. He soon attracted to himself a mob of bondmen and adventurers, to which was added the usual fringe of respectable trimmers. Simon, as is customary with leaders of democratic movements in the Levant, behaved like a dictator. He publicly proclaimed his intention of assaulting Jerusalem, in preparation for which he enlarged the caves in the vicinity of the famous Adullam, to serve as shelters and strongholds for his treasure. He had already overrun 'Aqraba, to the north of the Holy City, and now, pursuing a "pincer" policy, advanced to Tekoa, the village famous as the dwelling of the prophet Amos, which lies a little to the south of Herod's great fortress-tomb, the Herodium, and not far from Bethlehem itself. The Herodium was still in the hands of the Zealots; so Simon, thinking that his name and authority would be enough to cow them, sent one of his staff, called Eleazar, to demand its submission. The garrison were so disgusted at this display of arrogance, that they drew their swords upon Eleazar, who leaped to his death from the ramparts.

This setback was offset by the timely treachery of an Idumaean called Jacob. He undertook to persuade the Idumaean forces opposed to Simon, who were encamped at Halhul, the village on the ridge five miles north of Hebron, to disperse and to welcome Simon as their leader. In this he succeeded, so that Simon was able to enter Hebron—the sepulchre of Abraham, holy and rich. He was now master of Idumaea, and despatched his men to devour the countryside like locusts, for he had 40,000 mouths to feed.

This kingly conduct naturally annoyed the Zealots; but such

was Simon's authority that they dare not oppose him openly. One day, however, they laid an ambush in one of the valleys, and managed to carry off his wife and a number of her slaves. Simon, "like a wounded beast" swooped on Jerusalem, and lay in wait for all those who might venture beyond its walls. He either killed them, or sent them back with their hands lopped off. The Zealots returned his wife.

Within the city, what Abel calls "two regional chauvinisms" were at war: the Galileans of John of Gischala and the Idumaeans, many of them refugees from the bloody rapacity of Simon. The Galileans, posing as the patriots *par excellence*, united organized robbery with studied depravity. Scented, painted boys dressed as women, allured men to accost them, repaying the misplaced attention with a swift stroke of a concealed dagger. The Idumaeans prided themselves on being straight toughs. Growing tired of John's tyranny, they attacked his followers, killed many, and compelled the rest to take refuge in the palace of the Adiabenian princes, which Simon had made his headquarters. From this they were soon dislodged, and driven back into the Temple. The rumour now spread that the imprisoned Zealots intended to break out and set the city on fire. What could be done to prevent them? The priests, the men of property and the Idumaeans all agreed: the only thing to do was to call in Simon, already lord of Idumaea. Thus, at last, Simon entered Jerusalem, hailed as a saviour and protector. But he was master of the upper city only; before the Zealots embattled in the Temple, he was forced to fall back. They held not only the crenellated ramparts of the sacred precinct, but also four towers, which they had erected as artillery-posts, on the north and west sides of the enclosure.

It was now April, 69. Vespasian, who had declared his loyalty to Otho, felt that the situation was sufficiently favourable for him to attempt to finish off this tiresome war.

Being the prudent general he was, he refused to expose his troops to the dangers of the main Beth-Horon route. Instead, he went up, as he had done the year before, to Samaria, and thence came down on Jerusalem from the north, occupying the districts of 'Aqraba and Gophna (Jifnah) en route, and leaving garrisons in Bethel (Beitin) and Ephraim (et-Taiyibeh). At the head of his cavalry, Vespasian reached the neighbourhood of Jerusalem, killing many on the way, and taking a number of prisoners. Meanwhile, Cerealis, commander of the Vth, was cleaning up Idumaea. He swept down past Adullam, occupied Hebron, burned it and put its youth to the sword. Except for Masada, Machaerus and the Herodium, which were still in the hands of the *sicarii*, the whole country was under control of the Romans. The capture of Jerusalem was now their objective.

At that very juncture arrived the news of the defeat and suicide of Otho, and of Vitellius' first successes. Almost a year was to pass before Vespasian was recognized as emperor, his two sons, Titus and Domitian, as his heirs. Only then could the war be resumed. Titus had gone with his father to Alexandria. He now returned to Palestine, reaching Gaza in a five days' march from Pelusium, at the eastern mouth of the Nile. He moved on, by Ascalon, Jamnia and Joppa, to Caesarea, where, in the spring of 70, he concentrated his forces.

Meanwhile, affairs in Jerusalem went from bad to worse. The inhabitants resented having to obey either a Galilean, or else a Gerasene: was there no native-born son of Jerusalem to lead them? they asked. Eleazar, son of Simon, had forfeited much of the public's sympathy for having, with his colleague Zachariah, called in the Idumaeans against Ananus. Nevertheless, it was Eleazar who, at the very outset of the war, had humbled Cestius Gallus. He now aspired to become the sole master of Jerusalem. Supported by two notables, priests, no doubt, like himself, and by a band of enthusiastic followers, Eleazar succeeded in occupying the inner courts of the Temple, and making the shrine itself into their citadel. John was thus confined to the outer court and cloisters of the Temple, where he found himself between two fires, Eleazar and his Zealots in the sanctuary, and Simon Bar Giora in the city. Nothing daunted, John built towers with the great beams of cedar which Agrippa had brought from Lebanon for the repair of the Temple, and so was able to shoot not only at the forces of Simon, but also at those of Eleazar. The sanctuary was soon defiled with human blood; for the stream of pilgrims still came to the Temple, the priests still maintained the liturgy, the great altar still smoked, while priests and worshippers alike fell victims to the Zealots. Eleazar and his men supported themselves on the provisions laid up within the sanctuary, Simon controlled the magazines and markets of the city. John could feed his faction only at the point of the sword. He raided the granaries, which of course involved him in fighting with Simon. It was in these skirmishes that a large part of the food supplies of the city was burned, thus causing the awful privations of the ensuing siege. The region of the town immediately beneath the western wall of the Temple, the no-man's-land between John and Simon, was soon in ruins.

Titus' army consisted, first, of the three legions which Vespasian had commanded during the Galilee campaign, the Vth, at Emmaus, the Xth, at Jericho, and Titus' own regiment, the XVth. To these was added the XIIth, eager to avenge their disgrace under Cestius Gallus. From Alexandria, Titus had brought detachments of 1,000 men each from the IIIrd and the XXIInd, and 3,000 had been seconded from the garrisons on the Euphrates. In this way, the legions from which Vespasian had drawn the detachments that Mucianus had led against the Vitellians were brought up to strength. There were twenty allied cohorts, eight cavalry corps, and the auxiliaries furnished by Agrippa, Suheim, Antiochus and Malik of Petra. Thus, the total strength of the army now amounted to 65,000 men. As chief of staff, Titus had Tiberius Alexander, the former procurator, whose knowledge of the country and people, and command of their language, would be invaluable. He was, moreover, not without military experience, having been chief of staff to Corbulo during his campaign against the Parthians.

Titus, following his father's example, approached Jerusalem from the north, camping for one night at Gophna. The army then moved forward, and took up its position in the little depression four miles north of Jerusalem, between Gibeah of Saul, or Tel el-Ful and Beit Hanina. It was thus invisible to watchers on the walls of Jerusalem, towards which Titus, with a bodyguard of 600 horsemen, now made his way. Expecting no opposition, he had laid aside his helmet and his breastplate, but fortunately for him had retained his sword. When the party came almost up to the North Gate, of which the foundations still exist beneath the modern Damascus Gate, Titus turned to the right, his intention being to ride up the slope to inspect the great tower of Psephinus, which stood at the north-west corner of the city, on the site of what is now the Frères' College. Simon's men, who from the Towers of the Women which flanked the Gate had watched every move, now rushed out, and took the party in the rear. The horsemen were at a hopeless disadvantage in the maze of gardens and dry stone walls of what is now Musrara, below the great hospice of Notre Dame de France. Titus and a few others were soon separated from the main body. Wheeling his horse about, he laid about him right and left, and through his own prowess succeeded in getting clear of the mêlée. He returned to the camp unscathed. Two of his companions were less fortunate, being cut down by Simon's men, who captured one of the horses. The rebels were naturally elated at the outcome of this first brush with the Romans.

The next morning Titus brought forward two of his legions, the XIIth and XVth, to establish their camp on the southern slopes of Mount Scopus, or *Look-out*, for from it the towers and palaces of the city were visible, as well as the great mass of the Temple. The Vth, which had come up from Emmaus, camped a little further to the north, on the site of what is now the village of Sh'afat. The Xth, advancing from Jericho, took up their position on the Mount of Olives. From this eminence, across the cleft of the Kedron valley, the whole city is spread out, like a model of itself. In particular the whole of the Temple *parvis*, with the glittering sanctuary in the middle, and the cloisters beyond, could be kept under perpetual surveillance. It was of this view that the young Disraeli, beholding it for the first time, said "the mind, full of the sublime, required not the beautiful"; but in truth in the spring of the year 70 it must have provided both, so soon to be left desolate of either.

The camp was not to be established without difficulty. The sight of the Romans on the mountain, so close to the city, and in so strong a position, had the effect of uniting the three factions within its walls. They made a sortie, crossed the torrent-bed, and swarmed up through the garden of Gethsemane towards the summit. The Xth, who were quite unused to this kind of warfare, and who had not their arms to hand, gave ground. Titus himself, at great personal risk, rallied the bewildered legion, and succeeded in pushing the Jews down the slope. They soon recovered, and once again forced the Romans up the hill. The workmen engaged on the construction of the camp panicked and ran away. In the end, Titus was able to re-group his men, and under their protection the camp was finished.

Passover was approaching. Eleazar, who still controlled the Temple shrine, wanted to have the gates opened, so that the faithful might perform their devotions. John of Gischala, who was in possession of the gates, turned the request to his own advantage. He sent in a number of his own men, with their arms concealed, who succeeded in forcing Eleazar and his Zealots to hide in the *souterrains* of the sanctuary, such as that now known as Solomon's Stables. A number of innocent pilgrims were killed, but the two factions were thus united against their rival, Simon.

Titus now set about levelling the ground in the immediate

vicinity of the north and west ramparts, on which sides alone the
city was approachable. He was taking no more risks with stone
walls and garden plots. They must be swept away wholesale—
"bulldozed", as we should say now, but of course the task had to
be laboriously performed by hand. From the walls, the Jews
watched the work, and decided to interrupt it. This they did by a
ruse. Josephus, who was now on Titus' staff, had been sent the
previous evening to offer terms to the besieged, who had refused
them. They now sent a party out through the North Gate, who
were to pretend that they had been expelled for intransigence.
Their fellows pelted them with stones, and said that all they
wanted was peace, and offered to open the Gate to those troops
who were working near it. The Romans fell into the trap. They
approached the Gate, only to find it shut and themselves caught
between the two flanking towers, while the party of Jews who had
come out set upon their rear. Many were killed, more wounded,
and the survivors, pursued as far as the tomb of Queen Helena,
straggled back to their camp. Titus was furious at this new humiliation, threatened the offenders with death, but contented himself
with a warning against impatience.

The levelling operations were completed in four days, whereupon Titus brought up his strongest troops, and disposed them
opposite the north and west walls in seven lines, three infantry,
three cavalry and one of archers. This array, it was thought,
would prevent sorties by the Jews. Titus himself camped on what
is now the Russian Compound, two furlongs from the wall, and
opposite to Psephinus. The rest of the army dug themselves in
opposite Hippicus, the great tower of the upper palace. They, too,
were two furlongs from the wall (i.e. out of range), which would
place them in the Nikephoria quarter, near the French Consulate-
General. The Xth stayed in its camp on the Mount of Olives,
probably on the little knoll to-day known as "Galilee", the summer residence of the Greek Orthodox Patriarch.

It was now (by Abel's reckoning) the 10th May. Everything
was ready for the siege.

Chapter XX

JUDAEA CAPTA—FINALE

THE siege and destruction of Jerusalem, and of the Temple, has for centuries been a classic of horror. There are two reasons for this. The first is that the consequences of the calamity were so grave, so radical, involving the utter destruction of what Pliny had called the most splendid city of the whole East, and the end of a religious régime which had lasted for 1,000 years; the second is Josephus himself. His description is so vivid, so detailed, so three-dimensional that to this day it holds and appals his readers. But in reading it we must always bear in mind the purpose with which he wrote it: it was meant to terrify and to deter. Naturally, therefore, the author omits no incident that could serve his end. The more brutal it was, the better.

The walls of Jerusalem have already been described. The plan of Jerusalem shows clearly where they were situated. On the east and south, the valleys of the Kedron and Hinnom which coalesce below Siloam, made any attack out of the question. The towers and the battering-rams could never be erected on those precipitous scarps, and the altitude gave the defenders an invincible superiority. That is why on those sides the city had but one wall. Only on the north and the west is the approach to the city reasonably level. That is why the city had expanded on those sides (as it has gone on doing in our own time), and why, in addition to the old north wall which ran from the upper palace to the Temple, two further walls had been added, the second by Antipater, the father of Herod the Great, the third by Agrippa I. Titus' reconnaissance had shown him that on the north side this Third Wall was strong enough to resist his engines; he therefore decided to make his assault on the west flank, against the portion of the wall which ran from Psephinus to Hippicus, that is, from the Collège des Frères to the Jaffa Gate. That is why he had placed the camps of his troops and himself where he had. This part of the wall had not been completed when Agrippa died, and even now was lower than the rest. The Jews were continually sniping the Romans, and it was clear that they had no intention of yielding. Titus therefore ordered the construction of three ramps, on

which the towers would be rolled forward until they were within
range. The countryside was ransacked for trees, and the artillery
kept up a barrage of missiles to cover the workers. Even so, they
dare not approach the wall itself, but had to calculate their range
by casting a weighted line up to the rampart. The artillery of the
Xth was superior to the rest. They had machines capable of
throwing a stone of one hundredweight a distance of over two
furlongs. Simon's men tried to reply with the engines they had
captured from Cestius Gallus and in the assault of the Antonia
four years before; but they lacked the skill to use them. The most
they could do was to post sentinels to watch the Roman artillery,
and, when they saw that a stone had been released, sound the
alarm, so that, as the shining white missile sang through the air,
they could avoid it. "Here comes the stone," they cried, and
everyone took cover. The Romans soon learned of this, and so, to
make it harder for the Jews to follow the trajectory, they painted
the stones black—one of the earliest known examples of the use of
what would now be called *camouflage*.

Gradually, the towers, the *helepoles*, or city-takers, as they were
called, had advanced near enough to the wall to allow the three
rams to get to work.

The sinister din of these relentless weapons struck terror into the
defenders, and once again Simon and John agreed to act in con-
cert. Simon allowed the defenders of the Temple to come up to
the western wall, from which their combined forces attempted
to burn the Roman towers by throwing torches into them. This
proving of no avail against their protective armour, the Jews
made a sortie through a hidden postern near Hippicus, carrying
firebrands in their hands. Such was their fury that they would
have succeeded in setting fire to the Roman works, but for the
personal bravery of Titus, and his *corps d'élite* from Alexandria.

The rampart was now at the mercy of the three *helepoles*.
These towers were seventy-five feet high, and to manœuvre them,
on the improvised ramps, and under a rain of missiles from the
wall, must have required great skill and courage. It is hardly
surprising to read that on the night after the skirmish one of them
collapsed, causing panic in the Roman camp. Once again, it was
Titus who restored order. The two remaining towers pressed the
attack, and so did the rams, especially one which the Jews called
Nikon, or "Conqueror", because it carried everything before it.
At last a breach appeared, and in the small hours of the morning,
while the guards, tired and disorganized, had withdrawn from

the wall itself, the Romans entered. The Jews at once retired behind the Second Wall, thus leaving the whole of the new city in Roman hands. It was the 25th May, the fifteenth day of the siege.

While the Third Wall was being demolished, Titus advanced his camp to what was known as the Camp of the Assyrians, just inside Agrippa's wall, near the great tower Psephinus, which, like the wall, was now doomed to destruction. The few fragments of it which remain, incorporated in the foundations of the present Damascus Gate, testify to the solidity and beauty of its construction, not inferior to that of the Temple itself, Josephus says, of which the scanty remains exhibit the same kind of masonry and finish.

The Jews now faced the Romans on the line of the Second Wall. It is this wall which, better than the other one, justifies Tacitus' remark (*Hist.*, V, 11) that its oblique curtains and re-entrant angles left the attackers' flank always exposed, for, as the Map makes clear, its course was zigzag, from the upper palace to the Antonia. With a fortress at each end, and the tortuous wall in between, the Jews now had a good defensive line, of which Simon manned the upper, or western, section, and John the eastern, including the Antonia and the Temple cloisters. It was further reinforced by a great tower in the middle, guarding the gate which led from the city to Golgotha, which, of course, at the time of the Crucifixion was *outside* the City, the Third Wall not having been built by Agrippa I until seven years later. It is the remains of this tower and gate that are visible to-day in the Russian Hospice near the Church of the Holy Sepulchre.

This tower was now the chief target of the Roman rams. One of its defenders, named Castor, tried, by feigning readiness to capitulate, to delay its fall; but as soon as his ruse was exposed, Titus "perceived that mercy in war is a pernicious thing", and ordered the renewal of the attack. Just before the tower fell, Castor and his companions set it on fire, and leaped down through the flames into a cavern below it, through which they made their escape. This whole operation had taken five days only; but in the street-fighting that followed, the Romans, who were as usual at a disadvantage in such combats, were driven out of the city and back to their camp. Four days later, the Romans were back, this time for good. It was the 4th June. The interval between the two assaults had been occupied by a grand military review, attended by the whole army in full dress, with richly-glittering armour, and finely caparisoned horses. Legion by legion, they

came forward to receive their pay and rations. The pageant
lasted four days; it was watched by the Jews, who crowded the
battlements of the old First Wall to witness it; but despite the
eloquent appeal of Josephus it made no impression on their
resolution to go on fighting.

Titus, who had spared the Second Wall so long as he thought
that the Jews might yield, now gave orders that it should be
destroyed, all except a section on the extreme west, where it ran
north and south, which he preserved as a protection for his new
camp.

Titus now had before him the rampart of the First Wall, and
the Temple, to which the wall descended, in an almost straight
line from the upper palace, above the southern side of what is now
David Street. This bulwark, which had been first raised in the
early days of the Jewish monarchy, protected, as may be seen from
the map, a very large portion of the city, a much larger portion,
in fact, than either the Second or Third Walls. In addition, the
Temple area, protected by the Antonia, was a fortress in itself.
Clearly, therefore, Titus' task, far from being nearly completed,
was not yet half done. Meanwhile, the Jews had trained themselves in the manipulation of their artillery, of which they
possessed 300 catapults for darts, and forty for stones. Besides,
they were learning how to dig mines. In these arts they were
helped by co-religionists who had come from Adiabene and elsewhere and were skilled in every technique of warfare. Increasingly
the Romans were embarrassed and hindered by their attacks.

Thus it turned out that the Romans' first attacks upon the
Antonia and the First Wall were failures.

The Antonia was separated from the hill of Bezetha by a great
artificial ditch. Pompey had encountered it when he besieged and
took Jerusalem in 63 B.C. Since those days, it had been deepened
and widened by Herod the Great, when he constructed his great
fortress of Antonia. Portions of the counterscarp are still to be seen,
behind the Greek *Praitorion*, and the Franciscan convent of the
Flagellation in the *Via Dolorosa*. For Titus, as for Pompey, there
was only one course open: the fosse must be filled up. Otherwise
the engines could never come to close quarters with the fortress.
This involved the creation of *aggeres*, artificial causeways or
inclined ramps made of stone and wood and earth. Already
timber had become scarce. Nevertheless, three *aggeres* were soon
under construction. That of the Vth was raised in the middle of
a pool called *strouthion*, which had been created when the stone for

Herod's building had been dug out of the rock. It now formed part of the fosse, which at this point must have been some fifty feet deep, to judge from the remains of the pool which are still to be seen beneath the convent of the Dames de Zion. The XIIth built theirs alongside that of the Vth, and ten yards from it.

The double attack on the Antonia and the wall was to be synchronized. The Xth and the XVth, therefore, built their ramps right at the other end of the line, just below Hippicus, at the end of what is now Christian Street, so as to stretch the defence as widely as possible.

All the ramps were ready on the 16th June; but the labour of seventeen days was to perish in a night. On the Antonia front, John succeeded in undermining the ramps and filling the sap with combustibles, including bitumen, of which the Dead Sea provided a convenient supply. Waiting until the. ungainly towers were actually starting to ascend the ramps, John gave orders to withdraw the last supports of the gallery roof and to fire the mine. The roof crumbled, the ramps dissolved, the towers collapsed into the ditch, where their broken remains were soon consumed in the fire.

Two days later Simon scored a similar success on the northern sector. He made a sortie, set the *helepoles* on fire, as they, too, were about to be levered up the ramps, and, with great tenacity, held off the Romans who came to the rescue of their comrades, until the timber revetments of the ramps were also ablaze. Another detachment of the Jews actually attacked the Roman camp. Only the artillery now mounted on the ruins of the Third and Second Walls held them off, until Titus arrived to clear the field. Titus and his troops were disheartened, naturally enough, by this double setback. Was this city really impregnable, as men had said? It was now the height of summer, when, in Disraeli's words, Jerusalem is "a city of stone in a land of iron, with a sky of brass". The attackers were running short of water. The Jews controlled the one spring, down in Siloam, as well as the vast cisterns of the Temple. The Romans had to fetch water from distant sources, and the Jews were not slow to ambush the convoys, killing everyone they encountered. At the same time, they were able to bring in supplies by the many secret tunnels with which the city then abounded, as it still does.

Titus therefore won his staff over to the plan of making a *circumvallation,* or ridge wall in a complete circle, the whole way

round the city. It was a device that the plodding Romans often
used with success in their sieges. Starting from the Camp of the
Assyrians the wall, two or three metres in height, to judge by the
similar one at Masada, ran down east, through the upper and
lower part of the New City to the Kedron, crossing which it
ascended the slope of the Mount of Olives and the camp of the
Xth. Thence it went down obliquely past the site of the *Dominus
Flevit* Chapel to what is now Ras al-'Amud, where it turned west,
enclosed Siloam, climbed up to Deir Abu Tur and the site of the
Scots Church. Thence, turning northwards, past Herod's mausoleum, by way of the other camp, it returned to its starting-point.
The whole circle was nearly five miles long. It had its own towers,
thirteen of them, each 200 feet in circumference. This enormous
work was finished in the space of three days. From it, the Romans
could keep strict watch over the Jews, without coming within
range of their missiles. Titus, Tiberius Alexander and the regimental commanders shared the three night watches between them
by lot.

Finding themselves thus implacably surrounded, many of the
defenders began to lose heart. Josephus, with a skill that would do
credit to a modern motion-picture director, continually interrupts
his narrative to flash upon the consciousness of his readers yet one
more scene of despair, horror and crime. This was justified by the
plan of his book, which was to deter any would-be rebel against
Rome, while at the same time lauding the valour of his people,
and that of his patron and censor Titus, who alone had prevailed
over it. The most agonizing sufferings, the most cynical savagery,
the most disgusting assaults, even a circumstantially reported case
of a mother's cannibalism—these illustrate Josephus' narrative
of the all-consuming famine that now began to possess the city.
Many tried to escape. The first to leave bethought themselves of a
ruse to defeat the greed of their companions or captors. They sold
their belongings, and swallowed the gold they received, hoping to
recover it in due course by the processes of nature. The rumour
was soon spread that everyone who left the city had a belly full of
gold, and the wild auxiliaries from Nabataea and Syria ripped up
every transfuge they encountered in the hope of finding it. In one
night 2,000 people met this fate. Meanwhile, the Romans were
crucifying those whom they caught, at the rate of 500 a day,
trusting that the sight of so many sufferers would mollify the
determination of the defenders. Soon, "room was wanting for
the crosses, and crosses for the bodies". Titus then ordered his

troops to cut off the hands of those they captured, and send them back as object-lessons to John and Simon.

On one occasion Josephus, who was often employed by Titus to go round and harangue the people from below the walls, was hit on the head by a stone, and fell unconscious. He was rescued just in time by the Romans. He was hated by the majority of the rebels, and distrusted by the Romans, as so often happens to people who undertake such pacific missions. But Titus would listen to no petty slander against him. On the contrary, he showed him marked favour. One day, when Josephus was returning from Tekoa, where he had gone to choose a site for a camp, he saw to his horror among the day's batch of newly-crucified three of his own friends. He went to Titus, who immediately ordered that they were to be taken down, and cared for by a doctor. Two of them died, but one recovered. Titus also allowed Josephus at various times to beg off not only his own brother and family, but groups of his friends.

The clemency of Titus is in bright contrast to the vindictive rage of Simon. It was Matthias, a former High Priest, who had originally brought him into the city. Simon now had him murdered, together with three of his sons and other notables. A certain Judas, who was just about to surrender to the Romans the tower of which he was in charge, was seized, carved into pieces, together with his men, and flung down outside the wall.

It was now July. The sultry heat of the Jerusalem summer was at its height, its rigours aggravated by the stench of rotting bodies within and without the city. Titus reckoned that dissension and famine, reinforced by his inexorable encirclement, must by now have weakened the vigour and the resolution of even such fanatics as John and Simon sufficiently to justify his making a second assault. Besides, as Tacitus remarks, the splendid pleasures of Rome kept flitting before the eyes of the young Caesar. He was eager to get back.

Already four new ramps, far higher than the former two, were rising against the walls of the Antonia; for Titus had realized that to divide his forces had been a mistake: he must concentrate all his might on an assault against the Antonia, and then, having occupied the Temple, make his way into the upper city. Preserving their machines this time from destruction by fire, and doggedly braving a devastating hail of missiles from the fortress, the Romans at last effected a breach, only to find that John had constructed another wall behind it. This too must now be taken:

[*Anderson.*

41. This picture shews the famous candelabrum, the "seven-branched candle-stick" from the Holy of Holies, being carried in the Triumph of Vespasian and Titus, as represented on the Arch of Titus in Rome. In 533, it was to figure in a second triumph, that of Belisarius, who had brought it from Carthage (whither Genseric the Vandal had taken it in 455) to Constantinople.

Strictly speaking, "candlestick" is a misnomer: it was a lamp-stand, each of the seven branches supporting an olive-oil lamp. Josephus tells us (*War*, VII, v. 5) that the candelabrum had been remodelled for the occasion of the triumph—no doubt it had been damaged in the fury of the last assault on the Temple. The changes were two. First, the branches had been lengthened, and turned upwards, "so as to resemble a trident". They were now all in one horizontal line, having before declined on either side from the central lamp. Secondly, the lamp had been furnished with a new base—the pagan symbols it bears shew that it must be Roman work. The candelabrum in its Romanized form, as here represented, has been the model for Jewish replicas down to our own day.

The complete bas-relief, which bears representations of the golden Table of Shewbread and the silver trumpets, is reproduced on the dust-cover of this book.

[*L. Perowne.*

42. The lion, seizing an ibex, built into the wall of a fifteenth-century house, No. 1D on the north side of the Via Del Portico D'Ottavia, in the Jewish quarter of Rome. The Jews of Rome hold that it was "made in the days of Caligula, and brought from the Temple of Jerusalem by Titus" and that it symbolizes "Judah triumphing over her enemies" (see page 187).

Titus could not afford a second repulse. It was a Syrian volunteer, a shrivelled, black-a-vised warrior called Sabinus, who led the storming party, taking only eleven others with him. On the 22nd July, in broad daylight, he made his way to the very top of the wall, and seemed to have secured a foothold on it, when he stumbled and fell. He was soon done to death by the guards, and his followers as well. Two days later, a group of Romans, taking with them the standard-bearer of the Vth and a trumpeter, crept upon the exhausted Jews at two in the morning, cut the throats of the outer guard as they slept, and mounted the wall. Through the stillness of the night the trumpet rang out. The Jews fell back into the Temple, the Romans led by Titus and his bodyguard surged forward. The Antonia was theirs at last; but the battle for the Temple had only begun. John and Simon were determined to deny it to the Romans at all costs. Julian, a centurion from Bithynia, greatly distinguished himself; he put the Jews to flight, but when he came to the Temple Court, his hobnailed boots slipped upon the marble pavement, and he fell. Those whom he was pursuing at once turned on him. Titus, watching from the top of the Antonia, would have gone down to rescue him, had not his staff restrained him. When the engagement was broken off, the Romans had been forced back into the Antonia. The battle had lasted from two in the morning until one in the afternoon of that torrid, dusty day.

Titus had no desire to destroy the Temple. He would willingly have had it declared neutral ground. Later, he was to be accused of having given orders for the destruction of the shrine. The charge is repeated, for instance, by Sulpicius Severus, a Christian writer of the 4th century (*Chron.*, II, 30). Josephus might naturally be expected to clear his patron of so odious an imputation, and in fact he does. But the whole tenor of Titus' conduct, as circumstantially related, suggests that it was not the pagan Caesar but the sacrilegious Jews who destroyed the Temple of the Lord.

The 7th August saw the end of the Daily Sacrifice, which had been offered since the memory of man ran not to the contrary. The undying flame of the altar of God died that day; and the courts of the Almighty streamed with the blood not of sheep, nor of goats, but of the sons of men. The Antonia had already been reduced to rubble by the Roman engineers, save for an observation post from which Titus surveyed the carnage below, and a broad road had been levelled to allow the great *helepoles* and rams to enter the Temple area. The rebels tried to break through the fortifications on the Mount of Olives, and so gain the desert. They failed. It was in the Temple that, by their own folly and failure, their fate was to be decided.

The cessation of the sacrifice had profoundly shocked and grieved those Jews who were not of the rebel parties. Titus, when Josephus told him of it, bade him inform John that he was prepared to suspend his attack on the Temple if John on his side would abandon it and fight the Romans outside the city. Titus also sent Josephus once more to appeal to the inhabitants, his authority being reinforced by a number of notables and priests who had already gone over to the Romans; for it must be emphasized that the best elements in the Jewish polity had no sympathy with the rebels. Titus had treated them with kindness and consideration, arranging for them to be installed at Gophna where they might live their own Jewish life until it should be possible for them to return home. He now recalled them, and bade them exhort their brothers, who still tarried within the doomed city, to come to terms with Caesar. Above all, let them save the Temple.

The fanatics were at first disconcerted by the reappearance of these venerable men, whom they had advertised for lost to their gullible dupes; and a large number of the besieged now staggered across to the Roman lines. But the reply of the tyrants was to mount their artillery on the very roof of the Shrine itself, and thence to invite the inevitable vengeance of the insulted foe.

For three weeks the awful sacrilege continued. The rebels, on the 12th August, set fire to the cloisters that adjoined the now ruined Antonia. Two days later, the Romans brought up two of their towers, for which ramps had previously been constructed, one on the north and one on the west of the Sanctuary. On the 15th, the defenders, again outwitting the Romans, lured a number of them to death by firing the western cloisters beneath the feet of their deluded pursuers. But the rams proved powerless against the masonry of Herod the Great's masterpiece. Nor could the massy doors be forced with levers. Scaling-ladders were tried: those who attempted to climb them were repulsed. Titus, who was watching the struggle from the Antonia, now realized, says Josephus, that his desire to preserve a foreign shrine was causing grievous losses to his own army, and so gave the order to set fire to the doors— the doors only, be it noted (there were six of them, three on the north and three on the south), between the Court of the Women and the Court of Israel, but not to the Shrine itself. The flames consumed not only the wooden doors, melting the silver plates that covered them, but their frames as well, thus opening the way to the inner courts, and to the Holy of Holies itself. The defenders were stupefied by this new disaster, and did nothing to extinguish the fire. Titus, therefore, the next morning, sent soldiers to put out the flames, and to make a way through the débris for the approach of the legions. He then called a council of war. It was attended by the four regimental commanders, Fronto, the general of the Egyptian contingent, Tiberius Alexander and Marcus Antonius Julianus, the *procurator* of Judaea (the title being used here purely in its fiscal sense): the country was now under military rule. Should the Shrine be spared? asked Titus. Some were for destroying it, in accordance with the laws of war, others for sparing it, provided the Jews refrained from using it as a citadel. Titus declared that he would spare it, even if the Jews did not fulfil this condition. Tiberius (whose father had given the now demolished silver doors), Fronto and Cerealis, commanding the Vth, all agreed with Titus. On this resolution Abel comments as follows (Vol. II, p. 33): "Was the son of Vespasian speaking under the influence of a reverential fear, or to please his devoted Berenice, who, living in the Roman camp, exercised the same authority over his heart as Poppaea had possessed over Nero's? Although Josephus has drawn a veil over this liaison, it provides the only plausible explanation of Titus' decision. Even though the obstinacy of the rebels had involved the ruin of the *parvis*, the Shrine should be preserved despite them."

It was too late. On the eve of the day fixed for the final assault, when Titus had retired to the Antonia to snatch some rest, the Zealots, issuing from the Shrine, set upon the Romans who were extinguishing the fire in the outer courts. The Romans beat them back; then one of the legionaries, "being hurried on by a certain divine fury", climbed upon the shoulders of another soldier, and thrust a burning brand through one of the northern windows. The whole edifice was soon in flames. Titus rushed to the scene in an effort to stop the arson and the carnage. In vain: like the Duke of Wellington in a more recent war, he was unable to restrain in victory the passions of the men whom he had animated in adversity. The House of God became its own holocaust, to which its own brawling guardians contributed. In his own despite, it was on the smouldering ashes of the Temple that, when the sun rose through the smoke on the 29th August of the year 70, his rebellious and triumphant troops, after setting up their

standards against the eastern gate and there sacrificing to them,
saluted Titus as *imperator*. Within sight of the very plaques which
denounced death to every Gentile who entered the sacred courts,
the very ensigns which the Jews had adjured Pilate that they
would die rather than admit within the precincts of the city were
now flaunted and adored. The abomination of desolation stood in
the holy place unrebuked. Jewish tradition regards the preceding
day, which corresponds to the ninth day of the month Ab, as the
day of the Destruction of the Temple; in reality it was the tenth
that witnessed its end.

Titus could only acquiesce in the doom. When, five days later,
the last starving tenants of the gutted sanctuary gave themselves
up, he refused them quarter. "The time for pardon is gone by,"
he said, "it is well that the priests should perish with their
temple." So massive was the loot which the soldiery acquired
that the price of gold on the Syrian market fell to half its former
value.

The capture of the Temple gave the Romans a splendid *place
d'armes* for the occupation of the Lower City, that is, the area lying
to the south of the Temple, Ophel, the ancient Zion, Siloam
and the region to the south of the modern Southern Wall (see
Map). One gate led from the Temple into the Tyropoeon valley,
and two on to Ophel, each of them down steep slopes which put
the Romans at an irresistible advantage. In addition, the valley
itself, of which in those days the bottom was seventy feet below
its present level, was spanned by two viaducts, one just to the
north of the Xystus, and one to the south of it. The northern
viaduct, of which a portion of the great vaults still exists beneath
the street that leads from the Bab el-Silsileh, was hard against the
old First Wall, where it met the Temple, and may even have
carried that wall across the valley. The southern viaduct ran
from the Royal Basilica, and spanned the valley below the
Xystus, its site being marked to-day by "Robinson's Arch".

The defenders of the Temple, knowing that the circumvallation
prevented them from escaping to the desert, which would have
meant to Masada or Machaerus, withdrew to the Upper City,
and let Titus know that they were ready for a conference. Titus,
with his usual moderation, agreed to meet them. He appeared
at the Eastern or Temple end of the southern viaduct, while
John and Simon, with a mass of the emaciated survivors of the
population, who now longed only for peace, appeared at the
other. It must have been a dramatic contrast—the calm young

Caesar facing the fanatical gangsters, with the length of the bridge
between them, while Jews and Romans stared sullenly at each
other across the valley. Bidding his men restrain themselves, and
calling for an interpreter, Titus addressed the assembly. The
Romans, he said, were invincible: let the Jews make no mistake
about that. The strongest nations on earth had become their
subjects. "Even the Germans are our servants. Do you trust in the
strength of your walls? Pray what greater obstacle is there than the
wall of the ocean, with which the Britons are encompassed,
and yet the Britons adore the arms of Rome." Ever since the days
of Pompey the Jews had shown themselves rebels, despite the
magnanimity of Rome, which had allowed them their own kings,
their own laws, and the privilege of collecting Temple dues from
Jews in all countries, and thereby to amass a treasure which they
had spent not in the service of God, but in levying war against
Rome. They had sought allies "beyond the Euphrates", and to a
pacific régime had preferred slavery imposed by selfish tyrants.
Titus ended by saying that he had not sought to be entrusted
with his present command. At every stage, he had offered
clemency. He had protected those who came to him as suppliants.
He had done his utmost to save their Temple. If it had been
burned, it was their fault. After all this, what impudence it was
for them to appear before him in arms, as though they were con-
querors, and to seek to negotiate with him as an equal! Nevertheless even now, he was willing to grant them their lives, though
no longer their freedom.

This speech, though it is of course a "set piece", composed
under Titus' own direction some time after the event, is nevertheless of the greatest interest, as an exposé of Roman policy and
moral standards (*War*, VI, vii).

The rebels' only reply was a haughty rejection of Titus' offer,
whose terms, they said, they had sworn never to accept, and a
demand that they be allowed to pass through the Roman lines
with their wives and children, promising to leave the city to the
Romans. At this, Titus lost patience, and told his herald to
announce that henceforth no more deserters would be received,
and that no one would be spared: the laws of war would take their
course. The following day, the troops sped down into the Lower
City to kill, to plunder and to burn. Only the princes of Adiabene,
whose palace was destroyed, were spared to be taken to Rome as
hostages. One day later the devastation was complete, as far as the
fountain of Siloam, that is to the very southern limit of the city.

The terrorists now retired to the Upper City, where Herod's palace was their headquarters and the repository of their loot. While the four legions were bringing up their engines, for the last time, to batter the defences of the fortress, the auxiliaries were engaged in demolishing the wall which Simon had built on the west bank of the Tyropoeon, as a bulwark against John. The construction of the two ramps against the palace walls took eighteen days, wood being now so scarce that it had to be fetched from a distance of ten miles and more. (The Crusaders were to experience the same difficulty during their siege of the city in 1099.) Meanwhile, the Idumaeans had gone over to the Romans in a body, and Titus had once more relented: he spared 40,000 citizens, and allowed them to go whither they would. The soldiers were tired of killing, and preferred to make a profit by selling their prisoners as slaves; but they got very low prices for them, Jewish captives being by now a drug on a shrinking market.

Two priests, one of them Eleazar, the Temple treasurer, now came forward, and, as the price of their lives, handed over to Titus a large part of the Temple plate and vestments, which they had prudently buried when the fighting started. Candlesticks, bowls, tables, cups of solid gold, spices, tapestries, precious stones—all were now delivered. It was thus that they were able to be carried in the great Triumph.

At last, on the 25th September, the ramps were finished, and the artillery and rams got to work. The walls soon crumbled. This time there was little resistance. Those who could, escaped into the vaults below. Others made for Siloam, only to be chased back into the fetid ruins of the town.

On the 26th September, 139 days after the city had first been invested on the 10th May, the last resistance had been overcome. The victorious Romans planted their ensigns on the summits of the three great towers of the citadel, and saluted their general with cries of triumphant congratulation. The siege was over.

Chapter XXI

JUDAEA CAPTA—EPILOGUE

WHEN the usual massacre had been stayed, the survivors were rounded up. The aged and infirm—why keep them?—were killed out of hand, as were any men found under arms. The rest were herded like cattle in the Court of the Women, in the ruined Temple, and Fronto was sent down to dispose of them. The rebels were executed, every accused man being now ready to inform against his neighbour—again, a common symptom of a terrorism in collapse. Of the men, the tallest and most handsome were reserved for the Triumph; the rest, if over seventeen, were sent to the Egyptian mines, if under, were sold as slaves. Others were sent to the provinces and to friendly cities, to die as gladiators or in combats with wild beasts. Eleven thousand died of hunger, before they ever left the concentration area.

At last John and Simon gave themselves up. John, with his brothers, had been hiding in a cave. He was half dead from hunger, and surrendered unconditionally. Perhaps on this account, and because he was the first to lay down his arms, John's life was spared, and he was condemned only to life imprisonment. (It can hardly have been through any intercession of Agrippa, to whom the Galilean had caused so much damage, and who had himself been wounded by John's forces during the siege of Gamala.)

Simon did not appear until some days later. He had escaped with some quarrymen into a chamber beneath the Temple, and had thence tried to mine his way out. He was disappointed: the rock was too tough, the men too weak. He returned perforce, and donning a white robe with a purple cloak over it, gave himself and his companions up. He was sent in chains to Caesarea, to be kept for the Triumph, at the end of which, in accordance with Roman tradition, he would be butchered.

Titus held a victory review, on the site of his former camp well away from the reeking ruins, at which he distributed rewards and decorations and held a thanksgiving service. He then returned to Caesarea. It was now too late in the year to risk transporting so many prisoners and so much booty by sea, so he retired to the salubrious palaces of Caesarea Philippi, Agrippa's capital; and it was here news of Simon's capture reached him. Josephus does not mention Agrippa in this context, but there can be no doubt that he was there as Caesar's host, just as he had formerly been to Vespasian. We cannot, therefore, read without repugnance that among the festivities which marked Titus' visit were exhibitions of gladiatorial combats and wild beast shows at which numbers of Jewish captives were killed. It was Titus, says Josephus, who sponsored these "games", which no doubt exhilarated and pleased the pagan section of the population; but it is hard to believe that he would have done so unless Agrippa had at least acquiesced in the slaughter of men who, rebels though they might be, and in any case doomed to die there or thereafter, were yet his own country-men and co-religionists. More than 2,500 men perished at the celebration of Domitian's birthday, on the 24th October. Titus then moved to Beirut, where on Vespasian's birthday, the 17th November, the same scenes were repeated on a yet larger scale. What can have been the emotions of Berenice at all this blood-shed? Probably a feeling of utter impotence, to which Josephus may give the key where he says: "Yet did all this seem to the Romans, when they were thus destroying ten thousand several ways, to be a punishment beneath their deserts." Agrippa, no doubt, would have offered as his excuse the implacable brutality of the Romans, their determination to have their full measure of human flesh. Nevertheless, Titus, however he might treat his captives, refused to countenance any victimization of peaceful Jewish communities in other cities, notably in Antioch, although the Greek element of its population had given him a rapturous reception.

After extending his progress as far as Zeugma on the Euphrates, whither ambassadors from Vologeses sent him a golden crown, Titus returned to Antioch, and then went on to Egypt, passing by the ruins of Jerusalem en route.

Already the Xth Legion with its ancillary troops and cavalry had been installed as a garrison, their camp being the remains of the upper palace, of which Josephus says that Titus preserved the three great towers, as a memorial of his prowess, the plain truth being that he was unable to destroy them. A large portion of one of them dominates the city to this day. The remaining legions were dispersed, for already slanderous tongues were saying that Titus intended to set himself up as Caesar of the orient, in rivalry to his father. Had he not been hailed as *imperator*, and worn a golden diadem when he attended the rites of Apis at Memphis?

Titus, to dispel the malicious rumours, took the first merchant ship he could find, disembarked at Puteoli and hurried on to Rome, where he burst unannounced into his father's presence, with the characteristically disarming remark: "I'm here, father, I'm here."

The joint triumph of father and son took place in June, 71. For the Romans, the great pageant was a double celebration. Not only had Judaea been pacified, but Vespasian, like a second Augustus, had saved his own country and Rome itself from the horrors of civil war. The "year of the four emperors" left such a horrible memory, that when in 96 Domitian was assassinated, leaving no heir, the armies were content to let the Senate choose a successor. Not until 193 would the accession of an emperor again be a cause of civil war.

The two *imperators*—the term was just beginning to bear the significance "emperor" as well as "general"—spent the night preceding the festival at the temple of Isis, in the *campus martius* without the walls. Before dawn, the whole triumphal route was lined with expectant and joyful citizens. At dawn, Vespasian and Titus came out from the temple, crowned with laurel, and clothed in purple. After receiving the Senate, notables and knights, they mounted a tribune, where, seated on ivory chairs, father and son received the acclamations of the army. Vespasian then offered prayer (in which he was followed by Titus), delivered a short address, and dismissed the parade to breakfast, while he and Titus went to change into their triumphal garments.

The glistening pageant now moved forward: wave after wave of it, so that it seemed, as Josephus says, to run like a river. There were seventy richly clothed prisoners, there was a fabulous display of gold and silver, diamond-encrusted crowns, Babylonian tapestries and costly furniture. Then came the *tableaux*, depicting the capture of cities, and battles by land and sea. Some of these representations were three or four storeys high. The chief attraction was the furniture from the Temple, the candlestick, the table of shewbread, the silver trumpets, the censers, the veils and a Scroll of the Law. Finally, preceded by gold and ivory images of Victory, came first Vespasian and then Titus in their triumphal cars. Domitian, now aged twenty, rode beside them on a magnificent charger.

The proceedings were brought to a close by the shout of joy that hailed the execution of Simon Bar Giora.

The Temple treasures, which we may still behold in one of the reliefs of the Arch of Titus in Rome, were laid up in the Temple of Peace which Vespasian built after the Triumph, all except the veils and the Law, which he kept in the Palace. In the year 455, Genseric, king of the Vandals, carried the treasures to Carthage, whence in 533 Belisarius recovered them. Justinian sent them, or at least the candlestick, back to Jerusalem. We hear of it no more: presumably the Persians looted it when they sacked Jerusalem in 614. But the effigies remain, to remind us of that famous day, so bright for Rome, so dark for Jewry.

There are in Rome two other memorials of the Temple. One is the famous *Scala Santa*, the great marble stairway near St John Lateran, which is supposed to cover the original stairway of the Antonia, brought from Jerusalem by the empress Helena in the fourth century. This is a pious fiction: the staircase had been pounded to rubble under the eyes of Titus. It is, however, quite possible, and wholly in keeping with the spirit of the times, that the saintly British-born princess did remit to Rome some fragment of stone from the sacred site. Many others have since done the like.

The most poignant memorial of the Temple is to be found in what is now, and has for centuries been, the Jewish quarter of Rome, near the Portico of Octavia. There, set in the wall of the house of Lorenzo Manilo in the Via Del Portico d'Ottavia, is a fragment of carving, which shews a lion mauling a gazelle (see Plate 42). The style suggests a Syrian or even Assyrian influence. It cannot ever have adorned the Temple, since it represents living beings; but it must have been in its present setting at least since 1468, when the façade, as its inscription records, was last renovated. The Jews of Rome will tell you that it is a true relic of the Holy House brought back by Titus himself. "It represents," they say, "the Lion of Judah, ever-victorious over his enemies."

Chapter XXII

THE LAST OF THE HERODS

IN Palestine, three isolated fortresses still held out, Herodium, near Bethlehem, Masada, in the far south, and Machaerus in Peraea. Judaea was still, as before, a province independent of Syria, but in charge, now, of a military governor. After interim tenures of the office by the officers commanding the Xth and the Vth, Lucilius Bassus was appointed *legatus*. He took the Herodium without trouble, and then moved across to Machaerus. This splendid natural citadel could only be taken by a regular siege, and the necessary works, of which traces can still be seen from its summit, were accordingly begun. Fortunately for all concerned, the Romans captured a certain Eleazar, a popular young idol of the rebel forces. Bassus made as if to have him crucified before the eyes of the defenders, who then, as he had hoped, agreed to exchange the citadel for Eleazar. In the *faubourg*, which at Machaerus lies to the north of the fortress, and was excepted from the agreement, the Romans killed 1,700 men, and sold their women and children as slaves. Those Jews who escaped to the forest of Ajlun in the north, and joined their brothers who had managed to flee from Jerusalem, were rounded up and despatched, to the number of 3,000.

Masada was now the sole remaining rebel fortress. It held out, for almost two years more, and was only taken on the 16th April, 73, after a siege in which the constancy of its defenders was matched by the resolution of their opponents. Even now, so dry is the atmosphere in that remote region, we can discern the very works which the Romans constructed, and deduce from them the size of the besieging force, which has been estimated at 10,000.

Thus the rebellion ended where it had begun seven years before, at Masada.

Disturbances in Cyrene and Egypt, whither some of the Zealots had succeeded in escaping, were soon suppressed; and the temple built at Leontopolis in Lower Egypt by Onias, more than two centuries earlier, at a time when Antiochus Epiphanes had profaned the Temple of Jerusalem, was now first closed and then destroyed, lest it prove once again, but this time dangerously, an alternative rallying-point to the true Temple.

The Romans had restored tranquillity throughout Jewry, even though it was all too often the tranquillity of the grave. It might be thought that they would now adopt a policy of reconciliation. They did nothing of the kind: they had forgotten Virgil's noblest lesson—that if they were born "to rule the nations", and "to war down the proud", they must also "show mercy to the defeated".

Rome now inflicted upon the Jews three stinging humiliations.

The Jewish reluctance, on religious grounds, to use coinage which bore the representation of any human being has already been mentioned. The Jews were now to see, on the golden coins of their victors, the effigy of Judaea herself, her hands bound behind her back, or seated at the foot of a palm-tree, while the triumphant emperor leans on his spear above her, with the legend "*Judaea devicta*", or "*Judaea capta*". This unchivalrous, and thoroughly Roman, representation carried the shame of Jewry to the farthest bounds of the empire, and beyond. In Sabrata, where the name of Vespasian was familiar from his African days, a statue of the victor was erected, decked with a *Lorica* or breast-plate on which Victory is writing the fatal legend on a round target suspended from a palm-tree, with Jewish captives at its foot.

Next came the question of the Temple tribute. Titus was perfectly justified in claiming, as he had done in his last appeal to the rebels, that they had abused Rome's tolerance in devoting the funds, which were remitted to the Temple by pious Jews in all parts of the empire (often against the wishes of their gentile hosts, who objected to this drain on their gold and silver reserves), to the levying of war against the Romans. This, clearly, must stop. In any case, now that the Temple had ceased to exist, the tribute had no longer any *raison d'être*. Rome might quite equitably have declared the practice at an end, and have forbidden any further collection. Instead, the tribute was transformed into a special tax, levied on all Jews, and known as the *fiscus Judaicus*. There was a central treasury at Rome, in charge of a *procurator ad capitularia Judaeorum*, or steward of the Jewish poll-tax. The chief beneficiary of these Jewish contributions was to be the pagan deity, Jupiter of the Capitol. Suetonius (*Domitian*, 12) describes the indecent inquisitions by which this tax was exacted from every man who could be shown to have been born a child of Israel.

Finally, Judaea itself was simply confiscated. In the year 72, Vespasian sent orders to Bassus, and to Laberius Maximus, the imperial finance officer on his staff, to farm out the whole territory. He wisely refrained from founding gentile cities in it: only one little colony did he create, for 800 veterans, the village which still bears the name *Qalonia*, some six miles from Jerusalem on the Jaffa road. In Samaria, his hands were freer, and in this year was founded the town of Flavia Neapolis, which exists to-day as Nablus. On the ruins of Joppa, a pagan town arose. Caesarea became a colony, Colonia Prima Flavia Augusta Caesarea.

During all these proceedings, which were to affect his people for all time, we hear little of Agrippa. That he came to Rome, and was granted a Praetor's rank, we know from Dio Cassius (LXVI). That he continued to enjoy the friendship of Vespasian we know from a reference in Photius, who, in a tantalizingly vague note on Justus of Tiberius (cod. 33), says merely that the emperor "increased Agrippa's territory". A similar inference may be drawn from the fact that Josephus named his youngest-born Agrippa, which he would certainly not have done had not the king been still Caesar's friend. Beyond this, all we know, again from Photius, is that Agrippa died in the year A.D. 100.

With Berenice the case is very different. She accompanied Titus to Rome, where the young Caesar installed her as his mistress in the palace. What were his real feelings towards her? We cannot be sure. That he could be jealous we know from the fact that he ordered the assassination of a Roman general, Caecina, whom he suspected of wishing to share Berenice's favours. Whether he really loved her is another matter. It may well have been his sense of property that was outraged, his pride in the exclusive possession of the famous and exotic.

Berenice was now forty-three, Titus ten years her junior. He had chosen, after divorcing his second wife, to remain unmarried, and had in him, if we are to believe Suetonius, a streak of perverted lasciviousness which led him to find pleasure in male embraces. The rumour that he had promised marriage to Berenice originated, no doubt, with the Queen herself, who certainly aspired to become his wife, and began to behave as though she already was. For instance, Quintilian tells us (*Inst. Orat.*, IV, 1) that on one occasion when he was representing her interests in court, Berenice herself—a woman and a foreigner—took her seat on the bench.

This behaviour caused much offence among the Romans. For one thing, Berenice, so Juvenal says (VI, 156), was ostentatious— her diamonds were the envy of Rome—for another, her incestuous relations with Agrippa were only too well known. But even if it were possible to overlook these personal deficiencies (and Roman society of the day was one of the lewdest of which history has record), there was the overriding political objection. Berenice was an eastern queen, another Cleopatra. The recollection of the straits to which that woman's greed and lust had reduced Rome and one of her choicest sons, Mark Antony, made it out of the question for any Roman to countenance the union of his future emperor with a princess from the Levant, whatever her charms. The Cynics protested. One was executed, another flogged; but when Titus realized the state of Roman opinion, he dismissed Berenice, *invitus invitam,* in Suetonius' famous phrase "he reluctantly her reluctant" (see Appendix III). Poor Berenice! Seven years later, in 79, when Titus had succeeded his father, Berenice, with the pathetic imperception of an aging woman—she was fifty now—came back to Rome, and once again sought Titus' company. Once again he sent her away. We hear of her no more—in the mundane chronicles of mankind, that is. Like Cleopatra, she was to be immortalized by a great artist. Racine, with his flair for analysing human motives, shows us a Berenice infatuated not only with Titus, but with her own confidence that he loved her to distraction:

> *"Je n'écoute plus rien: et pour jamais adieu—*
> *Pour jamais! Ah Seigneur! Songez-vous en vous-même*
> *Combien ce mot cruel est affreux quand on aime?*
> *Dans un mois, dans un an, comment souffrirons nous,*
> *Seigneur, que tant de mers me séparent de vous?*
> *Que le jour recommence, et que le jour finisse*
> *Sans que jamais Titus puisse voir Bérénice?"*

"Mine ears are stopt! For evermore Farewell!
For evermore! My Lord, cans't thou not feel?
To one who loves, that fearful word's like steel.
A month gone by, a year; how anguish'd we,
When we're disparted by the sund'ring sea.
Come, dayspring, come: thou, night, thy shades restore:
Titus shall ne'er see Berenice more."

(*Bérénice*, Act IV, Scene 5).

What dynasty ever had a finer epitaph?
The family of Herod had held the stage of world affairs for

more than a century. It was now to disappear for ever into the obscurity from which it had come. What achievement would it leave behind it?

The first century of our era was the most formative in history. It was to see the rise of the two forces which were to generate, nourish and confirm the civilization of the western world, Rome and Christianity. The first tremendous clash between Caesar and God had engaged as God's champion, not the infant Church, but the Jewish theocracy from which it had sprung. The decision seemed to have gone irrevocably in Caesar's favour. In fact, it had not. Even at the material level, it is easy to exaggerate the effects of the destruction of Jerusalem. The moral shock was terrible; but it did not by any means involve the abandonment of Palestine by the Jews. Even in Jerusalem, seven synagogues had somehow escaped the general ruin, which according to Eusebius, a good historian, and himself a Palestinian, destroyed only half the original city. For certain Jews, the Messianic ideal was still re-stricted to a temporal restoration; and the fires of fanaticism, fanned by the blast of Roman rigour, were to break out in the next century, when again the indignation of the godly would be exploited by gangsters, to the worldly undoing of both. But for others the pure flame of the Torah remained the guiding light. No act of Vespasian, whose whole career was so mysteriously bound up with Jewish aspirations, has had a more lasting influ-ence than his establishing at Jamnia a colony of Jewish refugees who had come over to him before the siege of Jerusalem; for it was from this colony that there sprang the school, founded by Johanan Ben Zakkai and continued by Gamaliel the Younger, whose labours sowed the seed of what was eventually to flower as the *Mishnah*, the great codification of Jewish Law which is still the guide of the devout. Judaea, that is to say, had still a dominant part to play in the history of Judaism.

The Christian community, too, had returned to Jerusalem, where, under Symeon, it had established itself again in the little church on the site of the Room of the Last Supper. The Jerusalem Church was still Jewish. When, in the year 107, Symeon suffered martyrdom, it was not because he was a Christian, but because he was a Jew that he was killed—as a descendant of David, and so a possible focus of Jewish nationalism. Among the Gentiles, Christ-ianity was to win triumphs that, by its exclusiveness, Judaism had denied itself. But always Christianity would be the debtor of Judaism, even when they had so tragically parted company.

In the seventh century, a passionate re-assertion of the unity of the One God would arise out of Arabia. Islam, too, would regard itself as the fulfilment of Judaism, and of Christianity as well. It would revere Jesus, and His Mother, as it would honour the Patriarchs, so that to this day in Palestine, among the Moslem Arabs, the names Abraham, Isaac and Jacob, Moses, Job and Jonah, are more commonly bestowed than in any other land.

Both Christianity and Islam would be confronted with the problem of the balance of duty towards God and the State. Islam was from its very outset—and, we should remember, still is—a political no less than a religious communion. The Moslem Caliphate has found parallel developments in later Christianity— a Sovereign Pontiff, a Holy Roman Emperor, an Establishment. In our own uneasy age, when in so many realms the state, either openly or insidiously, has made such encroachments on the individual, the problem confronts more people more nearly than ever it did before.

The ultimate interest of the Herods is that they lived in the era that brought the problem to its first world crisis, and that, whatever their shortcomings, their follies or their failures, the best of them did try to discover a *modus vivendi*, a compromise, not of principle but of practice, whereby it should be possible for men to "render unto Caesar the things which are Caesar's; and unto God the things that are God's".

THE END

o

THE EMPIRE
IN THE
FIRST CENTURY

Appendix I

THE JEWISH LAW OF MARRIAGE
AND DIVORCE

I AM indebted to The Principal of the Jews' College, London, the Revd Rabbi Isidore Epstein (through the kind offices of Professor Bentwich), for the following note on the Jewish Law of Marriage and Divorce.

1. The Levirate Law (Deuteronomy xxv) still stands, whereby a brother may not marry his deceased brother's wife if there are children, and may not obtain her by divorce. On the other hand the brother is required to marry that wife if there is no issue, unless on the original marriage he had renounced his claim by the ceremony called Halitza.

2. The marriage of uncle and niece is legal by Jewish Law. (See the case of Wilton *v.* Montefiore in the English Law Reports.) The marriage of aunt and nephew is not legal.

3. A woman could obtain divorce, through the pressure of the rabbis on the husband to give her *get*, from the beginning of the Christian era. The Mishnah, which is the compilation of the oral law, made in the second century, has rules about that. If the rabbis were satisfied that the woman had a good cause for release from the marriage, they could apply religious sanctions against the husband to compel him to grant the bill of divorce.

4. Monogamy was the system favoured by the rabbis from the period of the Talmud. The Babylonian Talmud contains opinions of famous teachers of the third century against polygamy. For the Ashkenazi Jews, that is the Jews of Western, Northern and Eastern Europe, the rule became absolute by a decree of the famous Rabbi Gershon of Worms, in the tenth century. That rule, however, was not accepted as authorative by the Jews of Africa and Asia, including the Yemenites and those in Babylon (Mesopotamia). The rabbinical authorities of North Africa did lay down that the husband should not take a second wife, unless the first agreed or unless he gave her a divorce; and that provision was regularly inserted in the *Ketuba*—the marriage contract. But in practice polygamy has survived in oriental Jewish communities until the present day.

Appendix II

ARAMAIC was the vernacular of the greater part of Palestine; though in Jerusalem itself, pure Mishnaic Hebrew was used as an everyday language, and not merely as the tongue of scholars and priests. This would account for the tell-tale difference in speech between the Galilean Peter and the household of the High Priest (Matthew xxvi, 73).

Aramaic was also the *lingua franca*, the common medium of communication of a much wider region, corresponding to the old Persian empire. Its position was like that of Greek among the racially non-Greek inhabitants of Asia, such as the Syro-Phoenician woman of Mark vii, 26. An Egyptian, for instance, would dictate in Egyptian to his secretary, who would transcribe the letter into Aramaic. On its arrival in Persia, another scribe would translate it at sight into Persian for his superior.

In the Levant of the first century A.D. Aramaic was therefore (*a*) the *native tongue* of the greater part of Palestine, and (*b*) the *common language* of the whole area. It is still spoken near Damascus.

It is hard to say what language would be naturally spoken by a Jewish inhabitant of Palestine in the time of Herod. The older viewpoint, that Aramaic was the native tongue of the greater part of Palestine, is hard to hold. It becomes increasingly clear that Mishnaic Hebrew was not an artificial tongue used only by scholars, but a vernacular spoken naturally by many Jews: there is no reason for the phenomenon to be confined to Jerusalem, and our evidence is insufficient to establish in what regions each language was primary. Nor does the fact that Mishnaic Hebrew was spoken in Jerusalem prevent certain scripts from being written in Aramaic.

I am indebted to Mr John Strugnell for the substance of the foregoing.

Appendix III

"*Berenicem statim ab urbe dimisit, invitus invitam.*"

"He [Titus] at once sent Berenice away from Rome, he reluctantly her reluctant."

Mr Stephen Egerton has suggested to me that in this famous phrase Suetonius has consciously linked the Berenice who was Agrippa's sister with the prototype after whom she was named (see page 59).

Catullus, in his poem *On Berenice's Locks*, which is a translation of Callimachus' ode, describes (line 39) how one particular tress, as it is severed, cries out.

"*Invita, O regina, tua de vertice cessi.*" "Reluctantly, O queen, I quit thine head."

Virgil admired this line so much that he puts it with only one word changed, in the mouth of Aeneas (Aeneid, VI, line 460) when he is addressing the ghost of Dido:

"*Invitus, regina, tuo de littore cessi.*" "Reluctantly, O queen, I quit thy shore."

Both the Catullan ode and the Aeneid must have been familiar to Suetonius and to his public; it is difficult therefore to resist the conclusion that, by thus deliberately linking the two Berenices, he has heightened the effect of his famous epigram.

Table I

HEROD'S FAMILY

Note: This table is not complete. Herod married ten wives, by eight of whom he had issue, fourteen children in all, nine sons and five daughters. The names given here are those which come into this story. Rulers recognized by Rome as Ethnarchs, Kings or Tetrarchs are in italics. The date below each name is that of death where known. Herod-Philip, Herod's son by Mariamme II, first husband of Herodias and father of the younger Salome who is mentioned (though not by name) in the Gospels as having demanded the head of John the Baptist, is to be distinguished from Philip, Herod's son by Cleopatra of Jerusalem, who from 4 B.C. to A.D. 34 was Tetrarch of Ituraea, etc. It was their half-brother, Antipas, who was Tetrarch of Galilee in the days of Christ. For names to which a number is prefixed in brackets (see also Table II).

Antipater I *c.* 70 B.C.

Antipater II 43 B.C.

Phasael 40 B.C. — Joseph 38 B.C. — *Pheroras* 5 B.C. — (1) HEROD 4 B.C. — Salome = Joseph: Costobar: Alexas *c.* A.D. 10 — Berenice = Aristobulus

Doris (Idumaean) — Mariamme I (Jewess) 29 B.C. — Mariamme II (Jewess) — Malthake (Samaritan) — Cleopatra (Jewess)

Antipater 4 B.C.

Aristobulus = Berenice (d. of Salome the elder and Costobar)

(5) Herod-Philip = (6) Herodias

(7) Salome 7 B.C.

Antipater

(2) *Archelaus* A.D. 18 — (3) *Antipas* A.D. 39 — (4) *Philip* = *Salome* A.D. 34

Alexander = Glaphyra

Alexander — *Tigranes V* of Armenia

Herod of Chalcis A.D. 48

(8) *Agrippa I* of Judaea A.D. 44 — Aristobulus — Herodias — Mariamme

Tigranes IV of Armenia A.D. 36

Alexander in Cilicia

Aristobulus of Lesser Armenia

(9) *Agrippa II* of Chalcis, et A.D. 100 *c.*

(10) Berenice = 1. Mark (of Alexandria) 2. Herod of Chalcis 3. Polemo — (11) Drusilla = 1. 'Aziz of Emesa 2. Antonius Felix

Table II

This table shows the members of the family of Herod, of four generations, who are mentioned in the New Testament. The numbers prefixed to the names correspond with those prefixed to the same names in Table I.

1. Herod the Great . . .	Matt. ii, 1-22
	Luke i, 5
2. Archelaus	Matt. ii, 22
3. Antipas*	Matt. xiv, 1-10
	Mark vi, 14-28
	Luke iii, 1, 19
	Luke viii, 3
	Luke ix, 7-9
	Luke xiii, 31
	Luke xxiii, 7-15
4. Philip	Luke iii, 1
5. Herod-Philip	Matt. xiv, 3-11
	Mark vi, 17-28
	Luke iii, 19
6. Herodias	Matt. xiv, 3-11
	Mark vi, 17-28
	Luke iii, 19
7. Salome	Matt. xiv, 6-11
	Mark vi, 22-28
8. Agrippa I	Acts xii
9. Agrippa II	Acts xxv, 13-27, xxvi
10. Berenice.	Acts xxv, 13-27, xxvi
11. Drusilla	Acts xxiv, 24

*Often referred to simply as *Herod*. When Archelaus succeeded his father, he adopted the dynastic name of *Herod*, which appears by itself on his coins, with the title *ethnarch* on the reverse. When Archelaus was banished, in A.D. 6, Antipas became the senior reigning member of the family, and himself adopted the style *Herod*.

Their ancestor Antipater having been granted Roman citizenship by Julius Caesar, members of the Herodian family were accounted as being members of Caesar's *gens*, or clan, and as such entitled to the name *Julius*. Thus, Archelaus was called *Julius Herodes Archelaus*; Agrippa II, *Marcus Julius Agrippa*.

Table III

NABATAEAN KINGS

Aretas (Harith) III
87–62 B.C.

Obodas ('Aboud) II
62–47

Malchos (Malik) I
47–30

Obodas ('Aboud) III
30–9

Aretas (Harith) IV
9 B.C.–A.D. 40

Malchos (Malik) II
40–71

Rabbel II
71–106

Table IV

CHRONOLOGICAL TABLE

Year	Emperor	Legatus[1] of Syria	King, Ethnarch or Procurator of Judaea	High Priest	Important Events	Year
B.C. 5	C. Julius Caesar Octavianus AUGUSTUS, b. 63 B.C., Emperor 27 B.C., d. A.D. 14	P. Quinctilius, Varus 6–4 B.C.	Herod the Great, King, b. 73, King 37, d. 4 B.C.	*Appointed by Herod* Joazar son of Simon	Birth of[1] Christ	B.C. 5
4			Archelaus b. 22 B.C., Ethnarch 4 B.C.–A.D. 6, d. A.D. 18 Antipas Tetrarch of Galilee, 4 B.C.–A.D. 39 Philip Tetrarch of Batanea, etc., 4 B.C.–A.D. 34	*Appointed by Archelaus* Eleazar son of Simon Jesus son of See	Death of Herod the Great	4
3		P. Sulpicius Quirinius, 3–2 B.C. Caius Caesar, grandson of Augustus 1 B.C.–A.D. 4 L. Volusius Saturninus,				3
1						1
A.D. 4						4

	Events	High Priests	Procurators	Legates of Syria	Emperor
	banished	Simon (2nd term) *Appointed by Quirinius* Ananus son of Seth ("*Annas*" of N.T.)	Coponius, 6-9	6-7 (2nd time)	
9	Defeat and death of Varus		Marcus Ambibulus, 9-11		
12			Annius Rufus, 12-14	Q. Caecilius Metellus Creticus Silanus, 12-17	
14	Death of Augustus				TIBERIUS Claudius Nero Caesar, b. 42 B.C., d. A.D. 37, Emperor A.D. 14
15		*Appointed by V. Gratus* Ishmael son of Phabi	Valerius Gratus, 15-26		
16		Eleazar son of Annas			
17		Simon son of Qamhit		Cn Calpurnius Piso, 17-19	
18		Joseph Caiaphas 18-36		Cn Sentius Saturninus, 19-21	
19	Jews banished from Rome			L. Aelius Lamia, before 32	
26			Pontius Pilate, 27-36		

CHRONOLOGICAL TABLE—*cont.*

Year	Important Events	High Priest	King, Ethnarch or Procurator of Judaea	Legatus of Syria	Emperor	Year
29	Death of Empress Livia					29
32				L. Pomponius Flaccus, 32-35		32
33	Probable date of Crucifixion of Jesus Christ					33
34	Death of Philip the Tetrarch					34
35				L. Vitellius, 35-39		35
36		*Appointed by Vitellius* Jonathan son of Annas	Marcellus, 36-37			36
37	Death of Tiberius Birth of Josephus	Theophilus son of Annas	Marullus, 37-41		CAIUS Caesar Augustus Germanicus, known as *Caligula*, b. 12, Emperor 37, d. 41	37
39	Antipas banished			P. Petronius, 39-42		39

Year	Emperor	Legate of Syria	Procurators	High Priests	Events	Year
	Drusus Nero Germanicus, b. 10 B.C., Emperor 41, d. 54	Marsus, 42-44		Simon Kantheros son of Boethus	*Caligula*	42
42				Matthias son of Annas		
43				Elion son of Kantheros	Claudius in Britain	43
44			*Procurators* Cuspius Fadus, 44-46	*Appointed by Herod of Chalcis*	Death of Agrippa I	44
				Joseph son of Qamhit		
45		C. Cassius Longinus, 45-50				45
46			Tiberius Julius Alexander, 46-48			46
47				Ananias son of Nebedaios		47
48			Ventidius Cumanus, 48-52		Death of Herod of Chalcis Agrippa II made King of Chalcis, etc.	48
49					Jews banished from Rome	49

CHRONOLOGICAL TABLE—cont.

Year	Important Events	High Priest	King, Ethnarch or Procurator of Judaea	Legatus of Syria	Emperor	Year
50				C. Ummidius Durmius Quadratus, 50-60		50
52	Agrippa's kingdom enlarged	*Appointed by Agrippa II*	Felix, 52-60		L. Domitius Ahenobarbus, NERO Claudius Caesar Drusus Germanicus, b. 37, Emperor 54, d. 68	52
54	Death of Claudius					54
59		Ishmael son of Phabi (2nd term)				59
60	St Paul reaches Rome		P. Festus, 60-62	Gn. Domitius Corbulo, 60-63		60
61	Revolt of Boadicea	Joseph Kabi son of Simon				61
62		Ananus son of "Annas" (3 months) Jesus son of Damnaios	Albinus, 62-64			62
63		Jesus son of Gamaliel		C. Cestius Gallus, 63-66		63
64	Fire of Rome		Gessius Florus, 64-66			64
65		Matthias son of Theophilus	see note 2 (below)			65

	Jewish rebellion starts	Appointed by Rebels	Vespasian appointed as Commander-in-Chief in, and governor of, Judaea	*Legati*		
66						66
67	Vespasian in Judaea	Phannias son of Samuel				67
68	"Year of the Four Emperors"			C. Licinius Mucianus, 68-69	On Nero's death, in 68, Galba, Otho and Vitellius each in turn proclaimed Emperor. T. Flavius VESPASIANUS, finally becomes Emperor, b. 9, Emperor 69, d. 79	68
69						69
70	Siege and fall of Jerusalem			L. Caesennius Paetus, 70-72		70
73	Fall of Masada					73

NOTES: 1. The list of *Legati*, is neither complete nor established. In cases where Abel (published in 1952) differs from Pauly-Wissowa, *s.v.* Syria (published in 1932), e.g. over the successor of Cassius Longinus, I have followed Abel. I have also adopted his dating in other disputed cases, e.g. chronology of the life of Christ.

2. Judaea, for the time of the war, had become a consular province of its own: H. Seyrig, *Numismatic Chronicle*, 1955, p. 159.

INDEX